THE BEST SMALL FICTIONS

2020

NATHAN LESLIE
series editor

ELENA STIEHLER
guest editor

MICHELLE ELVY
assistant editor

SONDER PRESS

Sonder Press
New York
www.thesonderpress.com

ISBN 978-0-9997501-9-3

First U.S. Edition 2020
Printed in the USA

Best Small Fictions Founding Series Editor: Tara Lynn Masih.

Cover Design by Chad Miller
Distribution via Ingram

THE BEST SMALL FICTIONS

2020

CONTENT S

SPOTLIGHTED JOURNALS

NATHAN LESLIE

an introduction

WHAT TO SAY AND how to say it? How to find the words when it is increasingly difficult to say anything with any kind of assurance? As I write this, roughly two thousand plus Americans are dying every day. Typing these words is, itself, an out-of-body experience. As if we are trapped in some unlikely nightmare scenario from a dystopian novel, but we're not—this is reality. As you read these sentences, as we move into the fall and winter, I hope this tragically dire situation begins to abate. Perhaps a vaccine is on its way. Perhaps these ceaseless waves of death have slowed. Perhaps the economy has found its footing. Perhaps the pervasive, existential terror that clings to us is no longer omnipresent. This introduction feels like a message in a bottle: flung forward to a near future that may or may not be quite different than the one we currently inhabit. Nobody knows.

As I began assembling the *Best Small Fictions* selections for this year in February and March, the Covid-19 pandemic continued to spiral out of control. It was a disorienting and troubling time, to say the least—as schools shuttered, workplaces closed, professional sports associations called off months of competition, and the economy tanked. Throughout this time, the small fictions enclosed within these pages have been a source of comfort for me. Though literature cannot rectify such troubles, it can serve an important moral and spiritual role in times of crises—literature can point the way forward. Beyond solace and consolation, there is much wisdom to be found within these pages.

The written word has an uncanny ability to offer a semblance of order—to grant human connection and empathy—but also, and most importantly perhaps, to provide a direct link between writer and reader. It is a sort of permanent communication, something to hold, to live with as a kind of talisman. In this odd circumstance, a book contains not only more imminence but also a lasting resonance. You can take a book almost anywhere, the words within continuing to give and give. You can *reread*. One obvious indicator of the innate power of literature is that we refer to it—in celebration and distress—at funerals and weddings, graduations and memorial services. Something about the carefully constructed word allows us to build a bridge between our own disconsolate thoughts and those of others. Words offer awareness, empathy, guidance, wholeness.

One of the benefits of reading these works is that we can draw parallels between the words on the page and our own personal, or global, experiences. Even though the pieces contained within these pages (aside from the introductions and the interviews) were written pre-Covid-19, the parallels are uncanny. I found myself thinking increasingly retrospectively throughout the winnowing and selection process, especially when reading pieces for the second or third time. Amy Hempel writes in her story "Sing To It": "But what I said was, Sing to it…When danger approaches, sing to it." When reading the stories contained within this anthology, I harkened back to these lines frequently. Here was danger approaching. Here were the many powerful authors singing to it. These small fictions do not shy away; they face the threat.

Helen Rickerby's, "How to Live Through This", seems like an outtake from the pandemic itself—at least at first: "We will make sure we get a good night's sleep. We will eat a decent breakfast, probably involving eggs and bacon. We will make sure we drink enough water. We will go for a walk, preferably in the sunshine. We will gently inhale lungsful of air." Though often in the previous decade we have found ourselves ranting over political missteps or embroiled in the latest social media driven catastrophe, so much seems minor compared to the thousands upon thousands who have perished or were hospitalized by this devastating virus. We have quickly become both panicked and grateful. We take stock of the smaller things. We have learned to suffer in relative solitude—at home, away from society. We have embraced the benefits of isolation. We have become anxiously restless.

There is an inherent dreaminess to this year's selections, perhaps echoing a calm before the storm. Where the work within *Best Small Fictions* 2019 was jagged and volatile, the overall sweep of *Best Small Fictions* 2020 seems, to me, pensive and internal. Perhaps there is something in the water, in the shifting aesthetic sentiments. *Best Small Fictions* has always nurtured deep hybrid roots, open to genre-crossing literature. In 2020 especially, categories seem less and less meaningful to this editor. Words are words. Literature is literature. Constraint is stifling.

As was the case with last year's anthology, I made the final selections after consulting with the extensive *Best Small Fictions* team. The Guest Editor this year, our publisher Elena Stiehler, chose the terrific thirteen spotlighted stories from the overall selections (her introduction follows my own). Selections were chosen first and foremost from works nominated by publishers, but the Best Small Fictions team also did extensive online and hard copy scouring—in searching for the best of the best we never want to leave a single small fiction rock unturned. With a total of one hundred and twenty six inclusions in this year's *Best Small Fictions* anthology, we hope that we have represented small fictions with all due diligence.

I would like to especially thank assistant editor Michelle Elvy for her continued hard work and efforts, as well as for her moral support. Also, a huge thanks goes out to Elena Stiehler and Sonder Press for helping me negotiate the sometimes choppy waters an anthology of this size and breadth must traverse. A special thank you also to Richard Peabody and Chris Gonzalez who offered key advice and thoughts throughout the process. Lastly, *Best Small Fictions* 2020 would not be what it is without the key assistance of Jenny Drummey, Tara Campbell, Jen Michalski, Elaine Chiew, Ryan Ridge, Charles Rammelkamp and interns John Strohl and Gisele Gehre Bomfim. Hats off to you all!

I hope you enjoy these 2020 *Best Small Fictions* selections. I hope you find them both engaging and, in this terrible year, on some level, edifying, perhaps even consoling. And so now I drop this message in a bottle into these seemingly relentless waters. And I hope it makes its way to you, valued readers, safely and securely in what I also hope is a far less uncertain, dangerous and turbulent future. May we hope for a better, healthier 2021 and in the meantime, may the words which connect us, continue to sustain us.

Nathan Leslie
Series Editor, *Best Small Fictions*
Spring, 2020

ELENA STIEHLER

an introduction

WHEN NATHAN FIRST APPROACHED our press about taking on the *Best Small Fictions* anthology, I could not have been more honored, or excited. Nathan's vision for the future of BSF was inspiring, and also in line with my own passions: to celebrate not only the immense power of this genre, but also its timeliness—here is a form that in its essence adheres to none, that thrusts directly and deliberately to the heart. When I agreed to take on the publishing of this anthology I also understood, and was happy to accept, that it was just that. Nathan and his incredible team of editors and advisors would take on the awesome and difficult task of scouring submissions, making editorial decisions, and ultimately crafting, from thousands of pieces and hundreds of journals, this outstanding omnibus. My role on the other hand would be to bring it to life in physical form—to design it, print it, and work to champion it as much as possible.

It is for this reason that the fact that I find myself now stepping into the role of guest editor for this year's anthology is as unexpected as it is thrilling. The very reason I first began the small literary review that would grow into what Sonder Press is today was to celebrate short fiction in all its many and undefinable forms. To select and bring to life works which adhered to nothing but themselves, which had no rule or purpose beyond expressing the stark depth of humanity we find reflected within our own selves.

As guest editor, I approached the selections as I would any other piece I review. I read blindly, unaware of author or original publication, and focused solely on what I believe makes this genre exceptional: thoughtful, spare and deliberately crafted language; depth, not only despite but through brevity; embracing the function of form; and, ultimately, defiance in the face of definition. I read through the selections, then again and another time still, working each time to distill my selections further.

Finally, the thirteen stories I selected to spotlight were ones which not only exemplified the true depth and craftsmanship of this genre but its broad scope as well. I wanted to select pieces which showcased not only the delicate wording and thoughtful construction which defines this genre, but also the many undefinable forms, facets, and mechanisms it can, and should, embrace. These are pieces which are both short and long, which both push the boundary of form and let it be, which exist both within and without of our world. And yet there is a common thread. Ultimately what all of these pieces reflect is universal, full of life, encompassing: each selected piece shines back a light, mirroring our own, piercing the essence of our shared human experience.

Tina Barry's "Something Amber" is a masterfully poignant piece in which each word counts. It is a love story sketched in brief yet vulnerable moments, which creates, through deft, minimal prose, a fleeting chord struck in harmony with our own.

"Here is the Whole History of Us Part One" by Amanda Claire Buckley leans not only into the playfulness of form but embraces the abstract without sacrificing the universal. Each cadence is crafted with precision and nuance. It is a story which reveals both the evolution of family and the love held therein through the vision of a world not our own, but a reflection of it still.

It is the linguistic play of "Telling" by May-Lee Chai which showcases not only the subjective, and easily manipulated, nature of truth but also the powerful and often heavy burden of familial legacy.

Olivia Clare's "Some Female Cats and People" deals with a similar disconnect—the childhood gaze envisioned through adult eyes—while also subtly, and effectively, playing with the fourth wall as Clare names the very medium the reader is experiencing while recognizing the author as the ultimate master of that experience.

I found "Wishbone," by Rachel Heng, to be more traditional in terms of form, though it was no less thoughtful in terms of content—here is a work which weaves wryness with poignancy while exploring not only familial loss but the individual interpretation of experience, ultimately revealing both the power and division of inheritance.

In contrast, Micah Dean Hicks "The Listening Tree" leans heavily into the fantastical while still presenting a world known to our own. A world which we might sidestep into: revealing our capacity for manipulation, be it out of love or a desire for control, and the devastation that might be wrought from the simplest of secrets.

"Casper, Wyoming," by Blair Hurley, is again a piece which leans towards a more traditional form, but delivers a narrative style which underscores not only the blunt force of losing a parent, but the true cost and depth of love required to support the family that remains.

Holly Karapetkova's "Numbers" once again showcases the power of brevity within this form. Measured words paint an at once singular and universal experience, laying bare both the generational and societal struggle, and resilience, of women.

In lush yet bluntly honest prose and through the lens of a young woman's unfolding empowerment, Natalie Lima's "Men Paid Me to Eat" observes the primal nature of want, of satisfaction and our need to fill and be fulfilled.

Meanwhile, Perter Orner's delicately crafted "Pacific" is a brief yet richly layered narrative which contemplates not only the course of a life and of its ending, but the nature of that course and how it might be at once both monumental and minimal.

"A Writer's Guide to Fairy Tales" by Ellen Rhudy embraces a more experimental and evocative narrative style, but with such a restrained and thoughtful hand that the story is elevated even further as it contemplates the constructs instilled within us.

Suzanne Richardson's "Dollar Store, Yes" is immaculate in its prose—each word measured, each moment thoughtful—the piece itself a delicate crescendo demonstrating our desperate yearning to fully inhabit our existence, and the power that is seeing that desire fulfilled; reflected back to us within another.

Finally, Claire Standford's "The Earliest Memories of Ice" is sharply honed and stunningly conceived: demonstrating through the eyes of an element personified not only our intimate relationship with the planet that has born and supported us, but the eventual and painful reality of our callous treatment of that tender bond.

It is within this moment in history that we find ourselves at the great crossroad of our lifetime. A time that is as desperate as it is monumental, presenting us an opportunity for a great awakening or divide. It is my belief, a belief which informs the core of all I hope to do with Sonder, that stories like these, stories which break rules, which unflinchingly seek to expose the truth of our humanity, the bright and universal strands which thread through each one of us, are what we need to find our path. Stories are what have united us, guided us, illuminated us from our earliest beginning, and it will be these stories which guide us now because it is the work of storytelling to shine an unflinching light back upon ourselves—to throw into stark relief what unites and divides us, what stirs and fortifies us, what is right and what is wrong.

There is much that exists outside of our own control and understanding, but it is my hope that the pieces held within this year's *Best Small Fictions* anthology will bring solace; will inspire and invigorate. Though we find ourselves in a time filled with much darkness and doubt I see the work here as a beacon, slicing through the thick night to light upon the touchstones which unite and sustain us all. We are all human; we are all in this together.

-Elena Stiehler
Guest Editor, *Best Small Fictions*
Summer, 2020

SPOTLIGHTED

STORIES

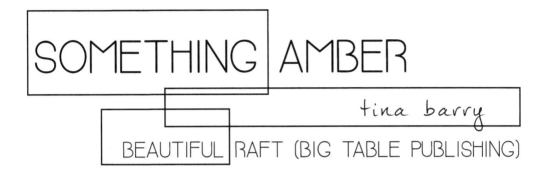

SOMETHING AMBER

tina barry

BEAUTIFUL RAFT (BIG TABLE PUBLISHING)

THE DARKENED ROOM SMELLS of baby, and cooked lamb. Over that, the scent of snow. You'd draw my head differently then I hold it now, cocked like a dumb bird listening. Jean's breath, not a sound really, just the opening of air. And David's slight baby rumbling. He's of you and of me but not. Serious somehow. Even in the few weeks of his life, I see that. You sketched him as connected circles, like the paper chain you cut from old drawings. We hung it over the table. Something festive to break up the winter. I like to draw your hand. The hand with that thumb. Such a thumb! Wide as the stump of an axed tree. Thoughts of you make me thirsty. I'll drink something amber. The glass's edge etched with your thin cardinal lips. And kiss you that way. My lips over yours.

Tina Barry is the author of *Beautiful Raft* (Big Table Publishing, 2019) and *Mall Flower* (Big Table Publishing, 2016). Tina's writing appears in numerous journals and anthologies including *Drunken Boat, The American Poetry Journal, Yes, Poetry, The Best Small Fictions 2016, Nasty Women Poets, Red Sky*, and *A Constellation of Kisses*. Tina is a three-time Pushcart Prize nominee and has had several Best of the Net nods. Tina is a teaching artist at The Poetry Barn, Gemini Ink, and Sloan Kettering's Visible Ink.

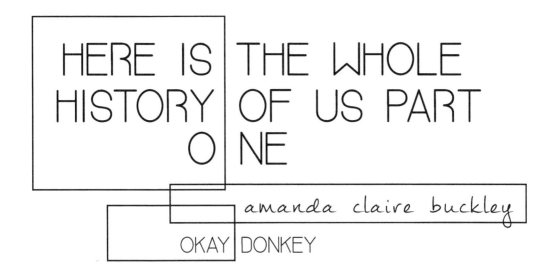

HERE IS THE WHOLE HISTORY OF US PART ONE

amanda claire buckley

OKAY DONKEY

WE CAME OUT OF the ocean. coming out of the ocean began with your attempts to get on land. you'd developed lungs. they were badly formed. no one had even thought to try to get on land before you. you said it was easier for you on shore. it felt better. i worried about you. *come down from there.* i called from the sea bed. *i'm ovulating.* we had a child who inherited both your lungs and my gills. i worried my gills would make her lungs even weaker. you died above us not long after she came out of me. it was too bright. your scales and your eyes had nothing on your lungs and your lungs were barely there to begin with. your lungs were small half-formed pockets that were continually ripping and sloshing with salt water. you'd cough up the saltwater on the beach. you'd tell me about how the sand got wet where you coughed. you'd leak our home out of your lungs. you'd say the shore wasn't so different from what we had down below. everything was just heavier up there. the sand. your body. our child is already swimming and your bones are where the light is. she asks about you. i tell her i remember very little. i tell her she will have to remember better. her brain is bigger. bigger than the both of ours. but she has your cough. i worry about her lungs. i put my ear to her chest and hope. our books say nothing about what to do with these new bodies. i have read them all. our child is already kicking. i can't believe it. she launches her body above the break of the ocean. into the air above us. then she crashes back down into the dark weightlessness. back to where we live together. we're a small family compared to the others. i beg our girl. *please stay near the seabed.* but she says it's easier for her up there. in the air. i tell her not to go on shore. i worry. she says she'll try not to go on shore but it's just so easy. it's so easy for her up there. away from me. she's growing. and growing. she doesn't need her mother to tell her anything anymore. i weave seaweed in my hair to make myself look younger. our child is growing faster than the others. i write the books i wish i could read to her. our child is grown. our child is grown and she is tan. one day she is late for dinner and i call her and ask her if she's alright and she tells me she's seen your skeleton on a nearby beach. *how long have i known.* she asks. i tell her i didn't want her to learn this way and she tells me she thinks she's going to stay on the beach above me from now on. it's just easier for everyone this way. by everyone she means her and her new child. my grandchild's lungs are so wide they can't help but float at the surface of our world. i would cry but I have not evolved tear ducts yet. i give a lecture to the others about paradigm shifts. the others say the world is flat. i tell them i've seen feet.

Amanda Claire Buckley is a writer, mover, teacher, and maker. One of five children born to Susan and Daniel Buckley, she grew up in a three-bedroom house in central New Jersey that was filled at all times with a wild menagerie: rabbits, parakeets, ferrets, lizards, skunks. She holds a BA from Bennington College and an MFA from Sarah Lawrence College. She is a contributing editor at the literary journal *Pigeon Pages*. She currently lives with her best friend, a cat named Yahz.

TELLING

CINCINNATI REVIEW

may-lee chai

WE WERE TOLD THE stories about Gramps in the Navy. We were told about the tour of duty in World War I. We were told he learned to be a gourmet cook in France, calf brains scrambled in eggs, sliced cold tongue on a plate, chipped beef on toast in a helmet on the beach. We were told that he was handsome. (*He looked just like Walt Disney.*) We were told he taught Grandma to cook. (*I was seventeen, I was just a girl, I didn't know anything.*) We were told how he remodeled the houses. (*First, he put on a porch. He fixed up the chicken coop for our bedroom.*) We were told how hard he worked. (*He never missed a day. He only drank on weekends.*) We were told how he loved to tell jokes. (*"Quick," he'd say if we farted, "catch it quick, paint it green, and sew a red button on it!"*) We were told he was restless, always looking for a new opportunity. (*We'd move in the middle of the school year. Sometimes just a few days from the end. My teachers never knew me.*) We were told he had gourmet tastes. (*He cooked the rabbits. He didn't know they were the children's pets.*) We were told how he liked his home kept. (*If there was ever just one little thing out of place. And you know with eight children . . .*)

We were told how he hit Grandma. We were told he did not hit Grandma. We were told how he punched Grandma, how he choked Grandma once, both hands around her throat. (*I remember it was the middle of the night. I ran to the neighbors. They said there was no need to call the sheriff. They made me hot cocoa to drink.*) We were told he was unsteady. (*We never knew where the next paycheck was coming from. We all had to work. Mother charged me rent.*) We were told he did not punch Grandma. (*Daddy would never do such a thing. It wasn't that bad.*) We were told he was steady. (*Such a good provider.*)

We were told how he loved his family. (*He always liked you best. He fixed up that car for you. He listened to you. He wanted to make you happy.*) We were told he never drank on workdays. We were told he was a hero. We were told he enlisted when he was seventeen. (*He lied about his age.*) We were told he was related to the Founding Fathers. (*We are related to George Washington. You should be proud of the white side of your family.*) We were told he had the family crest to prove it. (*He was always proud of his family.*) We were told we were ungrateful. We were told we were exaggerating. (*We come from a good family.*) We were told that's not how someone else remembered it. (*Mother provoked him. I had it worst.*) We were told not to tell.

May-lee Chai is the author of ten books of fiction, nonfiction, and translation, including her latest short story collection, *Useful Phrases for Immigrants*, recipient of the American Book Award. She teaches in the MFA program in creative writing at San Francisco State University. Her short prose has appeared widely including in the *Paris Review Online, Longreads, Prairie Schooner, Cincinnati Review MiCRo Series*, and *Kenyon Review Online*. Her writing has been awarded a National Endowment for the Arts fellowship, Bakwin Award for Writing by a Woman, Virginia Faulkner Award, Asian/Pacific American Award for Literature, named a Kiriyama Prize Notable Book, and recipient of an honorable mention for the Gustavus Myers Center for the Study of Bigotry and Human Rights Book Awards.

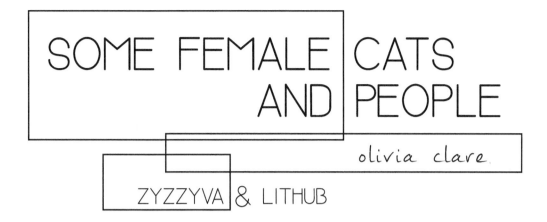

SOME FEMALE CATS AND PEOPLE

olivia clare

ZYZZYVA & LITHUB

FOR WE DID LOVE them, which is to say we watched them. Knew their habits and spoke gently and quietly about them. Loved them and did not ask for love in return.

Whenever we're some place waiting, my husband likes to hear small stories about my family. People knew my grandmother by her Siamese cats. She kept them in a room, on the third floor, and called it her cattery. For them I tried to play Mendelssohn, but the piano was on the first floor, a long way down. They could not—I was sure—even feel the vibrations. My mother worried to herself that my grandmother loved cats more than people. When my father came to this country and met my mother's family, he'd joke that the cats knew more English words than he did, but no one, he told me, would laugh.

You know already that when my mother claimed to worry about people she often meant herself. I worried about her. I worried about dying before my parents did. I imagined it, every now and then, so the story had somewhere to exist. What I imagined: them having to take care of a half-conscious, half-knowing me in bed. My body but brain not there, and them dragging up their old arguments, as old as myself, because I could not stop them, lying there. Dear God, my husband said, that's horrifying. I said, I'll go back to my grandmother.

She was a Biology professor, and she studied the bodies of cats. As she did with many creatures. In the summers we spent together in the Northeast I'd go to her office and sit at her desk and twirl her Rolodex and write with highlighters all the names I knew in rainbows. Here's the part I struggle to remember. In her lab there were dead cats sheathed in plastic. I was sure (was I?) they were not alive—unmoving, their fur flat and all about them, some eyes open, some closed, their tongues out—they couldn't be. They were the first dead red-blooded animals I'd seen. I had to say something to her. How could you? I began, meaning to ask how could she look at them. I made myself look. The way I made myself imagine my death. My inner eye has always made me see my sadness. The dead cats were together, hanging in plastic and on display, on hooks. Jesus, my husband said. You were just a kid to see that. So I'll change the subject now, I said.

Once I saw a cat come back to life. She'd been in pain, and my grandmother and I drove her at night to the family vet. He was in a tee shirt; he was eating a sandwich. This was in a very small town. I was young and you know I could have details wrong. He put her in a small aquarium and dripped anesthesia inside through a metal tube, and we watched her head drop and then her body thud down on one side of the glass. I wanted to leave the room, but my grandmother said, You should see this. Like the piano, like Mendelssohn. A part of my education. He was still chewing a bite from his sandwich when he took Ginny Woolf from the aquarium and laid her on the examination table and made a long cut and showed me her organs and ovaries and, on her ovaries, small cysts. He felt them and tugged at them with his fingertips. He twisted. Does she feel that? I asked. She'll be sore tomorrow, he said. He sewed her up and placed her back in the aquarium, and I sat and sat through four songs without words I hummed to myself until I watched her wake up and kept her sweet eyes open but down. God, we'll never put our child through watching things like that, my husband said.

I've never owned a cat, and my grandmother died a few Novembers ago. Last Thanksgiving we spent at my mother's. We were waiting for the rain to stop when her only cat came to rest herself in a swirl in my lap. She had wispy whiskers and a crooked tail and was small as a mixing bowl. No wonder, my husband said, and that was all, because he wanted me to ask what he meant by that. I said, What. No wonder that when we were ancient we'd worship them, he said. He stood and stretched. The rain's letting up, he said, and it's late now. We should start driving back. No, I said, that's not it. You know the story only ends when I tell it to.

Olivia Clare is the author of a book of short stories, *Disasters in the First World* (Black Cat/Grove Atlantic), and a book of poems, *The 26-Hour Day* (New Issues). Her novel is forthcoming from Grove Atlantic. Her stories have been published in *The Paris Review*, *ZYZZYVA*, *Granta*, *McSweeney's Quarterly Concern*, and elsewhere. She is the recipient of an O. Henry Prize (fiction), a Rona Jaffe Foundation Writer's Award (fiction), and a Ruth Lilly Fellowship from the Poetry Foundation. She is currently an Assistant Professor in English, Creative Writing, at the University of Southern Mississippi.

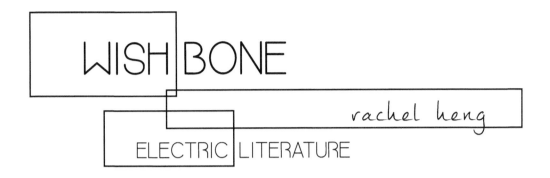

THE WISHBONE WOULD BE left to dry on a paper towel by the sink. Visual examination was permitted, but it was agreed one's back should be against the kitchen island at all times. There would be no touching.

These rules alone took an hour to hash out. Joyce, the eldest of the East Coast siblings, thought they should be allowed to handle the bone under reasonable supervision from the opposing side. She came up with an elaborate schedule of handlers and supervisors, but Lee Kwang, the youngest of the West Coasters, insisted it would be too easy for a supervisor to accuse a handler of having broken the rules. Here the discussion was sidetracked by Betty—East—remarking it was unsurprising Lee Kwang would think that way, given her history of rule-breaking. Voices grew heated, the issue of Ma's crystal swan figurine with the broken wing raised yet again, the old argument repeated.

She gave it to me, Lee Kwang said. It was a gift.

The East Coasters did not agree. Lee Kwang had broken the swan by accident when she was a child and had felt entitled to it ever since, just because Ma had told her it didn't matter because she would have it 'one day'. When the swan disappeared from Ma's display cabinets a year into her illness, there was uproar. The East Coast siblings guessed what happened at once, Joyce storming into Lee Kwang's home uninvited, finding the incriminating swan on her kitchen table. The West Coast siblings defended Lee Kwang's right to the swan, Ah Boon claiming he had been there when Ma bequeathed it to her.

You would say that, Betty said. We all know you've got your eye on the crystal poodle. Other objects began disappearing from Ma's flat: the faded watercolour of Venetian canals, a saucepot of delicate porcelain, an old, dusty Turkish lamp. Then things of greater consequence: lacquered side tables, Pa's calligraphy brushes from when he was a boy, the ancient jumbo rice cooker that no longer worked but which Ma had kept for sentimental value.

The seeds of the rift had been sowed decades ago, before any of them had been born. The year was 1965. Singapore, independent at last. The newly installed government was on a spree, shutting down Chinese vernacular schools under the guise of beating Communism, setting up new English-medium ones in the name of a new nationalism. Ma and Pa were practical about things. Half of any children they had would be sent to the former, half to the latter. They would alternate: English, Chinese, English, Chinese, and so on. Six children later, the family was evenly split down the middle. And so, the East and West Coast divide was born. It would only be decades later that the divide would be named as such, the English-educated siblings having left their childhood neighbourhood and moved to wealthier enclaves by the sea.

As they squabbled over weddings and money and perceived slights, the siblings still gathered each Sunday in Ma's flat, the one-bedroom she'd moved into after Pa had died. For a couple of hours, they'd put their differences aside, sit around the large circular table laden with garlicky greens, fish steamed in chilli and ginger, strips of pork belly that dissolved obscenely on the tongue. The siblings sat at their usual seats, steaming mounds of rice before them. They waited. Then, Ma would emerge with the oven pan, hands enormous in padded oven gloves, small biceps straining. It was her signature dish: a perfect, golden chicken. Skin done to a salty crisp that crackled between the teeth, tender white flesh that yielded its juices when prodded with a fork. The oven pan—red, cast iron, painted with scorch marks from years of chickens—was the very item the siblings were arguing over now, now Ma was far enough gone she no longer remembered their names or how to operate the stove.

The wishbone was dry and the visual examinations complete. It had come from a store-bought chicken they'd shared in surly silence. Each side picked their representatives: Joyce for the East, Lee Kwang for the West. Whoever won would get to choose first, thereby carrying off the the oven pan, the ultimate prize. The oven pan, of course, wasn't the only thing up for grabs. From then on they would alternate: Ma's favourite mug, the apron she wore when cooking, her gold reading glasses on a chain. Chairs with their threadbare seats. The stained dining table itself. The whole flat needed to be cleared out.

Joyce and Lee Kwang took up the bone. A shiver went through them. Reminded of all the times in their childhood they had assumed these very positions, arms outstretched, linked by the fragile joint. Reminded of what Ma had once told them: the wishbone held a bird's clavicle together, pliable but strong, essential for flight.

Rachel Heng is the author of the novel, *Suicide Club* (Henry Holt, 2018), which will be translated into ten languages worldwide and won the Gladstone Library Writer-In-Residence Award 2020. Rachel's short fiction has received a Pushcart Prize Special Mention and *Prairie Schooner's* Jane Geske Award, and has appeared in *Glimmer Train*, *Guernica*, *McSweeney's*

Quarterly, Best Singaporean Short Stories Vol. 4 and elsewhere. Her non-fiction has been listed among *Best American Essays'* Notable Essays and has been published in *The Rumpus, The Telegraph* and elsewhere. Rachel is currently a fiction fellow at the Michener Center for Writers.

THE LISTENING TREE

micah dean hicks

FAIRY TALE REVIEW

WHAT MADE ME WANT him? That supple, brutal kingsnake of a boy, wine-lipped and longhaired. He was strange. People talked, but nothing touched him. I wanted strength like that, to find iron in my thin bones. So when he grabbed my wrist and asked me to come, I went.

He brought me deep into the forest, to the listening tree. Even before our town, people had stumbled under black boughs to press their lips to the fleshy flowers. Anything could be whispered into the ears and they would close and bear fruit. The whisperer would forget what they had said. The fruit would be left to rot or eaten by the curious. How light we could walk, our secrets and shame given away, not knowing that we had ever been cruel.

I had never spoken to the tree, couldn't bear that someone might eat my fruit, might know shames that even I didn't know.

The boy cupped one of the tree's pale ears to his hot mouth and spoke. The flower swelled and folded inward, darkening like a bruise.

Hours later, he was done, eyes wet with pity for himself, already forgetting what had made him cry. Knowing I had given up nothing, he dismissed me with a look and left me behind. I waited until I understood that he wasn't coming back.

I wanted to hold the blossom he'd warmed with his breath, but when I went under the leaves—ears open all around me—I found that his flower had already swollen into fruit. It was rot-sweet and sagging, ready to fall from the branch.

Of course, I ate it. I wanted to know him.

What a tiny secret he had. Salt in a cut, knife-tip under a nail. What a small thorn to hurt so much.

He had loved someone years ago. They were swimming in the river when her foot slipped and the current sucked her away. Her head punched a stone and the breath burst out of her. He swam after, the river tumbling her end over end out of reach.

Something in me reminded him of her. But now that I had seen that gleaming girl through his eyes, I knew I didn't measure up. What a painful thing to know. I almost gave it to the tree, but I've always held my hurts close.

The next morning, the boy came to my house. He said that something important was missing. He felt hollowed out, half a person. He'd already been back to the tree, eating every secret he found, but none tasted like his. He had done this before, he said. He gave it away; he always went back.

Did I know what he had given up?

Of course, I told him. Put his arms around my waist and said, "You loved me, but then you betrayed me with someone else. I left you standing in the woods."

"I feel broken," he said. "Whatever we were, I need it back."

I knew then that I had taken his iron, given away the brittleness in me, that nothing could touch me now.

"One day," I said, "if you spend years making it up. Maybe I can forgive you."

He kissed me, told me he was sorry for ever wanting anyone else. He flinched from the truth in me, the secret that still stained my tongue.

Micah Dean Hicks is the author of the novel *Break the Bodies, Haunt the Bones* and the story collection *Electricity and Other Dreams*. He is the recipient of a National Endowment for the Arts creative writing fellowship, has been awarded the Calvino Prize, and is a two-time finalist for the Nelson Algren Award. His writing has appeared in *The Best American Science Fiction and Fantasy, The New York Times, Lightspeed, Nightmare*, and elsewhere. Hicks grew up in rural southwest Arkansas and now lives in Orlando. He teaches creative writing at the University of Central Florida.

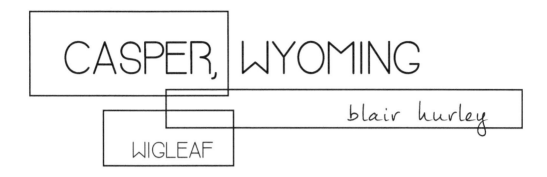

CASPER, WYOMING

WIGLEAF

blair hurley

IN CASPER, WYOMING, MY father fell off a horse and hit his head and was airlifted to the nearest hospital. My boyfriend and I were on vacation from Boston with him, trotting through hilly dry country that smelled sweetly of sage. We felt like grownups, lounging at the ranch house with wine in the evenings, our suncracked skin and dusty boots badges of honor.

When he fell off, he was right in front of me. I slid off my horse and ran to him; he was unconscious for a good thirty seconds, making an awful snoring sound while I shouted his name. I saw how he had landed on a sharp outcropping of rock and how his helmet was split all the way up the back like a melon.

My boyfriend and I drove the hundred miles across the dry sun-blasted expanse of the state to meet him at the hospital. We passed bleached white desert and billboards telling us to see the dinosaur bones and the jagged teeth of white-capped, unknown mountains.

When we finally reached the hospital, the doctor told us, He's had a small bleed but it's contained. He won't be able to form any new memories for a little while. Anything you tell him now, he won't remember. But in the morning, he'll be fine.

We went in to see him and he was sitting up in bed with a bandage ruffling his gray-streaked hair, looking a little confused but honestly all right. Where are we? he asked, and I told him, Casper, Wyoming.

What happened? he asked.

You fell off a horse. You're all right though. I explained what the doctor had told me and he nodded seriously, listening and attentive.

And where's Mom? he asked.

I looked at the nurse, who was standing in the corner keying something into the room's computer. Do I have to say?

You can say whatever you like, she said.

I didn't like to lie, and I'm a terrible liar anyway. She passed away, I said. She had cancer. It had been nearly a year since she died, and I still felt a small stab of pain whenever I allowed myself to think about it. Whenever I felt like punishing myself, I could bring up her face in my mind, her voice; the ache was reliable and sweet, something I could depend on.

He stared at me, and I saw the shock in his eyes. I don't believe it, he said. I don't believe it. He shook his head, and I saw the grief pass over him again the way I had in little flashes all year long, when someone said her name, or deliberately didn't say her name.

Then thirty seconds later he asked, Where are we? And immediately, Where's Mom? And I had to say again, She died.

His jaw worked. I was his younger daughter and I knew he was trying to stay calm for my benefit. Let me just try to understand this, he said. You're saying—

She died, I said.

I don't believe it, he said. I don't believe it.

And then, Where are we?

Casper, Wyoming.

Where's Mom?

I turned to the nurse, who was listening to this impassively, tapping at the keys. This is very upsetting, I said.

She didn't even look up from the screen. I'm sure it is, she said.

Again, and again, we went through the awful play. Each time I had the choice to say something else, I could have pretended for a little while, but each time I didn't; it felt like a betrayal of all we'd been through, the two years of her cancer, the pain and crushing, giant-sized sadness, to pretend that she was here, just in the other room, she'd just stepped away. My boyfriend held my hand and I said for half an hour or more, She died, she died, she died.

They told me he wouldn't remember any of it. And in the morning, after we'd found a motel for the night and returned, he was sitting on the edge of his bed, dressed and headachy and irritable, and we drove back to the ranch. I've never spoken to him of the night he asked again and again for his wife and I told him over and over that she was gone, we'd lost her. I don't know if he remembers any of it; I'm afraid to ask. The memory might be just mine and my boyfriend's to keep.

The fact that he asked for her immediately each time makes me think that he knew something was wrong, he had a kind of animal memory of her death, the way a dog will not know a fellow dog has died, but will stop hunting for it if he's shown the body. My father knew and did not know. He wanted me to answer, he held onto my hand and demanded urgently, Where is she? And I told him, again and again, what I knew.

Blair Hurley is the author of *The Devoted*, published by W.W. Norton, which was longlisted for The Center for Fiction's First Novel Prize. Her work is published or forthcoming in *Electric Literature*, *The Georgia Review*, *Ninth Letter*, *Guernica*, *Paris Review Daily*, *West Branch*, and elsewhere. She received a 2018 Pushcart Prize and two Pushcart Prize nominations in 2019.

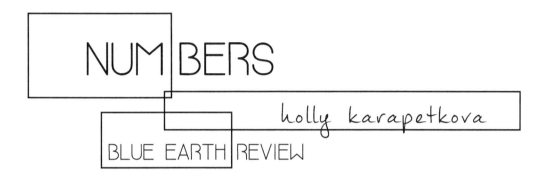

NUM|BERS

holly karapetkova

BLUE EARTH|REVIEW

THE MOTHER IS ALWAYS to blame: 40 years in the wilderness, count the decades on one hand. I am in my 40th year and life is a wilderness of children. I cannot count them all. The census lists the sons of the tribe. No one lists the daughters. The daughters list anxiety, depression, paranoia, phobia. They grow like the hairs on my head, heading for a world in which a woman is always to blame, sinking like a stone in the river of god. The test for an unfaithful wife is dust in holy water, the bitter water that brings a curse; if she then bears no child she has not sinned. I bear children, a long list of offerings, a long list of deserts. I spent decades following a husband who was following a cloud. I would like to speak with you alone, but this is impossible. I wander into rivers hoping to find solace or solitude. A door slams and I remember where I am: a desert. There is no water and someone will be blamed.

Holly Karapetkova's poetry, prose, and translations have appeared recently in *The Southern Review*, *Blackbird*, *Poetry Northwest* and many other places. Her first book, *Words We Might One Day Say*, won the Washington Writers' Publishing House Prize for Poetry, and her second book, *Towline*, won the Vern Rutsala Poetry Contest (Cloudbank Books). She lives in Arlington, Virginia, and teaches at Marymount University.

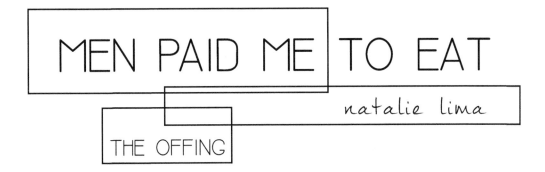

MEN PAID ME TO EAT

natalie lima

THE OFFING

OR, SOMETIMES, THEY PAID to eat food off of my body. The first time was in college. A boyfriend, or something between a boyfriend and a hookup, asked me if he could eat some peanut butter off my stomach. "You mean, off my boobs?" I said. And he said, "No, I really want to eat it off your belly while I squeeze it." At first I thought he was kidding but he was already unscrewing the jar of Skippy. I nodded, then pulled off my blouse and lay down on my bunk because I liked him okay, and because I knew that the remnants of the peanut butter would wash off easily in the shower. I let him lick the peanut butter off of me because, back then, I didn't know that I could ask for more.

The first time I requested payment for this, I was a few years older. The man I'd met online showed up with a bag from Wholefoods and pulled some food out of it. He placed a still-warm, broccoli-cheddar quiche on my stomach, then asked if it was too hot. "If so, I can put a paper plate underneath as a buffer." He said this as he caressed the part of my stomach that wasn't covered by the quiche. I could feel the calluses on his fingertips and as I lay there, I wondered if he played the cello in his free time, or my favorite, the viola. The quiche burned my skin a little but it wasn't scalding so I shook my head. "No, it's okay for now. But eat it fast before it actually hurts." I felt a surge of pleasure after speaking up, felt it buzzing all through my limbs.

I watched him steadily take bite after bite, watched him chew, grinning the entire time. When he finished the quiche, he lifted his head. With crumbs surrounding his mouth, he asked if he could watch *me* eat something now—like a slice of strawberry cake or some pizza from the options he'd brought. "Whatever you want," he said. "I just want to watch."

"Good. Give me the cake," I said and grabbed a plastic fork. Just before I dug in, he put his hand up to stop me. "Can you wait a second?" he asked and pulled out his wallet. He wanted to record the sound of me eating with his iPhone.

"Just the sound?" I said. "Sure, for five-hundred dollars."

I put out my hand for the cash, felt the buzz in my fingertips as I waited. He immediately placed the five bills on my palm, one by one.

He then watched me as I sat and tongued the sweet pink frosting from the slice, leisurely, like it was my birthday. Like this was all my idea in the first place. In the mirror, I noticed my posture was perfectly straight. Regal, even. When I finally took the last bite of the cake, I wasn't hungry anymore.

By the tenth time I required payment for this, a couple had solicited me. It was actually a man who had done the soliciting but claimed his wife was very open-minded. I charged double what I usually charged, and over the phone, I set immediate boundaries like: *No food on me hotter than 90 degrees* and *Nothing that'll be difficult to wash off or make me stink for a week.* The man agreed. The next day, a couple in their thirties showed up smiling at my door. They had blond hair and perfectly straight teeth, like a former prom king and queen couple. After they greeted me, the husband handed me some scented candles and purple flowers—a sweet gesture, different than usual, surely the wife's idea. I took off my blouse.

"So what's the meal du jour?" I said.

"Whipped cream," the husband said. "Nothing crazy, just some whipped cream. And my wife—my wife just wants to watch."

"Sounds good," I said and lay down on my bed. While he covered my belly with the cream, the wife searched her phone for music. She settled on classical—a surprise, but a welcome one. The husband licked the cream off of me like an eager puppy while the wife rubbed my hair. "Your curls are so beautiful," she said with the sincerity that comes from a woman.

"Thank you," I said and looked her right in the eyes, noticed a hint of crow's feet. The pressure of her fingers on my scalp was calming.

I closed my eyes and thought about that first time in college with the peanut butter and the boyfriend-hookup, and how this was immensely more satiating. Once the whipped cream was mostly licked up, the husband smiled, his mouth lathered like he was mid-shave. He got up and I pointed him to the bathroom to wash off. The wife poured some water from a bottle onto some paper towels and wiped my stomach clean, asked me if she'd gotten it all. "Yes," I said. "You got every last bit of it." We both smiled, and I stood up. She put down the paper towels.

I pulled her against me then and she kissed me. I kissed her back and I wanted to consume all of her, lift her up and place her body inside of mine, through my mouth or my stomach somehow. She put her arms around me and we held until her husband returned, car keys jingling in hand. We held, long enough to hear him exhale over the strings playing in the background. We held, long enough that I thought: *We could meld together like anglerfish this way.* We held so long that when I finally let go, I was more than satisfied. I was infinite.

Natalie Lima is a Cuban-Puerto Rican writer, and a graduate of the MFA program in creative nonfiction at the University of Arizona. Her essays and fiction have been published or are forthcoming in *Longreads, Guernica, Brevity, The Offing, Catapult* and elsewhere. She has received fellowships from PEN America Emerging Voices, the Tin House Workshops, the VONA/Voices Workshop, the Virginia G. Piper Center for Creative Writing, and a residency from Hedgebrook in 2020. To read her messy thoughts, find her on Twitter @NatalieLima09.

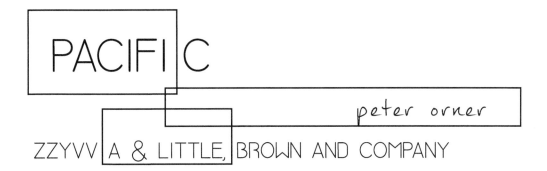

PACIFIC

peter orner

ZZYVVA & LITTLE, BROWN AND COMPANY

After Andre Dubus's "At Night"

SHE SAT CALM AND motionless in the living room while they worked on her husband upstairs. There's something so assuring about these people who tromp into your house out of the night. She'd always been a socialist and saw these men, and this one woman who's in charge, with their dark blue uniforms and heavy boxes and imperturbable faces, as physical proof of the ultimate (potential) goodness of government. She knew them. It wasn't the first time they'd come. Nor was it the second.

She sat in the living room amid their work. He was a sculptor; she was a potter. When people asked what the difference was, since they both worked with clay, she'd say, "The stuff I make is useful." And this was true. She made bowls. He made heads. Both of them always had day jobs. She'd been a librarian; he, an accountant.

The day jobs were a front.

On weekends, when they were younger, they'd attend craft fairs all over northern California. Sonoma, Napa, Solano, Contra Costa, San Joaquin. A few times they'd driven up to Humboldt. Once all the way to Oregon. They'd set up a card table and a couple of umbrellas. What better way to see places we wouldn't normally see! That's what she always told the children as she gently set unsold piece after unsold piece back into the trunk of the car.

She'd have to call them in the morning and tell them. Maybe not tomorrow morning, but soon. She sat in the living room, hardly listening to the commotion in the bedroom. She'd heard it all before. What fuss over a failing body as if it weren't designed to ultimately fall completely apart. To disintegrate. She gazed at their work in the half dark. The work of their hands. The rest of the world, she knew damn well, including their kids, thought them both a little bonkers. This room, the bedrooms, the kitchen, the bathroom, the front stoop. There was never enough room for their work. New pieces crowded out old pieces, heads and bowls, heads and bowls. After they retired, it was as though they'd been spurred on by a kind of delirious compulsion. Not to stave off anything, but simply because they'd had the stamina to go on working. Let it not make sense.

The kids, of course, would have to figure out what to do with it all.

"Ruby?"

It was Lucinda, the chief.

"Yes, dear?"

"Fred's medications, do you happen to—"

She recited them one by one, a litany, a chant.

The past few years they'd begun to shrink. In town, people said they'd become almost identical. This is often said of elderly people, but even she had to admit that in their case it was almost uncanny. They'd become dead ringers for each other. Same height, same wobbly gait. Really, from a distance, you couldn't' tell one from the other.

The dog died. The other dog died. Still, every morning they walked across the sewer ponds, through the fog, doubled back to Overlook, and wandered up Ocean Parkway to the place where the road crumbled down the bluff. You could stand there two hours; you could stand there five minutes. The Pacific didn't give a hoot about time. It would eat a year for breakfast. Is that why they'd always been so drawn to it? Is that why, still, they came and stood at the edge, day after day? Its blessed indifference?

Chicago-born Peter Orner is the author of two novels published by Little, Brown: *The Second Coming of Mavala Shikongo*, 2006 and *Love and Shame and Love*, 2010, and three story collections also published by Little, Brown: Esther Stories (2001, 2013 with a foreword by Marilynne Robinson) Last Car Over the Sagamore Bridge (2013), and Maggie Brown & Others (2019). Peter's essay collection/memoir, Am I Alone Here?: Notes on REading to Live and Living to Read (Catapult, 2016) was a finalist for the National Book Critics Circle Award.

A WRITER'S GUIDE TO FAIRY TALES

MILK CANDY REVIEW

ellen rhudy

YOUR STORY HAS A dead woman at its center. This is the first rule of storytelling. A woman in a tower, who doesn't yet realize she's already died. Maybe she will never realize, and maybe her years after the escape will be just as happy as if she had been alive. Maybe she will never catch the dank sweet smell of her own decaying flesh, or find in the mirror the empty space where her face belongs. You think she will be happy.

Your story has a man—that is the second rule of storytelling. A man who wants good things for himself and better things for the woman who is calling him. Nothing is more appealing or appalling to him than a woman who cannot decide whether she would like to climb down to his unknown arms, a woman who doesn't have likes or dislikes, loves or non-loves. Every day after he visits the woman who doesn't know she's dead, the man will wonder if there are other routes, ones to women who live and breathe. Or maybe he doesn't, because this is a story and one of the best rules of storytelling is that the man doesn't feel doubt, because he is there to act.

Here is the fourth rule of storytelling: the man and the woman fall in love immediately, before they speak, the moment they set eyes on one another. Love is a thing that can be created as quick as you can scratch its four letters on the page, and so when the woman climbs hand over hand down the fraying segments of her own braid, she is already in love with the man who waits for her with a broken comb and a hand swollen around a wretched brown thorn. I love you, she says, because this is what the man hopes for her to say, and because she knows it is what she must say. In some versions of the story he kisses her awake but in this version she is awake already, she kisses him first as though it is her choice, she waits for a spark, a glint, a sign of life to alight on her lips.

Over the nights to come the woman will lay beside him in bed, watching the close ceiling as he sleeps and trying to recall if sleep is a thing she knows. She will see her body crumpled at the base of her father's tower, again and again and again. She will hear the damp breath of her children in the next room, the snores of her husband at her side, and know that that was not the place she lost herself, if indeed she has lost herself, if she was ever even a thing to lose. And because this is a story, this is where you can leave her—not out of spite or authorial negligence, but because it is the only place a woman could find herself, in this world you've made her. It is a place where she might be happy.

Ellen Rhudy's fiction has appeared in *Split Lip*, *Story*, *Joyland*, *The Adroit Journal*, *Nimrod*, *Cream City Review*, and *Monkeybicycle*. She recently began working toward her MFA at The Ohio State University. You can find her at ellenrhudy.com, or on twitter @EllenRhudy.

DOLLAR STORE, YES

suzanne richardson

NEW SOUTH JOURNAL

THE CHECKOUT GIRL IS fecund with child and her neck is so finely dappled with the unmistakable constellations of hickies that when she asks you if you want more, (more chips because you have one bag, and it's two for one) you automatically say "yes," because clearly this girl is teaching you something in this moment about saying, "yes." Her body swelling, and puckering, and blistering, from the sucking and the fucking—so you reach for another bag, because *why not*? And that's what you want to say from now on, "why not?" Her body the lesson in "yes," in "yessing." So, you reach for another bag, and another, and you are stricken with her comfort. The way she moves in this dark purple necklace of hickies (as though it were Swarovski crystal) and her roundness, and her kindness, and her winking eyes tell you, "yes, more." Even as she scans the 2nd bag of chips and so you reach for a 3rd bag and a 4th bag, and she keeps encouraging you, "you can mix and match, you know, really grab any kind you want." And you keep thinking this girl is just so good at her job. This store with dollars, and trees, and flip-flops in December, and bizarre hotdog decals that no one needs for a cookout no one is having, and baseball cards from 1997, and vases, and stickers, and ribbons for gifts you don't have.

—And you're trying to think about the last time you had a hickey: that student who spent time in the military— the strange night he slept over in your broken bed. This was after you went crane watching in Socorro. You were taking a small break from sex, just coming up for air, and he went like a fountain, and you could see it in the moonlight on his cheek dripping down to his chin like a wound. So you instruct him more deeply to say, "yes" to this moment by kissing him, trying to show him "yes," "it's okay"—and that's really what we mean when we say "yes," we mean permission. The next day—too late to cover, too hot to wear a scarf, I teach with it. Yes, I teach with it. The "yes," on my neck.

The checkout girl says to have a good night, and you tell her to have a good night, and you nod at one another, *yes, do have a good night, do, yes.*

―――――――――――

Suzanne Richardson earned her MFA in Albuquerque, New Mexico at the University of New Mexico. She currently lives in Utica, New York where she's an Assistant Professor of English at Utica College. Her nonfiction has appeared in *New Ohio Review, New Haven Review, The Journal,* and *Prime Number Magazine.* Her fiction has appeared in *Front Porch,* and *MAYDAY Magazine, High Desert Journal,* and *Southern Humanities Review.* Her poetry has appeared in *Prick of the Spindle, Sundog Lit, Mas Tequila Review, Blood Orange Review, The Smoking Poet, PANK Magazine* and *BOOTH.* Her poetry chapbook, *The Softest Part of a Woman is a Wound* is out on Finishing Line Press. She is currently working on a memoir. More about Suzanne and her writing can be found here: http://www-suzannerichardsonwrites.tumblr.com/ Her twitter handle is @oozannesay.

THE EARLIEST MEMORIES OF ICE

claire stanford

MONKEY BICYCLE

CRYSTALLIZATION

THE ICE BEGINS AS a wrinkle at the edge of the lake, a threading of needles in the brush and the reeds. The slightest breeze will break its burgeoning corporeality, fracturing it into shards and then into nothing, causing it to rejoin the water, to resume that liquid shape. It is there, in body, at first dawn, and gone by sunset, straining to rebuild each night, crocheting itself around the edges of the land like a spiderweb, woven carefully in unseen corners, watchful, weary.

The ice knows it has been here before, in a past life. It feels a shudder down its spine, déjà vu. The shudder of a breeze that, this time, does not cause it to break. The surprise of survival. It gains confidence, clasps its neighbor, enlarges its reach.

Inch by painstaking inch, it turns the lake from liquid into solid, concentric circles closing in toward an indeterminate center, like the rings of a tree growing inward instead of out. The ice is growing stronger, but it cannot yet bear any more weight than a bird, on a break from migration. The ice tells the bird it must hurry, sending shocks of cold up through the bird's feet.

A warning.

ACCUMULATION

One morning, the ice wakes to find that it has coalesced. The fish look up from the reeds where they make their home and see only a prism of light where they used to see sky. The ice is tentative at first, but then it begins to test its strength. It roars back at the wind, it laughs at the sun. It tries to shimmy and shake, to identify the weaknesses of its body, but it finds, to its delight, that it has none.

Only the ice knows the day it covers the lake completely; only the ice knows the day that it can bear more than a bird's worth of weight. But humans will know soon; humans cannot help themselves. This the ice knows, too, somehow. Somehow, it knows the feel of human feet, the sound of human voices. Somehow, it remembers the approach of those first human toes, tapping its surface before every step.

The ice welcomes the humans. It opens itself to them. Skates and skis, ATVs and SUVs. Families with wool hats and rose-colored cheeks, frat boys drunk on Coors, joy-riding at midnight. Solitary beings who want, for an hour, to walk on water. The ice, too, feels full of joy, the pleasure of existing where it did not before exist.

Ice thick as cement and just as hard, a shock on the back of the skull, a cry. Ice that can sink ships, that can break bones, that can bring whole cities to a halt. The ice cannot help. It wishes it could. The ice does not like to be the cause of any pain.

SUBLIMATION

A day comes when the sun beats down, and the ice feels afraid. The fear is an instinct, deep-buried, but the ice cannot fight, nor can it fly. For months, it has withstood these rays, bathed in them, danced in them, shining like a disco ball. It had thought those days would go on forever, that it would go on forever, impenetrable. But a day comes when the ice begins to shed, to form thin slicks of water on its surface, minute puddles that do not re-freeze with fall of darkness.

A day comes and another day comes and another day comes, and the ice stops feeling human toes skating across its surface, stops hearing the human children exclaiming with shock and glee. It feels only a whittling, a calving, slow at first and then all at once, breaking into pieces that scatter like sea shells, that shatter like bones.

Come back, the ice thinks, come back to me. But it cannot stop the feathering of its body, its dispersal into air. The ice thinks of the birds, of how light they were, how free. The ice wonders if that is what it will feel like, when it melts into mist. If it will feel like flying.

EXTINCTION

There will come a time when ice will be only a memory. We will tell our children about the days passing into cold, about the clean smell of the air, its sharpness in our throats. We will tell them of the stillness and the quiet, the feeling every morning that the world had been re-made. We will tell them of trips to the lake, of that wobble in our soul, the lift of fear and pleasure when we stepped foot on that which should be liquid.

When the lake is a dry crater in the land, both liquid and solid will seem like science fictions, stories passed down from generation to generation. And that is what they will become – legends – but we will tell our children that we were the ones, the last ones to know the feeling of ice on fingers, ice on wrists, ice on tongues.

We will tell our children what it was to glide, how hard the ice felt on our backs when we fell. We will tell them of its brightness, its blinding purity. We will tell them about the sounds of ice, the primordial creaking coming from below.

There is a wildness buried deep within us, too, we will say.

Claire Stanford's fiction has appeared in *Black Warrior Review, The Rumpus, Third Coast, Redivider,* and *Tin House Flash Fridays,* among other publications. She holds an MFA in Creative Writing from the University of Minnesota and is currently a PhD candidate in English at UCLA. Born and raised in Berkeley, she lives in Los Angeles.

MAIN CONTENTS

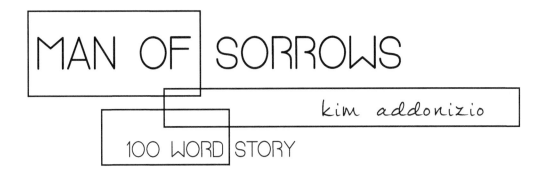

MAN OF SORROWS

kim addonizio

100 WORD STORY

— *15th century woodcut, artist unknown*

NOT ENOUGH TO GET crucified. You've got to be covered with red spots like an anti-vaxxer's kid's measles. Blood everywhere. Like when you clipped the cat's claw too close. A trail across the white comforter. Floor. Expensive white rug. Little fur-lined igloo where it hid, then ran across the rug again. The woodcut was meant "to shock the beholder into repentance." That spear—stuck through his neck? There's a whip, too. You've got to flagellate yourself repeatedly. It's your fault. About the cat and the entire marriage. God, at least, forgives you. As long as you remain really bloody miserable.

Kim Addonizio is the author of a dozen books of poetry and prose, most recently *Bukowski in a Sundress: Confessions from a Writing Life* (Penguin) and *Mortal Trash: Poems* (W.W. Norton). A new poetry collection, *Now We're Getting Somewhere*, is forthcoming. A book of stories, *The Palace of Illusions*, was published by Soft Skull/Counterpoint. Visit her online at www.kimaddonizio.com.

THE ASSIMILATION OF BOYBOY SANTOS

elison alcovendaz

LOST BALLOON

ON THE MORNING OF the Annual Santos Sibling Karaoke Contest, Boyboy told the police he was Justin Timberlake. Previously, he'd been other famous, white, American men: Bill Clinton, George Clooney, and, for one inexplicable weekend, Batman. He never dressed the part, not that it would've mattered; of my nine brothers, Boyboy was the shortest and the darkest and owned the flattest face. No amount of makeup or costuming could make him pass as a white man. In fact, he looked so Filipino that random strangers automatically spoke to him in Tagalog, as though he'd just arrived from Manila and hadn't yet adopted his new American skin.

Or maybe it was his name.

The genesis of Boyboy's name is one of contention. According to Junior, Dad's nickname was "boy" growing up, so he named him "Boy's Boy" though Mom, the stickler that she was, thought apostrophes didn't belong in people's names. Thus, Boyboy. Robert says that, since Boyboy was the youngest and the smallest, Dad thought calling him "boy" twice might someday make him a man. I, however, know the truth. When Boyboy was born, our family was months away from moving to the States. Dad and Mom, worried their youngest would have no ties to his Filipino roots, gave him the most absurd Filipino name they could think of. With that name, they said, there's no way he will ever become one of them.

I found Boyboy on the corner of Calvine and Mack dressed in a plaid shirt and jean shorts. He held a comb to his mouth as a microphone. He danced, too, though most people wouldn't call it dancing. The cops had arrived before me. They stood against their cars with their arms folded across their chests, laughing their white faces off. Boyboy smiled at the audience as he pumped his fist and spun on his toes. I stayed in my car and watched. It would be better for him to be arrested again, I thought. I drove off. Boyboy waved as I sped by.

None of us expected Boyboy at the Contest, but after we had already sung, he arrived. He didn't look at any of us as he strutted through the house, stopped at the microphone stand, picked up the remote, and selected his song. For five minutes, he sung without his usual accent. In fact, he sung so perfectly, all of us closed our eyes. When he finished, we opened our eyes to find our brother standing in the middle of the room, though he was tall and blonde and his skin was the color of ivory. Robert jumped off the couch and tackled him while Junior called 911, but all I could think about was that he finally did what Dad and Mom said he'd never do.

Elison Alcovendaz's work has appeared in *The Rumpus, The Portland Review, Rattle, Lost Balloon,* and other publications. He has an MA in Creative Writing from Sacramento State University and, until now, was worried he peaked in sixth grade, when he won a short story contest and the state free throw championship. To learn more, please visit www.elisonalcovendaz.com.

ORPHAN AN ORPHAN

kevin minh allen

OTIS NEBULA PRESS

EVEN WITHOUT A PAST the future will keep on snapping at your heels. If there were a cause, you'd be the reason, so we must insist that you not ask for what has not been offered. Keep on watching movies that watch you watching them speak all your lines with voices that sound all too familiar, except in a language we warned you to forget.

A burned-out house is a welcome mat with matching drapes and a sunroom where rain clouds keep each other company. Repentance is a broom closet, without the broom, but stuffed with unending chores with names like "Steven" and "Stephanie," "Robbie" and "Robin," and "Aaron" and "Josephine."

In the backyard you're forever mowing, an explosion lights up the sky and a terrifying whistle splinters into a hundred all at once, and then you see a plume of smoke far in the distance, over the horizon.

Against our wishes, you run toward the blackened cloud, your grass-stained gloves flopping off, and there is no one but you when you arrive. Burning fuel shoots right up your nose. Armless torsos wriggle away from the crumpled pile of metal and crawl under rocks, so surprised they were to see your face after all these years.

You instinctually look for the tail rudder to identify the aircraft, but it's missing. Apparently, neither of the wings want to show themselves in the wreckage. What is apparent remains hidden. A line of beetles follows you back to the yard, but you pay them no mind. They chat about the names they'll give their children and whether they could ever love them the way they ought to be loved.

Kevin Minh Allen was born Nguyễn Đức Minh on December 5, 1973 near Sài Gòn, Vietnam to a Vietnamese mother and American father who remain unknown to him. He was adopted by a couple from Rochester, NY and grew up in Webster, NY with his two younger sisters. He spent 17 years in Seattle, WA pursuing a life less ordinary and then returned to his hometown in 2017 to pursue something more extraordinary. Kevin has had two collections of poetry published in 2014 and 2017, respectively. In 2019, his first book of essays, *Sleep Is No Comfort*, was published in December 2017 by Rabbit Fool Press. In March 2019, Kevin had his first book of essays, *Sleep Is No Comfort*, published by CQT Media & Publishing.

WHEN I WAS NINE I LIVED

NIMROD

threa almontaser

in the middle of a dormant volcano // Fell in love with a falcon trainer's son named Waleed //
Stole a glittery birthday hat from a street vendor in Khormaskar // that I placed on the head of
a beggar girl selling juri flowers // Was called samraa for the first time // too dark // Mama
scolded by my aunts for not shading me // Stood in line next to Abu Bakr Salem's daughter in
a candy shop // who gave me gum wrapped in a cartoon sticker I kept // in my notebook //
Snuck into a boys-only classroom in Aden // to teach them animal names in English // Saw a
girl get snatched in a whirlpool // right in front of me in the Red Sea // her body found miles
away from the port by fishermen // who probably thought her a mermaid // In Yonkers NY
my locker and backpack turned inside out // classmates teaming up to look for bombs // I
was two days returned not yet resettled // wearing a pink practice headscarf the principal
confiscated // for breaking school dress code // Paired with Gina // the only other brown girl
in school // said to stink of something frying in a pan // so I slipped away from her side //
told everyone I was Dominican // In Yafaa where it was so sunny // my anklet burned my skin
// In Yafaa where the blue ceramic bathtub // held a giant desert lizard

so I had to bathe
with bucket of cold
well-water beside it

Threa Almontaser is the author of the forthcoming poetry collection, *The Wild Fox of Yemen*
(Graywolf Press, 2021) selected by Harryette Mullen for the 2020 Walt Whitman Award from
The Academy of American Poets, and a finalist for the 2020 Tupelo Press Dorset Prize. Her

work appears or is forthcoming from *The American Poetry Review, Passages North, Penguin Random House, The Rumpus, Adroit Journal,* and elsewhere. She teaches English to immigrants and refugees in Raleigh and is currently at work on her first novel. For more, please visit threawrites.com.

GIRL GOD

melissa bernal austin

LONGLEAF REVIEW

MY FAVORITE ITERATION OF God is 12-year-old GirlGod —
God of watermelon bubblegum and Dr. Pepper LipSmackers. Of hologram stickers and locked diaries. GirlGod of 1994. A God who never says anything mean about your bedroom when She comes over to spend the night. She can keep the secret about your brother's sadness and you can cry and cry and She won't be bored or make you feel like you have to say you're sorry for it. She smiles while running Her chipped, glitter polish fingers over the smooth spines of your books. Stands politely near the bed, uncertain about sitting until you say, *You can sit there if you want*, and 12-year-old GirlGod sits, relieved. She does my eyeliner like Hers, a little too thick, with a black pencil pocketed from the Walgreens on the corner. She leans in so close, I smell Her green apple shampoo, Her Windsong perfume. GirlGod holds my eyelid taut with one small hand, Her charm bracelet tinkling and catching the light. I can hardly breathe. When GirlGod is catcalled for the first time, we whisper about it during band. *He was old enough to be my dad*, She says, making that *gross* face 12-year-old girls do so well. If we tell Her father, he'll say he wants to *lock Her up 'til She's 30.* She rolls Her dark eyes, eyelashes fluttering like bird wings, descending. *As if he could.* My GirlGod is wise and beautiful. She is loving and kind. She shares Her cokes with me even though the health teacher says She shouldn't. *It'd be better to have mono together anyway.* We blow watermelon bubbles on the back of the bus. We play M.A.S.H. and only write each other's names on the list, four times. We lean close to share headphones. She winds and unwinds the cord around Her finger. I think She's really pretty and I know I love Her. I'm not even scared. GirlGod says She stole a new lip gloss from Walmart this time. She holds my chin steady to apply it. Hidden from everyone else, I am face to face with Her. When I smile without meaning to, She scolds me a little but it doesn't matter. We're best friends and I know it. And I smile again because She's looking right at me. Her lip gloss so shiny I can see myself in it.

MELISSA BERNAL AUSTIN

Melissa Bernal Austin is a proud queer, Latina, El Paso, TX, native writing and teaching in the Southwest. She is also an herbalist and maker who believes in the magic of self and collective care, plants, cats, science-fiction, and the seasons. Her work can be found in *Longleaf Review*, *CrabFat Magazine*, *The Narrow Chimney Reading Series*, *Funicular Magazine*, and more.

SUBTITLES: 50

matthew james babcock

ILANOT REVIEW

TAKE A MOMENT TO SILENCE all the days you weren't silent. If you need assistance, don't hesitate to ask yourself if there is anything you can do. To ensure a positive experience for everyone, refrain from forgetting that you hold a newborn child the way that in the flawed bowl of your hands you collect the chilly blue tones of a leafless February morning in Lafayette Square, the frumpy clumps of tourists in rumpled brown coats, Styrofoam cups of coffee steaming their red noses, bursts of sparrows strafing the sky. Your path is marked, located on either side. For your convenience, these safety features are found in your subconscious, so please take a minute and relive the sudden andante stroll of your blood the first time you saw your lover, the eye-widening shock of your only broken bone—digital phalange on your left ring finger, crushed under the gray boulder you were bearhugging when you stumbled the summer you worked the grunt crew at Deer Valley Ski Resort to pay off your fiancée's engagement ring—and the day it was your turn to bring snacks to school—and your mom, always the health nut—she dispatched you to First Presbyterian Church on South Buchanan Street where you attended kindergarten (the city couldn't afford another building), two brown paper sacks bulging with boxes of Sunmaid raisins under your arms. And when you and your older brother took a scrambling shortcut through the dry riverbed, you slipped on a stone shawled in papery pale green moss and the sacks went flying, exploding like perverse piñatas, sending red raisin boxes clattering into the dusty crevices of the riverbed. As you staggered doggedly ahead, cheeks streaked with a filthy paste of tears, the brown paper sacks in tatters, your older brother vamoosed, you dropped as many boxes as you gathered in your arms, eventually arriving like some hapless flea market merchant at the vacant bus transfer to find a stern woman in a slick floral raincoat and transparent vinyl rain bonnet volunteering for bus duty. When you said you missed your bus, your voice quivering like a raindrop on glass, without altering the scowl on her withered face she doddered with the stolid resolve of the grandmother of Frankenstein's monster into the office to call your mother, who arrived in her daisy-spangled kitchen apron, smiling and assuring you things would be okay as she drove you to school, and your contorted visions of trauma resolved into the knowledge that the world was a safe place where bigger people took care of smaller people, and that when you became bigger you would make the world safe for smaller people, too. Here at Skyways your sanctity is our highest priority. Please keep all insights clear, keeping in mind that your nearest regret may be behind you. Thank you for choosing to try with us. Make sure to leave all valuables where others can find them, and in the event of emergence, your exit, illuminated, is in front of you.

Matthew James Babcock is the author of two poetry collections: *Points of Reference* (Folded Word) and *Strange Terrain* (Mad Hat Press). His debut creative nonfiction collection, *Heterodoxologies* (Educe Press), was released in 2017. His debut fiction collection, *Four Tales of Troubled Love* (Harvard Square Editions) won first prize for short fiction in the 2020 Next Generation Indie Book Awards. His follow-up fiction collection, *Future Perfect*, is forthcoming from Engine Books.

THE CANDY CHILDREN'S MOTHER

a.a. balaskovits

OKAY DONKEY

I HAD TO SEND them away. They were children not born of me; they came rushing out between some other woman's legs, one right after the other, and I was told she lost so much of her liquid that, as soon as they squealed in the air, she had dried up, all broken apart, and pieces of her blew away with the gust of their father's grief. I had not known her, being so young myself when she died, barely out of my first bleeding, that when I was invited to her funeral, as the whole village was, I looked at the fractured remains of her bones with the curious pity one has for a dead animal. I expressed the appropriate grief to the father, my eyes cast down and my lips trembling, but he must have seen something genuine in me, though there was none at all, and he asked my father if I would be a suitable replacement. My father's hand hesitated to grant the blessing, but when a bag of coins found their way into his fingers, my father's hand was firm.

It was not so bad, at first. The children would not suckle from my breasts, but I warmed milk from the goat and dripped it into their mouths until their skin stretched over their expanding bones. They grew fast: the boy, Hansel, with his greedy appetite, and the girl, Gretel, long and thin like a branch, but whose arms knocked the china from the table if she did not get her way. They loved me, I suppose, as much as their father did, though when they saw my belly begin to expand they huddled together and whispered. When the rain forgot to fall on our small garden and the ground cracked, our lone goat's milk refused to be coaxed, and the four of us knew what would happen: a fifth would devastate us. Two of us would have to go. We would all starve if we remained together. I have not been taught numbers as men are, but even I know that three is less than five.

My grandmother once told me that once you go into the forest, you come back a changeling. Or you don't come back at all.

Gretel was awake the night I decided. Our small house had only one room for sleeping, and so all of us dreamed together. I climbed above their father and massaged his neck and behind his ear, as he likes. I pressed his hands to my belly and rejoiced at what we had created. In his ear I whispered that I would not die with its birth, for I was made of stronger things than dust.

It was difficult, after we finished, to fall asleep, for that daughter who was mine but not mine stared at me all night, the moon reflecting off her dark eyes.

They cried, of course, the boy more than the girl—his emotions reflected his appetite, and he could keep neither in check. Their father cried as well when he held the door open, but I held my hand on my belly—my only bargaining chip—and he gave them a little bread and told them they were old enough to make their own way, though they were young, too young.

At night, I asked them to forgive me, though they were already gone.

I bore him my daughter and I did not die. She suckles from my breast and squirms and laughs with all the happiness of a small thing. I see myself in her, that bit of myself that did not have to choose. With so few mouths to beg, the goat returned to its milk. We are saved.

Their father weeps for them, though quietly, as he knows it upsets me and my daughter. I don't voice what flows in my veins: I do not want them to come back, not my long-armed daughter nor my voracious son. If they come back, it is I who will pay the price for saving us, I who will pay the price for desiring my own daughter over them, I who will pay the price for making the difficult decision, though it was their father who held the door. After a few months, I suspect that they have died out there, and while I feel the ache of loss, I am also relieved that I will not suffer their retribution, even though they would be within their right.

One night, a little time before the birth of the new year, as I sit on the little landing with my daughter wrapped up against my breast, showing her snow for the first time, I see two figures make their way towards the house. Rather, I smell them first, the sickly stench of rotten sugar clings to them like a death. The boy is so big he makes the earth shake with each step, and the girl, tall and thin as she always was, has a red glint in her eye, and her teeth, when I they are near enough to see, are filed to uneven spikes.

They are almost upon me, and I hold my sweet baby daughter to my breast as I stand tall to receive them, these children that I have sacrificed to save my own, these children who are mine and not mine, these children who now sniff at my arms and neck, looking for the place to bite.

A.A. Balaskovits is the author of *Magic for Unlucky Girls* (2017) and *Strange Folk You'll Never Meet* (2021) from SFWP. Her fiction and essays have appeared in *The Missouri Review, Indiana Review, Story, Okay Donkey* and others. She is the co-editor-in-chief of *Cartridge Lit*. On Twitter @aabalaskovits.

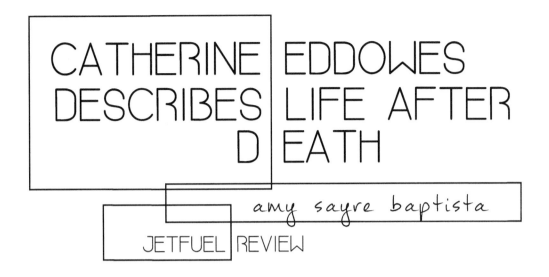

CATHERINE EDDOWES DESCRIBES LIFE AFTER DEATH

amy sayre baptista

JETFUEL REVIEW

THE SUMMER BEFORE I was murdered, I walked Brick Lane every day. Sewing a few days a week at a ladies shop, gathering scraps for the boot maker, and at night, I passed the evenings as I needed to. As we all needed to from time to time. Trading a man's pleasure to pay my bread and a place to lay my head. A place you might rest without being rousted up red bitten by fleas or prodded by a stranger for a shag in the middle of the night. I gathered my share of men's bruises and scoff, "bang-tail" they'd holler at me as I passed, or "step right, slag," as if they was the Queen's own brigade. The night he cut me open is just a shudder of light against the pavement, the wage I paid to pass there.

I wander these same streets, a soul half-lit, untethered.

Now, Brick Lane is populated by dark-skinned women in sari's and scarves brilliant as the finches and larks the bird-catchers used to sell here. And I am spirit covered in spice: saffron, curry-clouded. I cannot stop watching them, these bright Bengali women.

My life fed on the hope of a boiled potato, but my shadow trails the taste of sweet curd. The girl, Asha, works in the curry shop on the corner, just past where the Ten Bells used to be. As she pours mustard oil, I hold out my hands to be pierced by gold. Illuminated in liquid. I am a haunt mad-hungry for touch, and she, just a girl who forbids her own desire. Her smile is widened by scars purple as plums. Cuts made by a man whose affection she did not return and thought her face his knife's tapestry. Her name in Bengali means hope, but Asha tells her mum that her name is a lie. She says, "a ghost with a murdered face walks in my shadow." But I can't leave her side. Her mum says, "You will make me a grandmother one day." She repeats the words lighting incense, touching her head and heart, hoping the Goddess Kali will hear her and make mercy from smoke and ash. When her mother speaks of men and babies, Asha sharpens her knife and says nothing. The women cut and chop, cut and chop. Knives and spatulas crushing and rolling. Hands made for giving. Palms resplendent as sunrise. They use every root, peel, and stem. I love them. I worship every move, for nothing is waste, not even the tiniest scrap is judged trash and thrown out.

the sharpest blade never turns to hurt,

>   but cuts,
>   cuts, and cuts
>   to cook comfort.

—Catherine Eddowes, the third victim of Jack the Ripper, owned a coffee shop with her husband and sold penny poetry at public executions.

Amy Sayre Baptista's chapbook, *Primitivity* (Black Lawrence) won the Black River Chapbook Contest (Spring 2017). Her writing has appeared in *Jet Fuel Review*, *Corium*, *SmokeLong Quarterly*, *Ninth Letter*, *The Butter*, *Alaska Quarterly Review*, and other journals. She is a CantoMundo fellow, and a scholarship recipient to the Disquiet Literary Festival in Lisbon, Portugal. She is a co-founder of Plates&Poetry, a community arts program focused on food and writing. She has an MFA in Fiction from the University of Illinois, Urbana-Champaign, and teaches Humanities at Western Governors University.

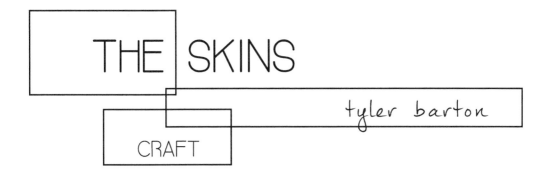

THE SKINS

CRAFT

tyler barton

THE PRODUCER WANTED WET hands. Sweaty and tense to where the sound really snapped. So my team detained the clappers in an overwarm anteroom beside the recording booth. Made them wait. Clammy, anxious, beating on the soundproof door—*We're still in here!* Eventually they were released, palms moist, only to find their mark at the mic and fail her. Each time, the producer sighed. The perfect clap was somewhere far off but—she assured my team and I—reachable.

She wanted trim nails. Short fingers. "I need *compact* percussion." At noon she called the bassist's handclap *languorous*. "I need hands that don't take all day to come together." We brought in children, but they had no strength. We brought in brawny wrestlers, varsity but rhythmless—and even though I could've made it match the beat in post, the producer wanted someone with an intuition she could sense. A soul she could hear on tape.

She wanted my team to stop bickering. A chat about the proper pop-filter had spiraled into a dispute over whether, in a finger snap, the sound was in the friction between thumb and middle finger, or rather in the finger's striking the palm. Battle-lines were drawn, mapping neatly onto two worldviews, neither of which the producer was interested in exploring. An intern was let go.

"What if you just do the clap yourself?" I asked her, trying to distract from the episode. "We'd probably have it in like one take." But this song was a part of her Selfless series, records with pages and pages of credits. *One is only built from a pile of others*, read the pull-quote from her *Vibe* interview, even though the album art was always, front and back, full-bleed headshots of the producer's stoic pout.

"No, Zeigler." She loved to put a touch of Dutch on the pronunciation of my name, even though I had never stepped foot in Europe. She had her own engineer in every country, refused to fly me out for tour. "It is not my role to clap," she said, pressing the delete key to erase an entire track.

So I brought in music students who cupped their hands in exotic ways. It didn't take. We got creative, idiotic—we had a policeman fire a gun. Blanks, but still. "It sounds forced," she said. One by one, my team began to flee, talking of union contracts, families, the sour taste leftover from the finger-snap debacle. "It's getting dark," they said. "Outside, too."

Hours meant nothing. What were hours? The coming lump sum would float my team through another summer. The payday was out there somewhere, invisible but within grasp. Marcus and I had decided not to adopt until I was established, until my name was a stock you could trade.

"You're getting all their information, right?" she asked from inside her stress-relieving VR headset. "The failures, I mean. I need each one credited." Yes, I assured her, and then made more calls. Calls. Calls until my phone died. I wandered down the street, past the café, past the poke bowl place, past the new lofts, and into the barber school. They didn't seem to understand my request, but I left an address. One man set down his scissors and shook my hand.

The producer ate dinner—a family-size bag of peanut M&Ms—right there at the soundboard. She'd suck the candy down to its furrowed core, pinch the nut from her tongue, and stack each one beside the mixer. It was times like these that I'd try to break a clipboard with my hands. I'm still working on it. Perfection, to me, is a pile of trying. The pile grows high enough to be enough. "You know, Ziegler," she said, "I'm not paying you for an opinion." And before I could sulk away to send some emails, she softened, turned to me, and confessed that perfection was immortal. "Omnipotent, yet quotidian," she said. "Like finding a dropped dollar."

"More like a million of them, all at once."

Our only agreement was that the handclap is the supreme snare. No drum, acoustic or digital, sounds immaculate as that: two hands brought together. To this day, I get a little kick when someone calls a set of drums the *skins*.

When the barbers arrived, the producer was sugar-crashed on the couch, facedown, so I led the session—instructing them through the microphone. "Just clap," I said, forgetting to hit record, and the four men began to applaud. My team was gone, so I cracked up all alone. My laughter woke the producer, who stood and leaned over the board, watching as they kept clapping.

"Who are these men?"

"Barbers," I said.

She touched the red button to capture their ovation. "They work with their hands," she said, raising her arms above her head—a victory, a stretch.

The song, you'll notice, is totally snareless. No claps, no snaps. No pillars prop up its structure. It marks the start of her Formless phase. You can hear a thread throughout, soft in the background—applause like rain. If you scroll through the credits, you'll find me buried there, beneath a sea of names.

Tyler Barton is a literary advocate and cofounder of Fear No Lit, home of the Submerging Writer Fellowship. "The Skins" is part of his debut story collection, which will be published by Sarabande Books in 2021. Other stories from that book have appeared in *The Iowa Review*, *Kenyon Review*, *Gulf Coast*, *Subtropics*, and elsewhere. His collection of flash fiction, *The Quiet Part Loud*, won the Turnbuckle Chapbook Contest and was published by Split Lip Press in 2019. He lives in Lancaster, PA. Find him at tsbarton.com or @goftyler.

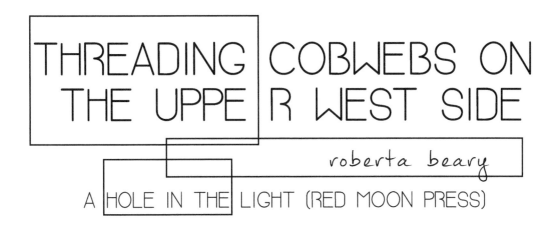

THREADING COBWEBS ON THE UPPER WEST SIDE

roberta beary

A HOLE IN THE LIGHT (RED MOON PRESS)

I LIFT MY ARMS and float over rooftops. Gerry Keating pulls me down into his camp tent. I know he'll marry Carol from Catholic school and die before 50 from lung cancer. But I don't care. Sparks from his Marlboro seep into me. He wants to do it right there and I let him. Our smoky afterglow drips sex. The doctor says look you can either put up with the hallucinations. Or take care of those cataracts. When the bandages come off my eyes climb the rooftops. Up down and sideways. Gerry Keating has folded up his tent. Gone back to his grave at Queens Calvary. The doctor says look it went as well as can be expected. At your age.

crushed spider
in my open palm
the future tense

Roberta Beary writes to connect with the disenfranchised, to let them know they are not alone. Author of two award-winning poetry collections, *The Unworn Necklace* (Snapshot Press, 2007) and *Deflection* (Accents, 2015), her micros and haibun stories have appeared in *The New York Times*, *Rattle*, *New Flash Fiction Review*, *100 Word Story*, *Cultural Weekly*, and *Best Microfiction*. She lives in County Mayo, Ireland, where she edits haibun for *Modern Haiku* and tweets micropoetry @shortpoemz.

THERMALING
digby beaumont
BLUE FIVE NOTEBOOK

MY BROTHER JOE TAUGHT me about crows. "They crave intimacy," he said. "They grieve for the dead."

A pair of the birds had nested on our roof. They would stare down at Joe through his skylight. When he played his violin, they cawed along with him.

Joe had this way of speaking—through his nose, puffing between words. His chest would rise and rattle, and his lips disappear, he pressed them so tight.

The night Joe died, Mum said, his airways just closed up on him. He was fourteen.

For weeks afterwards Mum sat in a lawn chair on the grass verge outside our house and waved at passing cars.

I'd hear squawking in the distance.

I often wonder about that night. If Joe felt alone in the world as he struggled for breath. Or if he looked up from his bed and saw those crows watching over him.

In my dreams Joe returns as a crow, gazing down at me through the glass. I reach up. "Don't be afraid," he says, before he leaps, and I'm not. I cling to his feathered back and we soar upwards into a tail wind. Gaining altitude. Our trail a whisper.

Digby Beaumont has had a long career as a writer. He has published numerous English language textbooks with Heinemann and Macmillan, including international bestsellers. His short fiction has been published widely in print and online literary journals and anthologies. In early 2020 he released a collection of flash fiction, one-page stories, *Dancing Alone and Other Lessons*. He is also an artist, working mainly on portrait and figure painting. He lives by the seafront in Hove on the South Coast of England. You can visit him at https://digbybeaumont.com/ or on Facebook: https://www.facebook.com/digby.beaumont.

GROWING UP

SOUTHERN REVIEW

talia bloch

On my father's desk sat a photograph, passport size, cracked and yellowed with age, tucked into the corner of a large frame. A boy's small face with round cheeks and large eyes peered out from it as I sat bent over my math homework, struggling through the numbers. The boy and my father had been friends back then. In the old country. They rode the tram together to school until, one night, it was burned to ash and glass, and they were forced to go to a different school. *Such a picky eater*, my grandmother used to say about the boy. *His mother had so much trouble with him. I made him spaghetti when he came to play, but even that he ate plain.* In the large frame was also a larger photograph of an old man sitting on a park bench in Upper Manhattan, wearing a cap and holding a cane. It was my grandfather, smiling at my father, now grown, holding the camera. When they left for America, my father was still a boy. There were three passports: one for my father, one for my grandfather, and one for my grandmother. For five days they took a boat across the ocean. In America they all lived in one room, but ate well. Passport size, but the boy's passport never came, so he stayed on as the burning spread and the ashes piled up to the skies. The murmurs of the murdered grew uncountable. *Even cheese and sauce he refused*, said my grandmother. Most nights I did my homework by the boy's photograph—thinking that he had died because he wouldn't eat.

Talia Bloch is the author of *Inheritance*, a collection of poems, published by Gold Wake Press. Recent poems have appeared in *Copper Nickel*, *Pleiades*, and *Prairie Schooner*. Her essays and feature stories have been published in places such as *The Brooklyn Rail*, *The Forward*, and *Tablet*.

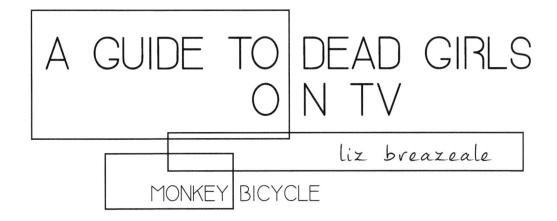

A GUIDE TO DEAD GIRLS ON TV

liz breazeale

MONKEY BICYCLE

1. Already Dead Girls

ALREADY DEAD GIRLS ARE easy to write; they do not require speech or action or emotion or growth.

They have been hoisted up, trussed, their hands starred out against a dark background. The men leave them dangling from ceilings or trees or hog-tied on the ground or yoked to bedposts, forgetting them as they forget roadkill, a rotted portion of scenery. The camera lingers on Already Dead Girls because their beauty is in their silence, in the space they do not take up, the bodies they no longer own.

Already Dead Girls are more dead than girl. They are lands waiting to be colonized. The husks of Already Dead Girls are the most valuable commodities in the world.

2. Dead Schoolgirls

A Dead Schoolgirl is Significant, forces Male Protagonist to remember his own Dead Child, his own Sorrowful Past. Proves Something Good still exists in him, the same way handing money to a homeless man does, or saving a cat from traffic.

Dead Schoolgirls never emerge from adolescence. Instead of blooming into young women, they blossom into bruises. They are the martyrs of Male Sins, so the brutality is more important than the girl. Because Male Protagonist needs something to react to, something to recoil from.

Even Male Protagonist is proven to be Sensitive, to be Good, by the deaths of Dead Schoolgirls.

The point of Dead Schoolgirls is to never exist. To be a void in a family photograph, an absence of footsteps, a house at which a school bus no longer stops. Their impact is in what they will not do, the women they will not become.

3. Sick Girls

Sick Girls are gentle creatures. They are brave. They look perfect in hospital beds, as though they have always lived there. They move so little that they are like jellyfish in aquariums, bobbing, strange and luminous and deflatable.

Sick Girls do not have wishes for themselves, only for their men, only after they are gone. Their victimhood is clear. They wear it draped over their bodies in lips so chapped it is like they are covered in spun sugar and faces made angelic by hollowness and veins the color of blue sky, veiled by translucent cloud skin.

For there is no ugliness in Sick Girls. There is only a suggestion of pain, a ghost of discomfort, a specter rattling pans and shifting furniture just out of sight.

4. Victims

Victims are white. They are vaguely Christian, probably virgins, conventionally pretty, with features that could be molded from any number of women. Sometimes they wear crosses on gold chains that are so thin they shimmer like seams of water.

Victims are not humans but receptacles of pain. And they have done nothing to deserve this violence, these unicorns of women. They are innocent in the way babies are—never quite actualized, never making decisions, never acting on their own.

Victims are the color of snow, the unpainted cheeks of dolls. They are checkboxes ticked by their relationships to men: Daughter, mother, sister, wife.

5. Not Victims

Not Victims are at fault, somehow, for walking alone or leaving their drinks unattended or going home with a stranger. Everything about them says they were asking for it, and this way no one actually needs to speak the words.

Their smudged lipstick, their dark nebulae of eyeshadow, all a Rorschach test, reflecting. The men do not touch them with care; their necks are like the necks of bottles, made of glass primed for shattering.

Police do not move urgently, not for Not Victims. An officer will joke about Not Victims' jobs or their appearances or what they were wearing. The others may not laugh, but no one says stop.

6. Actresses Who Play Dead Girls

When the day is over, the Dead Girl rises. She yanks on her clothes, snags her chignon on the back of her shirt, leaves the bun dangling, hair tickling her neck like fingernails. She snatches her purse, rushes off the set, across the lot, before anyone can remove her makeup, the constellation of injuries still patterning her face.

The Dead Girl claws her keys between her knuckles. She checks her backseat before entering her car.

It has been a long day. The Dead Girl laid in a morgue set for hours as actors, all men, perched their hands too long on her body, not violently, not angrily, but as though they did not notice her, this extension of their peripheral vision, this black-eyed set dressing. She could only take so much of it, sand castle body naked under the sheet, the air and the set and the fake morgue full only of men, their seafoam breath, their shark tooth words, their sea cliff bodies.

It reminded the Dead Girl, eyes closed, of other times she has pretended to be lifeless.

The Dead Girl stops at the grocery store. People ask, sweetie, are you all right? Do you need help?

The Dead Girl, for a moment, forgets the correct answers: Yes, she is fine. No, she does not need help.

When the Dead Girl gets home, she has no trouble recognizing herself in the mirror. She massages the palette of blue-black-jaundice yellow on her forehead, cheeks, circling her eyes, but it does not hurt, not in the way probing wounds should. It is a pressure, a dull fortified moment, and if the Dead Girl closes her eyes she wonders if she could tell who was doing the touching.

Because there were other times hands were laid on her, soft or calloused or empty or clenched, and each time she performed like today. Closed her eyes, focused without focusing on the patterns in the darkness, the swooping swirling pixels in colors shadowy and rich.

She begins to scrub. This seems like the correct way to bring herself back to life. Except it stains, the makeup, it clings to her skin.

Liz Breazeale received a 2020 Creative Writing Fellowship from the National Endowment for the Arts and won the 2018 *Prairie Schooner* Book Prize for Fiction for her first book, *Extinction Events: Stories*. She holds an MFA from Bowling Green State University and lives in Denver, where she works at the National Renewable Energy Laboratory and teaches at Lighthouse Writers Workshop. Her work has appeared in *Kenyon Review Online, Best of the Net 2014 & 2019, New Ohio Review, Hayden's Ferry Review, The Rupture, Pleiades, Fence, Fugue, Sycamore Review, Passages North*, and others.

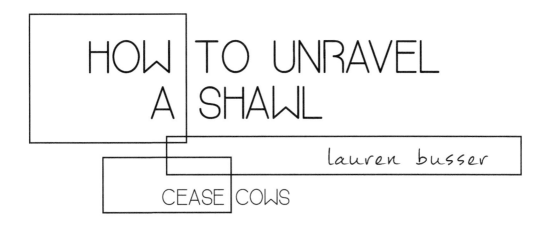

HOW TO UNRAVEL
A SHAWL

lauren busser

CEASE COWS

Size

THE SHAWL IS A scalene triangle that measures 80" in length at its longest point. You made it for her last Christmas after she looked at the similar one you made for yourself and called it pretty.

It was draped over a hanger in her otherwise empty closet with a note that it would have been "too sad" to take this with her. You assume the necklace you bought her for her birthday, and the novelty measuring spoons also fall into that category. So much for being like sisters.

It's splayed over your lap now with the long end over your left thigh and the right end on the floor. Your cat lays on the short side, her hair mixing with the hair of your former friend's dog.

Yarn

You bought two balls of expensive, naturally dyed merino wool and silk yarn for the project. It was spun into a thin lace weight that felt like the delicate crystalline strings of cotton candy when you worked with it.

She liked naturally dyed things. This one was dyed with indigo. It stained your hands so they looked like a large bruise as you worked, and you washed them frequently to try to hide the evidence.

Needles

The needles were dark and had impossibly low contrast to the blue yarn. It would have been easier with tips that allowed for sharper and more precise work, but that wasn't something that you thought of at the time.

Now you think of the hours spent working on this shawl and wished you'd made it easier on yourself.

Gauge

Gauge is important. It's always important. It helps with size and proportion, but you didn't pay attention and began knitting anyway. It didn't matter. You had 200 yards over what the pattern called for.

She and you were never exactly a match on paper. You were dark. She was light. You were calculated and organized. She was wispy and chaotic. You always imagined the twisted soul that put you together in a college housing office your freshman year.

She's the one that found this apartment. She bounced into the bar where you worked and showed you the listing. It wasn't an ideal part of town but the rent was cheap and she thought the bleak warehouse could be a home. You choked back your protests as she proclaimed her love for the space, and signed the two year lease with her.

Sitting here now, you're bitter you never spoke up. This will be your home for six more months.

Pattern Stitches and Techniques

You run your finger over the edge of the yarn. A picot bind-off made for a pretty, pointed edge. It reminds you of the way the roof leaked during the first big storm. Rain seeped through the cracks in the ceiling, collecting in pots that you found at a yard sale.

"We might be able to plug it up with a tampon," she said.

"Do you really think that's going to work?" you asked shaking your head.

During the next storm you came home to her attempting to plug the hole with a Q-tip.

"A tampon won't work!" she said.

She succeeded in something that looked like a plug twenty minutes later, throwing her hands up triumphantly. A line of raindrops ran down the cotton swab once it was saturated and continued to fall onto the floor.

Construction

At one corner of the shawl, fumble for the end you wove in. Slowly undo the slip-knot that holds this shawl together. Fold the end under the loop and away you go. Watch as the picot binding slowly unwinds until it doesn't exist.

Then the eyelets disappear.

Stop to wrap the yarn back into the ball periodically so that the delicate lace weight doesn't tangle.

Remember all the hours you spent reading the chart:

Purl across row.

Follow Chart B to introduce lace section.

Slip one, knit two, knit two together, knit to marker, make one right, slip marker, knit one, slip marker, make one left, knit to three stitches from the end, knit three.

The ball of yarn gets bigger in your hand and the shawl is starting to look a bit like a stingray.

Your memory is not so easy to erase. If only you can take back that night of crackers and wine and a giant game of Jenga. If only she hadn't fallen on top of you and giggled for a moment before brushing her lips against yours.

If only it had stopped there.

You watch each stitch come undone and try to forget the look on her face when she woke up the next morning. She wrung her hands and looked at you regretfully. And when you tried to talk about her feelings she clamped down and retreated into herself making excuses about being drunk and not herself.

The shawl disappears before your eyes and you mentally imagine that night fading with it. Think about the events of the night going backward like the picture on an old television set. The back further to the lease signing and meeting her at all, until the shawl is string again. Just potential. Nothing tangible.

Finishing

You set the backs of the two chairs together and move them a foot apart. Your cat jumps up and sits in the seat of one of the chairs as you wind the yarn around them. Soak the yarn for twenty minutes in tepid water. Wring out the access. Hang in a dry place with towels underneath it to dry, weighing it down with a hanger if necessary.

She didn't look at you for weeks after that, and then one day you came home from the bar to find her gone. Just a note.

The yarn dries overnight, and then you take it in two hands twisting it until it falls upon itself, tucking one end into another.

Store until the memories of her fade.

Lauren Busser is a writer of fiction and nonfiction. She is currently an Associate Editor at *Tell-Tale TV* where she reviews television and film. Her work has appeared in *Cease, Cows, Popshot Quarterly, Bending Genres, formercactus, five::2::one magazine's* #thesideshow, StarTrek.com, Bitch Media, and *The Hartford Courant*. She is a recipient of two awards from the Connecticut Press Club. When she's not talking about writing or television you can find her knitting or working on her novel.

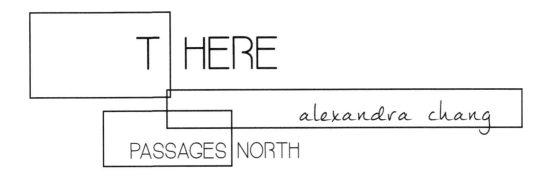

THERE

alexandra chang

PASSAGES NORTH

WHEN WE'RE IN HONG Kong, my dad points out places where his family lived and died. There's the pier where he first docked by ferry from Zhuhai, after a twenty-plus train journey from Shanghai. The communists couldn't reach you in Hong Kong—that 60 or so kilometers of sea, and the British, acted as a protective barrier. There's the hotel where an uncle and his lover killed themselves together, because she already had a husband and this was the 50s, when there was so much shame. I believe it was a room on the fourth floor, which would be appropriate, my dad says. In Mandarin, four and death are just an inflection away from one another. The mint green exterior peels with age, but once it was one of the best, most expensive hotels in the city. There are many suicides in this family, did you know? Another uncle killed himself in Shanghai around the same time, but at home, not in a hotel, and the reason was less apparent. He was just an emotional man. Back in Hong Kong, my father's grandfather had a gambling addiction and during one of his sprees at the casino, where everyone knew him by the way, where he spent a lot of money and was buddies with the owners by the way, he threw an angry, drunken fit after losing all his night's fortune and was asked to leave. Just as one of the owners was escorting him out, he had a heart attack and died on the casino floor. Would he have had the heart attack if they hadn't kicked him out? Who knows. The casino owners felt so bad about the incident that they paid for shipment of the body back to the mainland and for the entire funeral, where many friends and family came and mourned, but not my dad, who had already escaped by then even further to New York City after he'd jumped ship as a seaman with fifty dollars in his pocket and didn't return to Hong Kong for nineteen years, after the handover back to China, when the communists were less dedicated. Over there is where his brothers and mother stayed behind in Hong Kong and lived in an apartment in a district that used to have a lot of tea and noodle shops, but now is the expensive pet district where tiny pure-bred puppies sit in window displays, pressing their small bodies and noses against the glass. I take a hundred photos of the puppies, and two of my dad on a street corner where his family used to live in a little three story apartment building that is long gone and been replaced with a gigantic pink tower more than ten times the height. In the photos, he stands there beneath the street sign, pointing up at the words that signify this is the same place where he once stood, although nothing looks the same, expect maybe those thick, tall trees in the background.

Alexandra Chang is the author of the novel *Days of Distraction*. She is from Northern California, and currently lives in Ithaca, NY.

MONA LISA

rita ciresi

OVUNQUE SIAMO: NEW ITALIAN-AMERICAN WRITING

YOUR PARENTS DON'T KNOW Leonardo from Michelangelo. But like every other good *famiglia* on the block, they've got a chipped porcelain Last Supper plate hanging over the kitchen table. A plastic Pietà—purchased at the 1964 World's Fair—squats on top of the behemoth Zenith TV. And a warped canvas Mona Lisa smiles down from the dining room wall as you eat your fancy Sunday macaroni.

Since Mona Lisa hangs from a single nail without a frame, sometimes she leans to the left and other times to the right. *A destra, a sinistra. A sinistra, a destra.* Either way it doesn't matter. Mona Lisa creeps you out as much as the silver Jesus nailed to the wooden cross hung above the front door to keep evil spirits from entering the house. Jesus is skinny and Mona is fat. But at least Jesus is polite enough to look away when you steal another chocolate from the Whitman's Sampler that's supposed to be reserved for guests. Mona Lisa always has her dark eyes on you.

Mona sounds like *un pianto del bambino*, a baby's cry. *Lisa* reminds you of the only non-Italian girl in second grade—Lisa Ford, who has hair so blond that all the dark-haired girls surround her in the lavatory and fight for a chance to braid and comb it. Mona Lisa's dark hair looks like a bad wig. Her forehead is high as a nun's wimple. Her deep-set brow-less eyes remind you of basset hounds.

You don't want to look like Mona Lisa. You don't want to sit there and sorta-smile and watch people eat their Sunday ravioli. You want to be the one who gets to paint her. You want to be Leonardo sitting at the easel, dipping a brush into a palette of oil paints and shading the background blue and gray and mysterious purple.

You would give anything to be an artist and live in Rome where the hand of God reaches out to meet the hand of Adam on the ceiling of the *Cappella Sistina*. In Rome, you're sure even the pigeon poop smells better than the *cacca* you have to scrub off the window ledges here in America.

Oh, why did your family ever come to this country where the only real Italian things are fakes? You want to flee from the plastic Christ on the Pietà and apostles on the chipped Last Supper plate. This house is a jail and Mona Lisa the warden. She stares at you. She is watching *ovunque vada, qualunque cosa faccia*—wherever you go, whatever you do—and from her gaze you will never escape.

Rita Ciresi is author of the novels *Bring Back My Body to Me*, *Pink Slip*, *Blue Italian*, and *Remind Me Again Why I Married You*, and four award-winning story collections, *Female Education*, *Second Wife*, *Sometimes I Dream in Italian*, and *Mother Rocket*. She is professor of English at the University of South Florida, a faculty mentor for the Bay Path University MFA program in creative nonfiction, and fiction editor of *2 Bridges Review*.

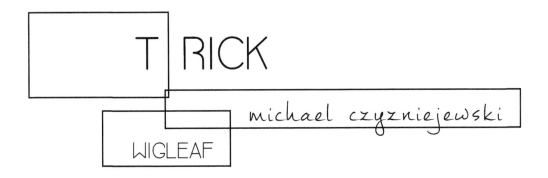

T RICK

WIGLEAF

michael czyzniejewski

MY FATHER ONCE TAUGHT me this trick: If ever I can't fall asleep, I should imagine undressing a woman. I should start with a woman I want to undress, which I knew would be easy, because there were lots. I should next imagine the woman in a specific room, the kind where we could be alone, my bedroom, or maybe the living room, when my parents weren't home. I should picture the time of day, the light quality, what time of year it is. I need to know what the room smells like, too, a robust candle burning, maybe some potpourri, make my brain smell its smell. After that, I should create a scenario, one in which the woman comes to this private, specifically lit, memorably smelling place. It could be a date or study session, or better yet, something more creative. Perhaps her car breaks down in front of the house and she needs to use our phone. Maybe it's raining. Then she'd need to get warm and out of her clothes. From there, I could begin. I should start with accessories, big rings and bracelets, any dangly jewelry, making sure to place it somewhere it won't get lost. Then the shoes—the woman should be wearing shoes, the kind that need untying and pulling off; boots would serve me best, the higher, the better. Next her belt, if there is one, and there should be. The pants should be a challenge—definitely pants, not a skirt and certainly not a dress, much too quick to remove, while pants need to be unbuttoned, unzipped, tugged from the hips. I should then undo her blouse, at least six buttons, if not seven or eight, letting the parted garment fall off her shoulders. This leaves her in just her bra and panties. At this point, I should take a step back and conjure a garter and stockings, fishnets or hose. While unclasping the stockings, I should take care to imagine the hardware, the workings of each clasp as it comes undone in my fingertips. Then go the stockings, one at a time, the woman's heel up on my shoulder. After that, the garter belt, pulled downward, careful to leave the panties in place. And while I'm at it, why not a bustier, or better yet, a corset, the kind with the x-crossings in the back, which have to be untied and unlaced? I should imagine each cross coming undone, the aglets pulling out of each and every eyelet until she's free.

My father stopped. I asked what came next, her bra or underwear. He didn't know: He'd never stayed awake that long. In fact, he'd been winging it since the pants, and he'd only gotten to the pants once. I asked how long he'd been using this trick and he said since he was my age; otherwise he'd lie awake and stare at his ceiling for hours. I asked him if this is why he slept in a different room from my mom. He said no, but immediately changed his answer to yes, then sort of. I asked if I could improvise at all, and he said I should definitely improvise—that's what the candle and jewelry and garter belts were, improvisation. I asked if I could kiss the woman as I undressed her. He asked if I meant on the lips, and I said sure, but other parts, too: her feet, her stomach, her neck and back. He said he'd never thought of that. I said, Really? He reminded me I didn't want to get agitated, that the purpose of the trick was to get me to fall asleep. I told him this was all pretty agitating already, me in my bed, candles lit, a shivering, grateful Mrs. Culkin (my seventh-grade social studies teacher) ready for my warming. My father said it wasn't about the ending but the process—all the eccentricities of women's clothing made undressing them complicated. That's why he chose undressing a woman over counting sheep or reciting state capitals: It was the process, not the reward, that would put me to sleep. Maybe I won't want to go to sleep, I told him. Maybe I'll want the reward.

My father shook his head, said that wasn't how this worked. I assured him that everything he told me was helpful, just not in the way he thought. I was sixteen—I stayed up until I couldn't stay awake anymore, then passed out the instant my head hit the pillow. You're lucky, my father said. Spoiled. He regretted sharing his trick with me. He grunted. I told him I would probably skip ahead, maybe to the garters, if not further, see what all this fuss was with bra hooks. I expected him to smile at this, but he was asleep, sitting upright on a stool at the kitchen counter. I considered helping him up to his room, but decided not to. He'd always made his way on his own, sooner or later.

In bed, I looked at pictures of women with their clothes already off. I couldn't help but think of my father down there. He could fall off the stool, hit his head, bleed out. I went downstairs, brought him halfway around, walked him up to his room. We passed Mom's door—she wasn't home yet. I rested my father on his bed, which smelled like wet concrete. I undid his boots, both a bitch to get off, then pulled off his socks. I peeled off his Carhartt bibs. I worked off his flannel and T-shirt. I tossed his ball cap on the nightstand. He was in his underwear and I was exhausted, felt my eyes growing heavy. I lay down beside him, too tired to move, unsure of what came next.

Michael Cyzyniejewski is the author of three collections of stories, *Elephants in Our Bedroom* (Dzanc Books, 2009), *Chicago Stories: 40 Dramatic Fictions* (Curbside Splendor, 2012), and *I Will Love You For the Rest of My Life: Breakup Stories* (Curbside Splendor, 2015). He is an associate professor at Missouri State University, where he serves as Editor for *Moon City Review* and Moon City Press. In 2010, he received a fellowship from the National Endowment for the Arts.

BOOK OF RUTH

kyle g. dargan

SHENANDOAH

THERE WERE HORSES ONCE in Weequahic Park. I cannot fathom their rippling chassis charging around the now paved half-mile oval, but this is true for many things Grandma Ruth told me about old Newark. My deficient imagination. Or my mind trained to see the city as I found it—one riot worse for wear.

She always spoke of that grandstand. Just east of it, the lake she watched me walk onto one winter as it was iced and snowed over. Falling in was my first physics lesson. Her arms pulling me out, my first salvation—the first of many things we'd learn to keep between ourselves.

The lake displaces the race track in my memory's legend. Tap that spot: *that's where I almost slipped under.*

Directly north from that point of recall, rose over the tree line, the brown-brick building where she lived. *I can run there*, I told her. Then begged her. Despite the spectre of me watching from under the lake's surface, she lets me trot the mile and half out the park and down Elizabeth Avenue—another thing between she and I. Her thunderbird curbing every few blocks to ask *you ok?* A decade later, I'd be a cross country athlete, but she hadn't seen the future. What she saw was will—the same that almost got me drowned in the lake—and she let it run.

Kyle Dargan is the author of five collections of poetry. His most recent collection, *Anagnorisis*, was awarded the Lenore Marshall Prize and longlisted for the Pulitzer Prize in poetry. He lives and works in Washington, D.C.

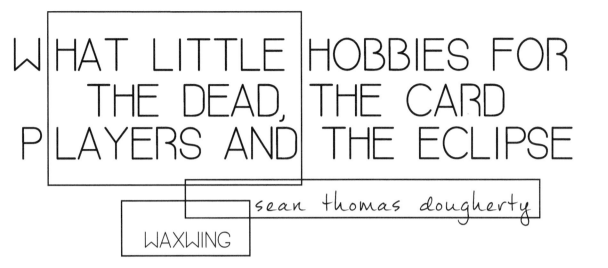

WHAT LITTLE HOBBIES FOR THE DEAD, THE CARD PLAYERS AND THE ECLIPSE

WAXWING

sean thomas dougherty

UNDER THE OAK TREE, the shadows of church going women hallalujahing, the Bingo players ecstatic shouts, all from the shades. The lungs begrudge me a smoke or two for letting them still breathe. I have nothing more to give away, except this evening's light as luminous as the last supper, our bones they speak in orchestrations as we were, I bend to shoot and the small crackling like the branches of a camp fire *to rise like an ember in the flame.* To hold the darkness of the branches in the backyard. Or a cold beer. I drink nothing less than the blues. I have no other habits left. Though sometimes at Wegman's bakery I stand there sweating, inhaling the breath of just baked bread. The only citizenship I claim is the mountain and the great lake. I have never saluted a flag or said a pledge, except perhaps *The Leaves of Grass,* or to Thoreau's diction to always resist. What do we care if all that is left is ruins, it is where we have always lived. Once though when I was small, and my mother took me to the coast of Maine, & I saw the wild sea roses rim the road and cliffs like a thorned crown. Or in the marketplace in Cleveland, the old Hungarian woman who handed me a great length of sweet sausage wrapped so quick yet carefully in white paper & then the day's newspaper tapped together with masking tape. Is that our true flag? The untamed and the stained? Who are our people those who emerge with poor unturned faces from doorways and windows, then run shouting despite the evidence each day I am waiting for a sign, a spark, I test the direction the wind might turn, & what will come with it? A Puerto Rican girl with barbed wire tattoos & a Social Distortion shirt, her plaid skirt hitched blatantly above her knee, a Syrian boy dribbling a soccer ball, not looking up for bombs, a bald white man laughing, chasing his wind-blown fedora? All of us tumbling down the avenues & roads looking for something, even the stray black dog, who trots around the corner, sniffs the air. His long and lopping expectant tongue. What does he taste? What does he *imagine* he will taste? & like birds who cursive across the sky, who are we if not something written with the body's ink across the page of the workday's dwindling hours, some testament to survival? Step by step, shift by shift, we pass even the saints. We become something closer to our dead. I ask for no wager except that others who come after to suffer a little less. In this life is another & another, & another that is this human nest. This daguerreotype divine or damaged—for what is damaged is closer to divine. I look up just in time to see the wafer of moon dissolve into the mouth of the dark.

Sean Thomas Dougherty is the author or editor of 18 books including *Not All Saints*, winner of the 2019 Bitter Oleander Library of Poetry Prize; and *Alongside We Travel: Contemporary Poets on Autism* (NYQ Books 2019)). His book *The Second O of Sorrow* (BOA Editions 2018) received both the Paterson Poetry Prize, and the Housatonic Book Award from Western Connecticut State University. He works as a care giver and Med Tech for various disabled populations, and lives with the poet Lisa M. Dougherty and their two daughters in Erie, Pennsylvania. More info on Sean can be found at seanthomasdoughertypoet.com.

WHAT YOU HAVE BEEN TOLD

molia dumbleton

FLASH FLOOD

COMB A STRAIGHT LINE down the scalp. Sweep half to one side.

Wrap elastic 'til the tiny pigtail stays in place, then do the other side.

Say, There. Good? Now teeth.

Wet the toothbrush, tuck it into the small, open mouth.

The eyes—her father's—are on you.

She says, Mama, too rough. Scrub each tiny tooth more gently.

Give the rear end a pat. Say, Pick out your clothes. I'll button you up.

Watch her go. Scrub your own face 'til it hurts.

Pour cereal, pour milk, set a spoon.

Unlatch the back door, light a cigarette, hear the highway.

See your dog paw at the gate. Feel even the smoke leave you.

Hear, Mama? Crush the cigarette, wave the smoke away, wave the dog inside.

Say, Yeah, baby? She wears a plaid sweater dress, open at the back, and knee socks.

She says, Buttons, please. Marry each small button with its tiny hole.

Then dress your self. Brush your own teeth. Marry your own fucking buttons.

Get there.

At school, from the top of the yellow jungle gym, feel the gaze of cruel-eyed girls.

Remember what you have been told:

Never let a child watch you leave. Let the child leave you first.

Feel the small hand inside yours, a hand you are responsible for, squeeze.

She says, Will you stay? Say, Yeah, baby.

In the bright light of the yard, see the hair's crooked part, the missed button, the spot of milk on the jumper.

Molia Dumbleton's first collection of short stories was a finalist for the Iowa Short Fiction Award, and individual stories from that collection have appeared in *Kenyon Review, New England Review, Cincinnati Review, SmokeLong Quarterly, Witness, Bath Flash Fiction Award Anthology, Bridport Prize Anthology,* and elsewhere, and been awarded various honors including the Seán O'Faoláin Story Prize and Columbia Journal Fiction Award. She is an Assistant Fiction Editor at *Split Lip Magazine* and a member of the Curatorial Board at Ragdale. She writes and teaches in the Chicago area.

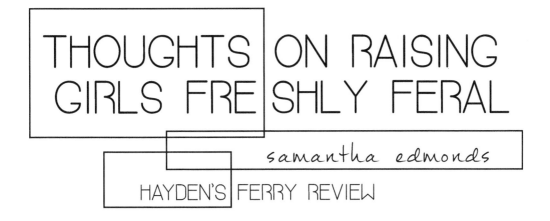

THOUGHTS ON RAISING GIRLS FRESHLY FERAL

samantha edmonds

HAYDEN'S FERRY REVIEW

THEY ARE CHILDREN OF the wood. They belong to the pack, the band, the herd, the flock. They know how to stand on four legs a shoulder's width apart on a mountainside and bellow, bear-like. Some leap mad as squirrels, loud and wild. Some stalk silent through sticks and bark, arm hair raised like fox hackles. Yet more bound after deer through yellow grass, faster on four legs than adult men are on two. Others grip tree limbs in horn-toughened toes and cackle-scream, jump so surely you will swear they are flying. They are a tangle, a tumble, of grass-painted skeletons, wearing crowns of leaves in their hair in a kingdom of branches.

Your job is to bring the girls home, teach them. When you arrive in their forest, booted-feet covered in mud, baseball cap on head, hair sticking to the back of your neck and flies too, the girls scream and flap skinny arms. Or they snarl and crouch on hands and knees, hunkered necks low. Or they rear on two legs and paw the air and blow through the nose, slap the ground with open palms. The men who led you here are dirty, experienced, unafraid. They look at their quarry and smile, clap each other on the back and say, *We're losing the light. Be easier to round 'em up in the morning.*

They build a fire and you sit near it, so close that your cheeks and calves start to burn. The forest is full of the children's night-noises: howling, snuffling, shaking tree branches. You scoot closer to the fire, even though the embers spark on your knees. The men sleep. You don't. You never close your eyes, not ever, in the dark around strange men. In one boot, you have stuck a can of mace. In the other, a pocket knife. Still, you stick close to the light. Your red nails are black from the dirt. Your cell phone doesn't work out here. You want to check your voicemail for a new message from your doctor, anxious to be unreachable but glad, too.

In the morning, the sleeping men will help you bring the children, girls all, to the city. To capture them, the men will have to get close to them, even though they stamp and stomp and scream and snarl. The men will come close and the men will touch them though they do not want to be touched and the men will put them in nets and cages and you will take them home, where you've been hired by an adoption company to teach them people things. You usually teach addition, subtraction, picture books like *A House for Hermit Crab*. But you need the money, you rationalize, remembering the voicemail you hope isn't there. These girls do not need math. They need you to teach them many things about being girls instead of bears deer squirrels stallions ravens beasts. You need the practice raising unwanted children.

Start by teaching them how to be afraid of the dark. They are not yet, not like you have learned to be, after years of using the bathroom in a group, never leaving your drink unattended at a party, locking your car doors in a late-night drive thru. Not them. They were raised by, and have become, creatures of the dark woods, hunters at home in the night, equipped with claws, a sense of their own capability, teeth that they do not use for smiling. Like you, they have had their survival depend on their awareness, scuttling through the trees, and, unlike you, they are alert, but not afraid. Unless you teach them to be, like you were taught.

No one knows for sure how they got here, in this tall national park a few hours from the state line. But you think you know. You can imagine the panic of new mothers holding daughters for the first time, thinking about everything this baby must un/learn to be a woman. How tempting it would be to never teach them, to instead leave them in leaves where they will never be touched except to sleep nose to tail with a fox, to lose oneself in the thick mat of bear fur, to pick insects from feathered backs. They will know the feel of soft moss under fingertips and what it is like to walk through the night and not be frightened of men. This way they are more rocks and branches and sharp edges than girls. A mother might wonder if it is necessary to teach them to shrink, to shy, to shake. Surely not these girls, they of the forest caves and cliffs and cold rivers and prickly brush. Perhaps as you wait you may start to wonder if you, too, should leave them—join them, even—right where they are.

Samantha Edmonds is the author of the chapbooks *Pretty to Think So* (Selcouth Station Press 2019) and *The Space Poet* (Split/Lip Press 2020). Her fiction and nonfiction has appeared in *The New York Times*, *Ninth Letter*, *Michigan Quarterly Review*, *The Rumpus*, and *McSweeney's Internet Tendency*, among others. A PhD student in creative writing at the University of Missouri, she currently lives in Columbia, MO. Visit her online at www.samanthaedmonds.com.

FLY SEASON

elizabeth erbeznik

FICTION SOUTHEAST

IN A ROOM WITHOUT furniture, the flies have nowhere to land. They flit from wall to wall, winged dirt, smearing the air around them.

Alice stops in the middle of the room and drops her bags to the floor.

The village, her guidebook says, is drab and hot as blazes. It has the distinction of being a big producer of manioc root. Its name, in Malagasy, means "waiting for a wife."

From her front porch, she watches flies crawl across an old woman's face as she naps beneath trees. Alice cannot name this strange flora. The landscapes of the southern hemisphere are illegible to her.

The old woman's mouth twitches in her sleep.

They say it is too hot for fleas. On the plateau, where temperatures dropped to the low 50s in July and she had shivered through rushed bucket baths beneath unfamiliar constellations, there had been fleas.

Her empty house was once a classroom. It smells strongly of chalk.

From her backpack, Alice pulls out a stack of photos and a roll of tape. She arranges photos on her wall, centering them in the dark rectangle where a chalkboard used to hang. She stops midway through the stack and looks at a photo of a man drinking coffee on a porch. She sets it aside, then changes her mind and hangs it up with the others.

The windows of her barren room have no glass. The flies let themselves in. Outside the window, past a printed cloth tacked to the wooden frame, she smells pigs. The first morning, she hears pigs squeal in the darkness. Their joy at the slop bucket sounds like pain.

After a month, furniture is delivered to her house in a cart. A bedframe, a table, two chairs and a bookcase. The bookcase is of course an indulgence.

Underneath the new bed, the rats make a nest. They scurry across her mattress in the dark of night. And it's not noise, but movement, that wakes her. Between her and the rat there is only the thin gauze of a mosquito net. The rat's eyes glow in the beam of her flashlight.

Routines are established. Alice wakes to the screaming of pigs. And sleeps to the scampering of rats.

She gets lice and buys expensive shampoo to treat it. Her ankles are ringed with the scars of infected flea bites.

Alice can't sleep when it rains. She listens to rain drum against the tin roof. A corner of her latrine crumbles beneath the onslaught of water. Mud bricks are left exposed.

The mail plane arrives on Wednesdays. She goes to the post office during the mid-day break at school, waiting for letters that, mostly, don't come.

He writes: I met someone. (I'm sorry).

She places a trap beneath her bed. Four nights in a row, she is startled awake by the noise of it snapping shut. Four mornings in a row, she bribes children to dispose of the bodies. A student gives her a kitten. It is the size of a full-grown rat.

She writes back: I hear rain in the middle of the night and wonder whose house will fall down next.

Bats settle into the rafters of her classroom.

There is nothing to do after nightfall. Wooden shutters are barred over every window. Stray dogs have empty streets to themselves. Insects hover around the naked bulb suspended from her ceiling. She sweeps them up each morning.

The smell of chalk clings to her clothes and hair.

Alice is twenty-three years old and strangers come to her for help. She learns to say "I'm not a doctor." She cleans their wounds anyway. She removes dirty bandages and peers at rotting flesh. Antibacterial ointment is poured over infections. A man knocks on her door and walks into her house with a razor blade. He hands her the blade and she understands that he wants her to cut a worm out of his foot. It is visible beneath his skin. She cannot help any of them. She gives away hydrogen peroxide, butterfly sutures and Band-Aids. She repeats that she is not a doctor.

There is no glass in her window to keep out the smell of pigs. Photos fall to the floor as chalk dust dries out the tape.

In the village called "waiting for a wife," people ask why she is unmarried. Some name eligible bachelors. Others wonder if she's been cursed.

A whistle hangs above her bed. Children play with it each day. Each night she wipes it clean.

One morning, she finds a cockroach in her coffee filter. It disappears into a corner, behind a tank of propane gas. She rinses the filter, fills it with coffee, and lights the stove with a match. The kettle does not whistle. Sweetening her coffee with condensed milk, she takes it outside to drink on the porch.

In the heat of the day, she brushes away the flies that land on her hair. On her face. On her legs, stretched out across the bed for a mid-day nap. Days it is too hot, too close for the mosquito net.

"Fly season," says the director of the elementary school.

Each day begins when she unbolts the shutters. Voices, and light, and flies stream in through the window. What sounds like pain is just the rapture of pigs.

Elizabeth Erbeznik grew up in California and currently lives in Austin, Texas. She earned a PhD in Comparative Literature and works in the field of international education. "Fly Season" is her first piece of published fiction.

OSTERIZER CLASSIC SERIES 10 CYCLE BLENDER

emily everett

ELECTRIC LITERATURE

I HIGHLY RECOMMEND THIS blender and came here to say so. Since people buy for their homes on Amazon now, I thought I should leave my review where the most shoppers will see it. I have the original version—Oster have rereleased it this year in their "Classics Collection," but I'm sure the new one is just as good.

My husband and I received this blender for a wedding present in 1975, in a color called Harvest Gold, though it's really more chartreuse than gold. My mother-in-law ordered it from the Sears catalog with a 10-year warranty—she told me, I think, to make sure I knew just how much she'd spent on it, how much she could *afford* to spend on it. But I can assure you we never needed that warranty (and the joke's on her in the end, since the Osterizer has far outlived her).

A lot of things in our kitchen at that time—all around our home for that matter—were second-hand, so the blender was quite a novelty. But with my husband and I both working full-time I can't pretend it got a lot of use. Mostly we used it to crush ice for drinks, to be sipped while dinner was in the oven. Everyone was drinking Harvey Wallbangers at that time, OJ and vodka with Galliano floating on top. Crushed ice made them seem fancier, and in the early days of a marriage it can be important to pretend things are a little better than they really are, even to each other.

I wasn't much of a cook, but when our old college friends came over I'd try to make something really special so it didn't feel like we were just playing at being adults. I learned to make fondue—blending cottage cheese, cheddar, and heavy cream—from the Standard Osterizer Recipes cookbook.

It was the '70s—we could've been doing a lot worse than chipping ice for our mixed drinks. But we were still young in our own quiet way: we read poetry aloud in the den, Frank O'Hara and John Ashbery, and sang Beatles covers around an acoustic guitar. Surrounded by friends, everyone swaying into the couch cushions—I always felt so pleased with us in those moments. Later when the house was quiet, arms full of cups and ashtrays, I'd tell my husband what a nice night it had been, and he'd say that every night with me was a nice night.

It seems like I was always chipping ice for one thing or another. Snow cones were a lifesaver. Our twins always wanted a big birthday party, all their friends and a scavenger hunt around the house and our little yard. Since I'd stopped working by then, I could make my own fruit juice syrup instead of buying so much ice cream, and crush the ice fine as dust in the Osterizer. Almost a decade of birthday photos show the girls stained nose to chin with wine-colored juice—faces turned up to the camera lens, both arms twisted around each other's shoulders.

As they got older, I found more time to cook. I applied myself to the Osterizer and its recipe book, and it rewarded me with quick breads, soups, salsa, even pancakes for slow Saturday mornings. Our kitchen was modest, and each year the new Sears catalog tempted me with shiny steel Oster appliances we couldn't afford. But eventually I did save up for just one: a toaster that fit eight slices at once—perfect for the four of us. I've heard people say that you should always eat dinner "as a family," but in my house breakfast was our time. At the table, before the frantic dash for books and bagged lunches, I soaked up their company. It was something to inhale, like a breath kept swelled inside until they returned from work and school and sports.

The year we both turned 60 my husband and I decided to start eating healthy and walking more, so only frozen fruit and leafy greens went into the blender. But his health seemed to get worse, not better. It was hard to find something to cook that didn't bother his digestion. Then, the same week my daughters brought the grandkids for a visit, a doctor diagnosed him with stomach cancer. It was triggered by a very common bacterial stomach infection, a very treatable thing had we known it was there.

The details are not important for the purposes of this review, but I will say that the Osterizer is very good for pureeing foods. Anyone who has ever taken care of a loved one at home knows that there's a time when swallowing becomes difficult, and from then on neither liquids or solid foods are advisable. And there's a time too when blending food to mush is the only thing you can do for someone, and so you do it with fierce concentration as if it were the most challenging recipe you'd ever prepared. There's even a time, though it seems impossible, when you will miss this unappetizing task, and all the other tasks, and long to do them again.

I hope this review will urge some newlyweds to buy this blender, or put it on their wedding registry. I have been to a fair number of weddings in my life, and I always gift the couple an Osterizer if I can find one. I suppose it's my way of setting them up for all of it, the best way I know how. My daughter, I remember, playfully rolled her eyes at us when she unwrapped hers, but the next week invited us over for margaritas straight from the blender. We brought over old records to play on the new turntable, another gift. It was a perfect night, and I told my husband so as we brushed our teeth before bed. Every night is a perfect night with you, he told me.

———————————

Emily Everett is managing editor of *The Common* magazine. Her work appears in *The Kenyon Review*, where it was selected as runner-up for the 2019 Short Fiction Contest. Other short fiction appears in *Electric Literature*, *Tin House*, and *Mississippi Review*. She lives in western Massachusetts, where she is working on a novel about a family farm during World War II.

OF CHINWOKE

adachioma ezeano

FLASHBACK FICTION

PAPA DIDN'T DRINK THE pap I passed him. Papa just picked six pieces of the bean-cakes and pushed over his plates. Chinwoke would have run to Papa. He would have taken the remaining bean-cakes, carried the pap, run. He would not want me to get to the food before he does. Chinwoke would eat them, lick his lips, make faces at me. He ran with food as if he knew he would not be around to have much of it in this life. Chinwoke isn't here today. Chinwoke wasn't here yesterday. Chinwoke will not be here tomorrow.

I packed the plate and poured the pap away. I was cooking yam, serving the sympathisers. Foamy water spilled from the yam on fire, pushed up the pot cover while boiling, forming ball-like clouds. Chinwoke would describe the process as evaporation or something like that. Smoke from the firewood goes to heaven. I wish it sees Chinwoke. I wasn't multi-tasking as Mama would love me to, but Mama didn't snap at me as usual. If things were as things should be, Mama would pull my right ear, say, stop being lazy. But not today. We feared death. Death hovered around. We heard it on the lips of a new widow. We saw it lie in the eyes of a new widower, new orphans, new fatherless and motherless. We knew it as something that happened to others. We didn't expect it to find us.

In our life before, by this time, Mama would have spread her legs on the raffia mat. And we would surround her, listening to her stories that tasted like our favourite foods. Papa too, would lie on his wooden seat, sniffing and staring. He gave orders sometimes, maybe to Chinwoke, maybe to me. Fetch me water. Get my tobacco. Bring me stool. Where is my mat.

However, tonight, the moon hid behind the dark and nobody told tales. Even Chinwoke, who always has something to tell, is silent too. Did Professor not promise to take him overseas? The

Professor said Papa was also that brilliant when they were in elementary school, but Papa had to leave school because Papa's Papa fell from the palm tree and died, and Papa's Mama suddenly became sick and died. People said her husband, Papa's Papa dragged her with him.

Papa did not let Chinwoke go overseas with Professor. He didn't say a particular reason. He just kept saying you don't know this boy, as my only son, will bear my name? But the day the Biafran soldiers came, carrying guns and swear words, took all the young men for conscription, Papa said nothing, and when they brought back Chinwoke's corpse, Papa still said nothing. He shook his legs till Chinwoke was lowered in his grave.

Mama asked if I had brought the yam down. I stood up, dusted ash off my wrapper, brought down the yam, and sieved hot water from the yam. I served the food, kept a share for Chinwoke.

Adachioma Ezeano works with First Bank of Nigeria during the day, writes at night. She is an alumnus of the 2018 Purple Hibiscus Trust Creative Writing Workshop taught by Chimamanda Adichie. Her works have appeared in *McSweeney's Quarterly*, *Deyu African*, *Brittle Paper*. By Fall, 2020, she would be moving to the University of Kentucky for an MFA.

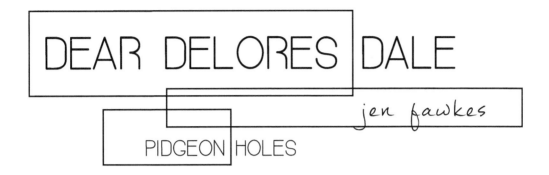

DEAR DELORES DALE

PIDGEON HOLES

jen fawkes

I REPRESENT THE ESTATE of one Walter K. Brennan, owner of a popular Midwestern chain of fast-food eateries. Twelve days ago, Mr. Brennan lost a brief but grueling battle with esophageal cancer, and I have now disposed of his assets as instructed, with the exception of a single item—an item he bequeathed to you.

I know you never met Walter Brennan, Mrs. Dale, and are probably wondering what I am playing at. If I am some psycho merely masquerading as an attorney. Let me assure you, nothing could be further from the truth . . . though at times I think I might prefer institutional life to shaking hands and arguing cases, to sitting in snarled traffic and sighing and making occasional love to my dear wife.

Walter Brennan saw you only once, at a Dairy Queen fifty-eight years ago, and in his words you "stole his heart." So that is what he left you.

Obviously I cannot excise Mr. Brennan's heart, cure it, and ship it to you. I was his attorney for sixteen years, but I never saw the man cry or even smile until the morning he sat across from me describing your lips as they curled around the stripy straw through which you drank a vanilla milkshake six decades ago. On that morning, Mr. Brennan broke down, sobbed so hard I was forced to lend him my favorite handkerchief.

And last night, when I asked my dear wife how on earth to honor Walter K. Brennan's strange bequest, she smiled sagely and asked me one question.

What did you do with that handkerchief?

Please forgive the state of my handwriting, Mrs. Dale. I have never before composed a piece of correspondence upon a hankie.

Yours Most Sincerely,
Paul Wainscot, Attorney-at-Law

Jen Fawkes's debut story collection, *Mannequin and Wife*, is forthcoming in September 2020 from LSU Press. Her fiction and nonfiction have appeared in *One Story, Crazyhorse, The Iowa Review, Shenandoah, Joyland, Michigan Quarterly Review*, and elsewhere. She is the winner of the 2019 Pinch Award in Fiction and the 2019 John Gardner Memorial Fiction Prize from *Harpur Palate*; her stories have also won prizes from *Salamander, Washington Square*, and others. Jen is a four-time Pushcart Prize nominee and two-time finalist for the Italo Calvino Prize in Fabulist Fiction. She lives in Little Rock, Arkansas, with her husband and several imaginary friends.

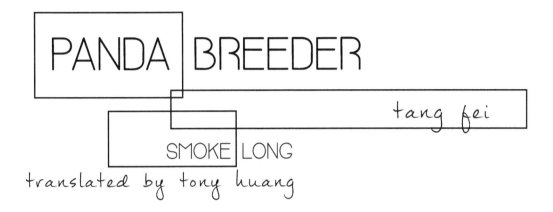

PANDA BREEDER

SMOKE LONG

tang fei

translated by tony huang

THE PANDA BREEDER CAME to the zoo earlier than the panda. This was a dangerous forced landing. Unprepared. Everyone was shocked when this howling baby appeared in a lion's cage. He was naked, energetic, unashamed, like a beast. His crying penetrated the clouds and could even scare the gods in heaven. The lions dismissed the idea to add a meal, and the zoo director decided to break the long-established employment policy.

The panda, which was only five months old, was brought to the panda breeder. They hugged tightly, prattling, drinking the same thick and gamy milk, and growing up together in an imaginary green bamboo forest. From a distance, it is difficult to tell which is human, but if you venture to get closer to this pair of untamed animals, you will see the gloomy green light shimmering in their eyes. The zoo director was satisfied with this arrangement, and felt he should be able to retire with peace of mind. A week later, the kind old man left the zoo with a sense of loneliness that was exclusively possessed by people outside the cage.

Four years later, the old man returned to the zoo, this time as a visitor, for some ineffable, yet reasonable reasons. He held his excitement down and visited other animals one by one before his beloved panda hall. Surprisingly, he did not see the two intimate figures in the artificial green bamboo forests. After many inquiries, the old man learned the following fact:

On a Sunday afternoon, in front of the zoo visitors who crowded the panda hall, the panda breeder blatantly bit and killed the docile and sophisticated animal he raised. When this happened, the panda, just like what it often did, was showcasing all the talents a stout animal like it could have. It rolled on the floor, stood straight, bowed, walked on string, and stood on rollers. While showing its deftness, it also spent the same effort pretending to be clumsy, to be tempted by the food, to be intoxicated by the applause, to stumble and to struggle to stand up.

Exactly at this moment, the panda breeder dashed toward the panda and slammed the poor, and still clowning, animal onto the floor. Amid frightened screams, the breeder bit into the throat of the animal and tore it into pieces.

In court, the panda breeder confessed to his crimes. In order to evoke the breeder's conscience, the defense lawyer tried to remind him of the life of the panda, but the breeder just briefly took it with a few words of contempt. He laughed at the animal's weakening body, mocked its becoming gluttonous, and claimed that he had never taught the animal to juggle or play the fool.

Finally, when asked about the motivation, he answered, unexpectedly, "I just want to see if in the body of this beast hides the soul of a dog."

Tang Fei, SFWA member, is the author of "Wu Ding's Journey to the West" and "Addiction," etc. She is also the author of a short-story collection, *The Man Who Sees Whales*, and a novel, *The Unknown Feast*. Many of her short pieces have been translated and published in the UK, the US, Australia, Japan, Korea and Italy. Her recent work "Wu Ding's Journey to the West" is a runner-up of Favorite SFT from 2019. She also writes literary criticism and poems, and is interested in photography and other art forms.

Tony Huang is the founding editor of *The Hong Kong Review*, an international literary journal that is based in Hong Kong and Tianjin, China. He is also the founder of Metacircle Fellowship, Metacircle (Hong Kong) Culture and Education Co., Ltd. and Metaeducation. His poems and translation have appeared in *The Hong Kong Review*, *Tianjin Daily*, *Binhai Times*, *Nankai Journal*, *Large Ocean Poetry Quarterly*, *SmokeLong Quarterly* and other places. He teaches British and American literature and literary theories at Nanka.

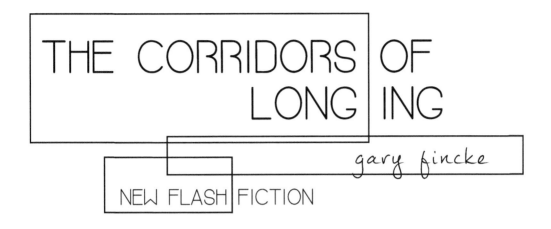

THE CORRIDORS OF LONGING

NEW FLASH FICTION

gary fincke

1

AT TWILIGHT, DRIVING ROUTE 8, my father refused the headlights, saving, he said, the bulbs. Three lanes, that road, passing a dare. Always, the oncoming cars would flash the code for fear, but still he blinded us, ready, traveling Route 8, to hoard the minutes and challenge the darkness, proving, by the mile, he could see to drive by passing the brightly lit.

2

She was flicking the headlights on, then off, sending some signal into the game lands where we'd parked, creating, before I opened her blouse, the evening and the morning of the first day, telling me we were alone as Adam and Eve, reciting the passages about births from clay and rib, God's recipes so simple, yet perfect, flicking the lights again as if she wanted God's finger pointing at us as I found her breasts in the dark, secretive as the newly created, in love with the knowledge of her body, saying "yes" to whatever she believed about dirt and bones.

3

Twice in twenty years my father had laughed. I admit that he may have chuckled when I was absent, when he became his secret self, free of the need for work and the God of restraint. More than once, more often than he smiled, my father said he felt sorry for me, meaning I would live to experience the world's end by God or man. Hopeless was a thing he saw in others. What's said and done was proof.

4

Because she sang soprano in a church choir, my father worshipped her visits and never tried my room's closed, but unlocked door. He blessed our privacy, turning up his television so we could hear approval played by the champagne music makers while her thrumming pitched into a shriek I fractured with my urgent hand.

5

When the road seesawed, narrow and choked by forest to the shoulder, my father slowed for stories, each one ending with "I meant to" as if expecting a huge migration of the dead to cross the road from one wooded darkness to another, his parables meant as headlights. "Wives are meant to be widows," he said, the night shaking its shaggy head as it shredded a skinny album of ancient photographs.

6

Always, she said, the worst thing is safety. Warnings are exhausting, I said, and watched the road testify, tirelessly perjuring itself. Always, I thought, the worst thing is loneliness. That day's driving was an examination. My symptoms were caution and concentration, the radio loud and without mercy until she unzipped me and sang "speed" to my body.

7

My father dreams my bones, wakens to trace my face with his fingers, telling me how scientists reconstruct the faces of the ancient dead from their salvaged skulls, and I overhear his wish to be a curator for immortality, arranging selected photographs throughout our house until my mother is perfectly displayed,

8

Sometimes, I've learned, the eyes of birds weigh more than their brains. Sometimes their bones weigh less than their feathers. Sometimes, while touching her face, I became a boy who believed her eyes exclaimed "Yes, go on," because, sometimes, undressed, she felt so light her body lifted toward me, extraordinary as the moment she became an etched inscription on a mausoleum plaque—she was, she loved, she would have—an odd conjugation of loss, a wound in the private museum of the past, the corridors for longing where light is interrupted by the stunned levitation of her accident.

9

Even as we park beside the house sold twenty years ago to strangers, even in the front yard so small a child could hop, skip, and jump across it, I can't hear one word from my father who has made me drive here to remember. Traffic coughs its constant jargon. At the end of the street, two houses down, the world ends at a cliff blasted one lot closer for a widened highway. My father, from where we're standing, tries to distinguish an old path become a wide, astonishment of air.

10

Where my father and I are now, the wires are down, and the rain manages the back road. A channel opens beside us. The squall hoards our light. Pulled over on the shoulder, shuddering in the dark, I am asking Siri for directions. *Please repeat*, she says, *I do not understand you.* My father whispers, "Who is that, someone you know?"

Gary Fincke's books have won The Flannery O'Connor Prize for Short Fiction, The Robert C. Jones Prize for Short Prose, and the Elixir Press Fiction Prize. His latest collections are *The Sorrows* (Stephen F. Austin, 2020) and *The Out-of-Sorts: New and Selected Stories* (West Virginia, 2017). His stories, poems, and essays have appeared in such periodicals as *Harper's*, *The Paris Review*, *Ploughshares*, *Poetry*, and *The Missouri Review.* He is co-editor of the annual international anthology *Best Microfiction*.

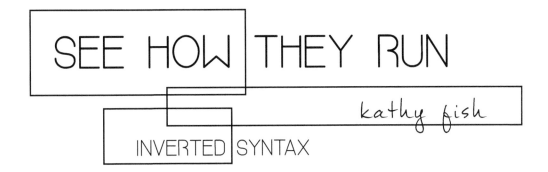

SEE HOW THEY RUN

INVERTED SYNTAX

kathy fish

SEE THE GIRL FIRST. See her large family moving in next door. How it twins your own. One girl, so many brothers. How they are different. How they are so thin and pale. How their faces look like masks of children. How even at five, you see that you and yours are stronger, wilder. How your brothers are already collecting rocks and loading them into the Radio Flyer. See the girl's strange shoes, like the stiff, white booties they corkscrew onto the formless feet of babies. How she is your age, maybe. Watch and wait. Let them approach first, says your brother, the tactician. How your backyards share the long, tall fence along the alleyway where rhubarb grows. Establish the battleground. Roll the wagonload of ammo behind the houses. Come out, come out you cowards. How they call back like girls, We don't like you at all, at all, at all. How they go door-to-door holding what look like soup cans. How the mothers stand warily behind screen doors, nodding. How you offer to go stomp on the girl's ugly shoes. How your brothers deign to swing their gaze your way. Do it! She won't even feel it. How they wager you won't have the guts. But you do. How she lowers herself to the grass, then. How calmly she unlaces her shoe, rolls down her anklet, examines the blood. If you could just have a moment, you'd sit next to her and explain about wanting to be seen. Her brothers, though. Screaming. Your brothers, though. See how they run. How your mother yanks you up by one arm and flails like she's shaking out a rug. Your mother. If I ever see you harm that girl again...How you never end up playing with those kids, that girl. No battle ensues. How the mothers, one afternoon over coffee and cigarettes, broker a detente. They barely leave their house, then, those kids. Until the day an ambulance rolls up the alleyway and hauls their mother away. See their hands, raised up over the top of the fence like morning glories, waving goodbye.

Kathy Fish is a member of the Core Faculty, Mile High MFA, Regis University, Fast Flash Workshops. She is the author of *Wild Life: Collected Works* from 2003-2018 and a Ragdale Foundation Fellow. She has stories forthcoming in *Copper Nickel, Washington Square Review, Literature: A Portable Anthology* (Macmillan), and *The Norton Reader* (W.W. Norton).

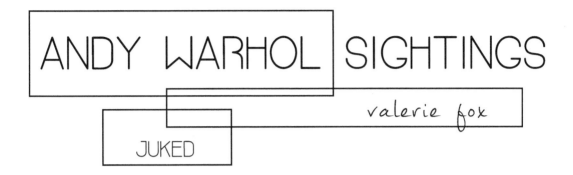

ANDY WARHOL SIGHTINGS

valerie fox

JUKED

IT'S ANDY WARHOL, WEARING a black, woolen cape, in a hamburger joint in California and chatting up a college kid. He's being personable and seems to expect the student to pay his tab. Not that Andy Warhol isn't good for the cash, but he isn't sure how to go about settling the check. Should he wait for the waitress? Should he approach the counter? Hm. Up until this point no one has asked him for money. Is it because they want to give him his Coke and hamburger for free, like he has a special coupon?

Andy Warhol cocks his head. He sticks up for a local indigent vet, also in the hamburger joint, who has forgotten his money. He gets his new friend the college kid to pay for the vet's meal. Andy Warhol has a lot of compassion for those returning from the war, or even for those who were stationed up in Alaska. Up there it's so cold people can rarely go outdoors in the morning and enjoy cappuccino and talk with friends. He and the vet take a picture together. Andy Warhol's regular entourage is unable to film the encounter because they are at the Amish market taking part in cheese-making.

Andy Warhol takes his stuffed lion out for a walk. No one stops him to make dumb cracks about Pittsburgh, his hometown. He rests in the town park on a bench near a vintage statue of Theodore Roosevelt. He takes over the local newspaper, known as *The Daily Trout*, one hand tied behind his back, and goes fishing. Andy Warhol visits the elementary school and talks to the children about what life used to be like before we all had electricity.

Meanwhile, back in the city, when Andy Warhol is shot, there is this sudden absence. Somebody has to temporarily take Andy Warhol's place in the lively diorama lodged in the minds of art lovers all over the world, next to other lions.

The mercury-colored cloudlike balloons Andy Warhol favors wander mote-style across his closed eyed, hidden by dark sunglasses. These are the same sunglasses donned by Andy Warhol that time he was going down the Mississippi in an old riverboat. This is the tie Andy Warhol wore when he was having lunch with Andy Griffith, who was not wearing a tie. Andy is giving Andy some sound advice about a quandary in his love life. Just ask Elvis with his cowboy gun. Time, Andy, fleeting, etcetera, etcetera.

Valerie Fox's books include *The Rorschach Factory*, *The Glass Book*, and *Insomniatic*. She's published prose in *Cleaver, Reflex, NFFR, The Cafe Irreal, Ellipsis Zine, The A3 Review, Across the Margin,* and *Literary Orphans*. A story she wrote is included in *The Group of Seven Reimagined: Contemporary Stories Inspired by Historic Canadian Paintings*. Valerie has co-written work with Arlene Ang (poetry, fiction). Recently, she published *The Real Sky*, a handmade artist's book (sketches, words) in an edition of 26, with artist Jacklynn Niemiec. She teaches writing at Drexel University (Philadelphia), where she's a faculty writing fellow with Writers Room.

XO TRAINING

molly gabriel

JELLYFISH REVIEW

THE EARLY BIRDS GET there right at 3:30 p.m. Those of us hosting the shower set our boxes of centerpieces and gifts aside. I wipe snow from my hair. My face tingles with heat. The principal stands at the front of the gymnasium with the fabric of her red dress pulled tight at her belly.

"Today's meeting is actually a training," she begins. We wait for those stragglers to file in from the back of the gym to their chairs. They sit still muttering to one another. "Given the circumstances." The circumstances. (The shooting.)

"The district sent a video. We will watch it together. I've been asked to give you the following information before viewing."

The information: the video illustrates the shooting using symbols. "They want us to understand *how* it happened," she says. "They want us to ensure that we *learn* from this tragedy." They. The district. The families. The government. The news.

"The symbols are simple—just like in football plays." Some of us murmur since we have never understood football, let alone its plays. She provides us the verbal key. A few of us take notes.

X is the shooter. O is the victim. A white O is *blank* meaning undamaged. (Safe.) Yellow indicates shot and injured. (Hospitalized. Bills to be paid.) Red symbolizes, the principal clears her throat, expired. (Dead.) She provides this key as she absently rubs her belly. She turns to the screen dragged in for our meeting. Presses play.

First is the schematic of the building. Free of Xs or Os. We are given a bird's-eye view. Hallway. Classrooms. Bathrooms. Stairwell. I recognize the floorplan from my time there as substitute right after college. I lay my pen beside my notebook. I force myself to breathe.

X appears in the hall. He moves. His pace is slow but energized like a jungle cat prowling the glass of a cage in a zoo. A herd of circles emerge from the stairs. Seeing X, they flee. X stops. Red O. Red O. Red O. The yellows dart around the corner with a few remaining whites. One yellow remains astride the reds. X approaches. Yellow blooms red. X looks after the escaped O's. We feel him sniff the air. Red O's pimple the now emptied hall. X resumes his hunt.

The video has no sound. The gymnasium thrums with stillness like held breath. Gasps. A few men talk in faux casual tones. The woman next to me whispers, "I'll fucking run. I will not leave my son to my ex-husband. I'm not playing hero." I glance away from her. I'm sick about the cake.

Os now understand. Os huddle in corners of classrooms. The video emphasizes X moving to doors and Os quickly metamorphosing to yellow to red again again again again again again.

The video times out with ten red Os left on the first floor. We know, from local news, that there are seven still not shown. We forget how many yellows have been depicted or ignored. The principal clears her throat. She picks up a sheet of paper from the table at the front. "The shooter killed himself after slaying seven more students. He shot and injured more than twenty."

I put my face in my hands. (*That fucking cake.*) "We expect a swift reaction." She looks up from her script. District orders, her eyes indicate, but also moral decency. We are *expected* to play hero. The woman next to me chews at her thumbnail.

"From our training today, we expect you to go to your classrooms and cover your windows." Complaints rise up and float through the gym. *What will paper really do?* "We don't want him to be able to see our students and get a good shot." Him. X. Our still-to-be-determined shooter.

"We also ask that you mark safe corners with X's of tape as a visual indication to students that they are safe from view. The best place to hide in an event of"
it hangs there. We complete it in our minds. *A shooter. An emergency. The end.*

She says more. I hear her voice, but over it *x marks the spot x marks the spot* runs through my mind.

I try not to cry for the cake.

The men mostly drift away after the presentation though I wrote in my email that *all* were invited. We push tables and chairs closer together. We lay down pink and red tablecloths. We stand up centerpieces: baby bottles stuffed with pink bouquets of posies punctuated by balloons that read *Oh, Baby!* in bubbled text.

I hold my breath as Ms. Boddie carries over the white baker's box. She opens it. *XOXO Baby Valentine.* The swirling, sugared longhand now jeering and grotesque.

Principal Valentine forces a smile. She lifts her hand from her taut red dress. She smooths her hair, says, "Oh ladies, I love it."

Someone sings, "Who wants the first piece?" A knife is produced. I shake my head, declining the honor of cutting my shame cake. Ms. Boddie offers her hand. The knife grows longer in her tiny fingers. She sinks the blade into the *XO* and its buttercream backdrop. She drags the knife to the edge. She frees a square. The yellow flesh, once exposed, makes our mouths water with fear.

She lays it gently, as if on a stretcher, obscuring the *Oh, Baby!* at the plate's center. Hands it off.

Molly Gabriel is a writer and poet whose work has appeared in *Jellyfish Review, Hobart, Okay Donkey Magazine,* and as Flash Fiction Editor's Pick in *Barren Magazine.* She is the recipient of the Robert Fox Award for Young Writers. She lives in Cleveland, Ohio with her husband and toddler. She's on Twitter at @m_ollygabriel.

RUNNING AWAY DIARY

avital gad-cykman

LIFE IN, LIFE OUT (MATTER PRESS)

Monday

I LEFT A LITTLE late for work and hurried to the bus station, when I realized I couldn't remember where I worked. I looked at the route map and chose to go downtown. In one of the alleys, I met my son. He asked me what I was doing there. I told him I was at work. He said he was at school. We hooked our elbows together and went to an Arabic bar to have a coke.

Tuesday

An old friend from high school, Rona Cohen, sent me an email full of memories I could not remember. I did not want to insult her, since she had been one of my best friends. I wrote her back, inventing more memories about people whose names she had mentioned. I wrote: "Do you remember how Arnon rang the bell of an old man's house like a madman? The old man chased after him screaming he'd kill every trespasser and they ran until I couldn't see them anymore.

She wrote back: "How could I forget? The old man died from a heart attack in the middle of the chase. It really marked me."

Wednesday

I carried a plastic bag full of sour cheese to the garbage can where I would not smell it. As I passed the gate, two boys chased a dog right at me. Its paws ripped the plastic bag, and the cheese covered us both. The boys ran away and the dog licked my shoes. I caressed its back until it finished eating.

Thursday

My daughter said we were out of water. I showed her the mineral water standing beside the yellow mustard.

She peeked at it and said, "We're out of everything."

Friday

A baby-girl with soft cheeks raised her large eyes at me. Her mother was smoking and drinking coffee by a café's counter. I picked up the baby and held her to my chest. She rested there with trust for a moment, then started screaming.

The smoking woman snatched her away. "What is it with you?" she asked.

I said, "I'm sorry. I could not help it."

Friday

When I looked up, the family was gone. I turned on the TV and watched a woman having a breakdown in an open field. I turned off the TV. Instead, I read a short story by an American writer, whose name was lost for me. It was about adultery. I took the daily paper. The weather prediction was that of too much rain.

Friday

The telephone rang. Before I said anything, a man said, "Sorry. It's a wrong number."

Thursday

A man with a brown stash of hair started following me. He went everywhere I did, keeping a few steps behind me, and when I was home, he waited behind the thick bushes and peeped into the house. I didn't mind it. I opened the window to invite him in for dinner. But when I looked out, the bushes were gone, and the street stretched long and empty.

Friday

I kissed the postman. I kissed the man who delivers the gas cylinders. I kissed the Sedex man. I kissed the neighbor who came to collect money. I kissed the mirror. All the lips were cold.

Saturday

I bought myself a birthday card with a little joke about going over the hill to pick flowers. I signed the card and went to the post office to send. I never received it.

Sunday

I passed by a glass door and saw myself, with a prettier face, playing ping-pong inside. I wanted to go in and play, but knew I would lose, so I left.

Friday

I finally got mail. It was a rejection of my application for a Philosophy course at the local university, UFEE. I had not applied anytime I could remember, but suddenly it seemed like a good idea. I looked the university up in the telephone book and Golden Pages, and then at Google. Such university did not exist.

Thursday

Nothing happened. I mean: nothing. Not the slightest wind, a barking dog, a passing man, nothing. The clock was stuck on 7:25. If I died then, nobody would have noticed.

Sunday

I was resting in bed when I heard steps in the empty house, crossing the room from the left to the right, the way it would sound through a sound system at a good cinema. The steps grew quick and urgent. I opened my eyes. The sound did not come from anyone walking, but from my own feet.

Avital Gad-Cykman is the author of *Life In, Life Out* (Matter press) and the upcoming *Light Reflection Over Blues* (Ravenna Press). She is a six-time Pushcart nominee, the winner of *Margaret Atwood Studies Magazine* Prize, first placed in The Hawthorne Citation Short Story Contest, and twice a finalist for Iowa Fiction award. Her stories have appeared in *The Dr. Eckleburg Review, Iron Horse Literary Review, Prairie Schooner, Ambit, W.W. Norton's Flash Fiction International* anthology and many other magazines and anthologies. She was born in Israel and has lived in Brazil for the past three decades.

BREAK BLOW BURN

JUKED

daniel galef

YOU COULDN'T KNOW, HOW optimistic and lucky you've been, all. We actually worked on the thing. Champagne in the desert, eyes still re-adjusting, the world singing day-night like an eclipse. It was the first time I didn't flinch when the cork popped out.

After we scattered like fallout. Some to RAND, to NASA, some hanged up their aprons for unbloodied academics. Fat men lecturing little boys. No point if there isn't time to grow up.

The mushrooms were all over like real mushrooms or grass. Tried those. Didn't work. Flicks, comics, the Twilight Zone. After Pigs in 63 I guess we none of us thought She had another decade left in her. Understand, at the start we didn't think there would be another left to waste. Understand, we didn't.

Engraved in my retinas like they say the last thing a murder victim sees, I still carry the flash fading in the blacks of his goggles as Oppenheimer pours my glass. I carry that. It's light as air, but I carry it. Light as light.

Daniel Galef's small fictions have appeared in the *American Bystander, Jersey Devil Press, Nanoism,* and *Flash Fiction Magazine*. He is currently seeking a publisher for his debut poetry collection, *Imaginary Sonnets*. He lives in Tallahassee and is listed in Webster's dictionary under "interfaculty."

NEW SHIRT

FICTIVE DREAM

louis gallo

IN 1954 MY UNCLE Alphonse took the bus to Goldberg's Men's Clothiers on Poydras Street where he bought a new Arrow dress shirt, sparkling white with stern isosceles collars. It cost three dollars, a lot of money in those days. He unfolded it, picked out each pin meticulously and flapped it back and forth for airing. He hung it on a sturdy wooden hanger and told Aunt Cecile he would wear it only on special occasions.

He didn't wear the new shirt to his birthday party in 1954, four months after he bought it. He said the shirt was more important than any birthday, especially at his age. Nor did he wear it on Easter Sunday to church nor to his fortieth anniversary of marriage nor to Christmas mass or the New Year's Eve party. Uncle Alphonse did not wear his new shirt in 1954 but he dropped some moth balls into its front pocket and routinely admired its texture, brilliance and fresh starchy smell. In 1955 he did not wear the shirt to his first grandson's baptism—and again, not on his birthday, Easter or Christmas.

He didn't wear the shirt in 1956 or 57, 58, 59, to observe the death of Stalin or the Korean, War, Ike's re-election, Elvis on Ed Sullivan, the invention of tranquilizers, Civil Rights, the Interstate Highway program, the launching of Sputnik. 'He's waiting for the new decade,' Aunt Cecile chuckled. But on New Year's Day 1960 Uncle appeared in one of his fuzzy, old and slightly faded flannels. 'This isn't the right time,' he mumbled gloomily. The shirt had become a family joke by now. Uncle Alphonse did not celebrate Kennedy's election, the Beatles in New York, Viet Nam, the assassinations, Chicago, Watts, the hippies, Neil Armstrong's giant leap, not in his new white shirt anyway.

In the seventies Uncle did not wear the shirt when the war ended, when Nixon resigned and Jimmy Carter lusted in his heart, when Disco killed rock and roll or during the Bicentennial. He had become morose and secretive about the shirt, hid it in the darkest corner of the closet, sealed it in black plastic, sprayed it with mist to stave off dry rot. He did not wear his shirt to Ronald Reagan's inauguration, nor to the baptisms and confirmations of more grandchildren, the funeral of his mother and Aunt Cecile's operation. When the Soviet Union collapsed, the shirt still looked new, flawless and elegant, though perhaps a bit quaint.

And here's where I come in—Uncle first let me see it around this time. He'd taken a fancy to me and sensed I would understand—I did, even if it's hard to explain. When the fishhook started to shred Uncle's gut and Chernobyl exploded, he turned yellow and coughed a lot, told me in a rare moment of levity that his skin would never match the shirt now. And something else: 'Don't let them bury me in it. What's so special about death? Wear a new white shirt only when something really grand happens.' They buried him in a black suit and blue turtleneck sweater. Aunt Cecile had already given me the shirt. 'He wanted you to have it,' she said. 'I thought we might see him wear it to the Resurrection, but I guess I was wrong.' Now it hangs in my closet, pristine as moonlight, immune to time, beautiful. It won't surprise me to wait forever but one of these days something really grand is bound to happen. The moth balls are still pungent.

Two volumes of Louis Gallo's poetry, *Crash* and *Clearing the Attic*, will be published by Adelaide in the near future. A third, *Archaeology*, has been published by Kelsay Books; Kelsay will also publish a fourth volume, *Scherzo Furiant*, in the near future, and a fifth volume, *Leeway and Advent*. A novella, "The Art Deco Lung," will be published in *Storylandia*. His work has appeared or will shortly appear in *Wide Awake in the Pelican State* (LSU anthology), *Southern Literary Review*, *Fiction Fix*, *Glimmer Train*, and many others. Chapbooks include *The Truth Changes*, *The Abomination of Fascination*, *Status Updates* and *The Ten Most Important Questions*. He is the founding editor of the now defunct journals, *The Barataria Review* and *Books: A New Orleans Review*. His work has been nominated for the Pushcart Prize several times. He is the recipient of an NEA grant for fiction. He teaches at Radford University in Radford, Virginia.

THREE FILIPINAS

harrison geosits

CINCINNATI REVIEW

1. THEY ARE BORN and raised in monsoon season, brushing humidity through their raven hair like all the other island girls do. They are eight, five, and four, the perfect ages for climbing trees, slicing mangoes, playing make-believe. On the veranda, they are separated from the jungle-city by only the bug screen; when the nannies are not looking, they creep out into the world, they explore, they meet the man in the van on the road outside their home, they almost get in. When the nannies stop them, they do not know why.

2. They are the only island girls at school. When they say *We are Filipino*, the Texans say *How exotic, How far away, How crazy!* Their oldest sister *is* crazy. When she runs away from their new home, her sisters follow her in the car; they are watching the road, they are shouting her name out the window, they are doing homework in the back seat. Their mother does not care if the oldest sister comes back, if she is pregnant, if her Camel-smoking boyfriend is slapping her around. They are still three little girls, seventeen, fourteen, thirteen. They eat Filet-O-Fish sandwiches until they are American.

3. They get all-white husbands, half-white babies, almost-white lives. They are island girls only on Sundays now, when they dip tapa in vinegar in their parents' kitchen, or maybe it is the condensed milk in their coffee. They have stopped aging at thirty-seven, they dye gray hairs brown, they do not see the oldest sister anymore. They leave their husbands, they lose their jobs, they raise their grandchildren. They stay up until 5:00 a.m. playing card games. They are living the American dream, they never wonder why they left the island, they never make plans to go back.

HARRISON GEOSITS

Harrison Geosits is a peddler of creative nonfiction, a native Texan, and an all-around decent guy. His work can be found or is forthcoming in *Split Lip Magazine, SunDog Lit, Redivider, The Cincinnati Review* and *Wildness,* among others. He prefers wine from the box. You can stalk him on Twitter at @HGeosits.

POMEGRANATE

SPLIT LIP MAGAZINE

pia ghosh-roy

ELIZABETH WHITE IS WHITE like her name. First time in our Bengali-medium, central-Calcutta school American woman is teaching. She is volunteer only. Come here, teach English one month and go. They're trying many-many things for making students speak English. Posters here-there in the corridor: No English, No Future. Even in the staffroom Principal is not wanting Bangla. Very strict. You must set example, she is telling teachers every day. Speak English, think English.

Miss White is coming from New England. Every day she's telling everyone New England is not in England, New England is not in England. But who is listening? Everyone is calling her British Madam, British Madam.

Yesterday I speak to her, first time. Before that I only was smiling, passing in the corridor and smiling. Yesterday in the staffroom I give a smile and say, You are looking extremely exquisite, my dear Elizabeth. I am only using my best words because first impression is last impression. But you know how she is answering? That's not very professional, Mr. Saha. In the middle of staffroom, she just said like this! Imagine! I am a senior teacher, she is only volunteer.

All the lady teachers are laughing and saying, She gave you good, Mr. Saha! I'm not replying anything. Afterwards I ask to Mr. Ranjan, What is the problem with little compliment, baba?

Mr. Ranjan tell me Miss White did not like that I moving my hands like this, like making shape of womanly figure. Arre, I do this shape in the air only, for to say exquisite, like this see: You are looking *extremely exquisite*, my dear Elizabeth. For adding little drama, little style. It is man's job to make beautiful woman smile. With full respect only, mind it. Appreciate the flower from far. Yes? Yes. Then why all this "not professional" business?

Poor girl, this is why she's spinster, I am telling Mr. Ranjan, she is not having very feminine nature. You understand? Women like her, very lonely. She is coming to India for finding herself. So many foreign tourists coming and searching for own self in India. Tell me—how you are losing your good self in India when you are living in America? Is it magic or what? If I am losing my spectacles in my house, I will find it in my house only. Why I will find it on Howrah Bridge? I am simply not understanding, please to explain, Mr. Ranjan.

But Mr. Ranjan is only shaking his head and laughing and saying, Arre, leave it no, Mr. Saha.

After this for five-six days I am passing Miss White in the corridor, but I am not smiling. She is smiling like normal, as if nothing.

Today is very last day for Miss White. Everyone is giving flowers, taking photo with Madam. The lady-teachers, they give her a sari. *Bara bari!* Why you did not give pyjama-punjabi to that Indian chap who volunteer before? I'm not asking them this, only thinking myself.

I hear Miss White telling the teachers she is very happy today, so happy, she saying something, some student…

Oh, he wrote these gorgeous words! I'm so proud of him, and on my last day, it's such a gift.

Who? I ask Mr. Ranjan.

Abhijit Mondal, Mr. Ranjan say to me.

What, that useless rascal in 7B? Always getting dubba in Mathematics? How he is making Madam so happy, baba? Normally Mr. Ranjan is understanding her English better. I am only catching few-few words.

So Mr. Ranjan is listening what Miss White is saying and repeating same to me slowly: I asked them to write a sentence…on childhood…you know… Abhijit, he couldn't express *anything* in English…but now look at this!

Miss White is showing the paper. Words in careful handwriting. *My childhood is full of joy and pomegranate.*

Which is pomegranate? I'm forgetting, I ask to Mr. Ranjan.

Bedana, he answer.

Bedana, hmm. Yes, I must admit the sentence is having feeling. I have to give the Mondal boy credit, I admit. Very nice picture it is painting.

Young boy, sitting on branch of pomegranate tree. In his two hands a fruit. The fruit is open. Inside is like gemstones, small-small sweet red jewels. Hiding. Like precious secret. Ah, that is childhood, yes. *My childhood is full of joy and pomegranate.* Bah, good, good! Joy and beda…beda… Wait. One minute…one minute. In my head something is coming. Bedana, and, and, bedona!

Arre, the fools! The boy is not meaning bedana, pomegranate. He is meaning bed*o*na.

Sadness. What is the other word, sow…sorrow. MY CHILDHOOD IS FULL OF JOY AND SORROW. He is only copying the wrong word from Bengali-to-English dictionary! Thinking Bedona and looking Bedana.

Oh, this is funny. I turn to say to everyone, Arre baba, listen. It is only a mistake. But everyone is talking. Mr. Ranjan is smiling. Miss White is smiling. Everyone, smiling.

Miss White is saying, Oh, these words, they just sum up India for me you know. So evo—. (I don't catch, very quick word.) She is putting the paper proudly, very neatly, in her bag. Her joy is sweet and beautiful, like inside of pomegranate.

What were you saying, Mr. Saha? Mr. Ranjan ask me.

Nothing, Mr. Ranjan, leave it, I say.

Pia Ghosh-Roy grew up in India, and lives in Cambridge (UK). She has received the Hamlin Garland Award for the Short Story and the Cagibi Macaron Prize for Non Fiction. Her work has been short- and long-listed for the Bath Short Story Award, Berlin Writing Prize, Brighton Prize and Fish Short Story Prize amongst others. Pia is working on her first novel. www.piaghoshroy.com.

ZONES OF CONTACT

eugene gloria

SIGHTSEER IN THIS KILLING CITY
(PENGUIN RANDOM HOUSE)

I.   *Saudade*

BAUDELAIRE WROTE THAT THE only way to inhabit the present is to revisit it in a work of art. "Go to Europe," my runaway sister whispered in my ear. My sister who later landed her dream job as a flight attendant bought me a ticket from SFO to Heathrow. Having graduated to the present, I found myself on a flight deadheading to unemployment. [*Exit above.*] Language is an inadequate vessel. Take the word *saudade*, which comes from a land of shipbuilders and navigators. Say it within the context of empire long gone, of important battles depicted on ceramic and tile. I traveled by rail on the continent. And on the slowest train in the world, I went for two whole days from Paris to Lisbon.

II.   *Supertramp*

Twenty years later, I am taking a train in northern Spain to see in person how ceramics inform Frank Gehry's design of the Guggenheim in Bilbao. Imagine a set of functionless bowls in the rain. [*Enter several strange Shapes.*] Twenty years earlier, I was running away from a pint-sized case of heartbreak. I thought I was going to stoke an old flame, a German classmate I met in Jacob Needleman's religion class at S. F. State U. She was a potter. Her work verging on the impractical I first thought. I had a standing invitation to visit her in Hamburg. She was an ideal host when I did. She put me up for a couple nights, and I had hopes of staying longer. But her square roommate who loved, *loved* Supertramp was growing impatient with a guest she didn't invite. Who could blame her? I was a bum. Her profound admiration for the song "Breakfast in America" was a testament to her world of disembodied arrivals. Imagine a nagging ringtone in a darkened theater whenever that song comes on the radio. The roommate's irritation with my visit crystallized when my Hamburg host introduced me to her new boyfriend. The Libyan boyfriend she met on the train.

III.   *Santa Apolónia Station*

I want to believe that *saudade* has something to do with arrival, a pause that lingers like homesickness for a place where you've never been, or the difference in the equation between arrival and departure. And if you round out all my miscalculations, my bad math might end up with a fraction of burnt flesh from my hobo heart. Oh, loveless me, *O sole mio, yada, yada.* I was in my twenties brimming with unnecessary drama. *Saudade?* No. I know it now. *Saudade* is a progeny of music, a wayward emotion that slips into wordlessness, a thing of *AnOther* culture. [*Burden, dispersedly within.*] And if saudade is only a feeling, then it must be the only thing that keeps me moving—. The sonorous grind of the potter's wheel, hands shaping clay from memory, that momentary catch in the throat.

IV.   [*Enter Song.*]

I heard a composer explain that in opera, when dialogue suddenly shifts into overdrive, emotions are climbing toward a heightened moment of arrival when spoken words are simply not enough. After two whole days of not speaking, I heard a small human hand tap on my door. It was the innkeeper's daughter holding a tray of coffee, hard bread with jam and butter. The coffee came in a cup and saucer, but it was her nervous gaze I recall, and her skin smooth as a celadon vase. I laugh now recalling my volcanic excitement for her chore of delivering my breakfast, which I regarded as a supreme act of kindness. I must have frightened her with my gestures of gratitude. She was only a child with her white socks and Mary Janes. I blurted the only word I knew in Portuguese, *obrigado*, I said over and over again, *obrigado* before she left the room without a word.

Eugene Gloria is the author of four books of poems—*Sightseer in This Killing City* (Penguin-Random House, 2019), *My Favorite Warlord*, winner of the Anisfield-Wolf Book Award, *Hoodlum Birds*, and *Drivers at the Short-Time Motel*, a National Poetry Series selection and recipient of the Asian American Literary Award. He is the John Rabb Emison Professor of Creative and Performing Arts and Professor of English at DePauw University.

THE VISITORS

anna granger

FLASH FRONTIER

NOBODY COMES OUT HERE except the birdwatchers. They have no particular ages or faces and they dress to blend with the beach and the water. Cradling their binoculars like precious babies, they don't talk or laugh among themselves. But if you ask them about the birds, they will tell you their special names, the desolate and beautiful places they travel from, and the many shades of their feathers and beaks.

The birdwatchers crave the salty smell of the mudflats. Every September they gather on the chalky drifts of dry shells and scan the sky waiting for the first migrants to arrive. They say they never get tired of watching how a flock of waders comes in to rest on the shells after their long flight, all facing the same direction with their heads tucked under their left wings, and how later they rise together in a quivering grey cloud, turn in unison and fly to the shallows to feed.

For many weeks they remain, resting and feeding, unafraid of those watching them, until one morning in late summer the birdwatchers come when the water flickers silver and the whole horizon is a still palette of soft greys. Then they will find the dazzling white shell banks deserted, and only a shimmer of mirage on the shore where the sand meets a strip of glittering water. And later in winter, when even the red-billed gulls have gone, they comb the silent estuary, slowly sifting the beach for the delicate white bones, papery skulls and lost feathers of those left behind.

Anna Granger is a New Zealand writer whose very short stories have won prizes and literary awards, been published in magazines and anthologies and broadcast on radio.

LIKE SHIT ON A CRACKER

claire guyton

VESTAL REVIEW

LIKE A FINE MERLOT. That's what he said; that's what he called me. And that wasn't enough to put me off.

When a man says you're like a fine Merlot and still you get in his car, make small talk about the famed restaurant where he reserved a table in the back, let him take your hand as you glide through the parking lot… you sort of have to say, yeah, I asked for it.

Like an apple in autumn, the blush in my cheeks. My eagerness at the menu—sure, I pointed; I love crab—like a schoolgirl on prom night. My smile like a cool slice of melon in August.

Like a script, I thought.

Like butterfly wings, my dress; like the shade of a weeping willow, my eyes.

Yeah, like a *bad* script; like a man fond of his own voice; like a date from the 1950s.

I reached for the actual Merlot, drank the whole glass down.

A bit like a black-hat with his shot glass, he says like it's funny; but also like a woman who takes what she wants, mmmm, but then again like a kid with a lollipop—too impatient not to bite.

Look, too many damn similes, I said, I did; I called him on it. But he just smiled.

Like a spoiled teenager at her tiara party, he said then; like a little girl who takes the head off her chocolate Easter bunny.

I said really, how about like a frat boy who thinks he owns the world because his daddy gives him too much money; like a quarterback who always calls the wrong play in the last two minutes of the game?

When a man pulls his mouth tight and slams his glass on the tabletop and you don't get up while the wine's still sloshing and toss your linen dinner napkin, then stalk through the flickering votives, lobster tail, unobtrusive string quartet, triple-decker dessert cart…then you have to accept that you wanted this fight. You chose that volume, that heat.

Like a slit-eyed cat mewling for more cream, he said, his face as red as the wine; like a used up old bitch having a flashback—and that dress? Like a hooker late on a slow night and behind on her rent.

I slapped aside the vase of flowers between us and pointed at his face. Like a teacher who bullies the fat kid, like a preacher who screws the flower lady, like the Senator with a little intern problem, like a cop all hopped up on bullets, like a dictator with fake medals across his chest; LIKE MY FATHER.

When you go from a kiss as velvet plum as a fine merlot to seeing your father's rage hurled at you across the crab bisque with corn kernels and chives... That's when you push, you push hard, for something, anything original, anything to *End Scene*.

Like a cracked tooth, I whisper. Cracked right down to the bone.

Claire Guyton is a southern transplant to Maine, where she works at her city's library, co-organizes a reading series at the local bookstore, and teaches workshops in very short fiction. She's been a Maine Arts Commission Literary Fellow and a finalist for the Maine Literary Award, and her work has been nominated for a Pushcart. Her short fiction appears in *Crazyhorse, Mid-American Review, Atticus Review, River Styx, New World Writing*, and many other journals, as well as in the Maine anthology *Summer Stories*. She's a co-founder of *Waterwheel Review* and holds an MFA from Vermont College of Fine Arts.

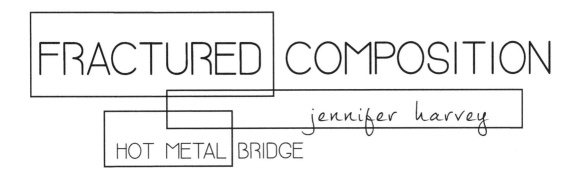

FRACTURED COMPOSITION

jennifer harvey

HOT METAL BRIDGE

1.

SHE ONCE TOLD YOU a lie. This was before you understood that lies could also be an expression of longing, a way of seeking out connections.

She told you a lie because she sensed, long before you did, that you held within you a need to believe such things were possible.

You told her: "I had the strangest dream. There was this turquoise circle of light, that's all it was."

You told her: "I was floating, and the light was behind my eyes, all crystalline and blue. All peaceful."

You didn't tell her how it shimmered and flickered. You didn't tell her that it left you feeling dazed and buoyed, as if you had been touched by grace. You didn't think she would understand that.

But she had surprised you. She had nodded and said: "Oh, I know, I know," and then left you to believe you shared this vision with her. And you were happy to believe it. But that was before you discovered the many ways it would linger. As memory, as premonition, as foreboding. No, it was anything but a dream.

2.

And if it was a memory, was it this?

Years earlier, in some park somewhere, you are playing hide and seek. You tell her to count to ten while you run and hide, but she is small still, four or thereabouts, and so she messes up the order, goes from three to ten in one jump, then cries, *"coming ready or not!"*

You're not ready, and so you jump to the nearest sanctuary, some shrub or bush. And down, down you go, into the dark and dank and gunk of a drain. Popping close to the surface a moment later. Above, the light, frayed at the edges. You call and hear your own voice echo and bounce. Then a face there, above, looking down and saying something. Then, laughter. You can't remember who pulled you back to the surface. But someone must have. All you remember is the look in her eye. Curiosity mixed with fear and a gleam of something else.

It's not a shared experience, this one. Not yet. She has yet to go under. You have yet to watch her sink. For now, there is only that gleam. And the lifelong shiver the memory will contain.

3.

The premonition is darker, no light this time. It starts in the old house. In a room with a flimsy curtain that floats in the breeze. It lets the light in but shrouds the scene outside in a gauzy haze which makes you think it's always raining outside. You can't help but look at it and wonder what purpose it serves. Better to leave the window bare, have the sun—when it's there—pour into the room. It's cleansing, so they say, a fact you find rather pleasing as you lie there not wanting the day to begin. Because now something has been illuminated. You can feel it.

That curtain wafting in the breeze, like the remnant of something long forgotten. You remember seeing it before and knowing straight away where you were in a dream. The dream of the old house, the one you never want to go back to. Just the idea of it, had filled you with despair. And it was despair. It wasn't melancholy or nostalgia.

"Please, not there," is what you had thought.

And how does it make you feel, to be back here again, back in the room, back in the house and watching the curtain waft? To know that dream was more of a vision, a casting of the die. It brought you here once more. Left you longing to slip back into sleep, into dreams. To get away. Far, far, away from here.

And the curtain flutters and lets the light in. Just long enough to illuminate something: *"You don't know what you're doing, where you're going. There is no away."* And the truth of it makes you turn to face the wall.

But it doesn't help.

4.

It's the one thing they never tell you.

Memories will come unbidden, and always when you are least expecting it. You are galloping on a horse. You feel the pull in the muscles and lean forward, you and the horse, fused sinew to sinew. And then there it is, you remember her and understand the effort it will take to forget. How you will need to pull away from her again and again and again.

And you squeeze your heel into the belly and kick, but know the pull you feel, the rush as you try to push it all away, is but a momentary relief.

But still, you do it. You listen until all you hear is the thud of hooves on the soft ground, beating the rhythm of your retreat. Away, away, away.

5.

Before the turquoise light, before that shared dream, she tells you of a different dream she had once. No lie this time.

"I'm a block of ice and I'm melting," she says.

And you think about that. You never stop thinking about it. It will always be the first thing you think of, when you think of her. That she called it a dream. Not a nightmare. That was the moment you knew something was wrong.

Though you never dared ask her, "Who wants to melt away like that?"

She did, apparently. And you need to find a place for it, for the impossible certainty you have, that if you'd said something back then, things would be different. You would be different, because you had asked her why she dreamed such things.

Instead all you have is her laughter. "It's just a dream. Just a stupid dream."

You could have told her, "No, it's not. It's more than that."

But instead, you turned your face to the wall again. Away, away. Gallop far away.

6.

A day trip to a waterfall. You hear the rumble of it long before you get there and though neither of you say a word, you hold hands in the back of the car as your father drives closer. All you can think about is the edge, the place where it becomes inevitable, the tipping point where falling cannot be halted. Over and over and over you go.

Memory, premonition, foreboding.

You close your eyes and try not to think of it, squeeze her hand a little harder than you mean to, so she pulls it away and squeals, "Ouch! That hurt!"

And when you open your eyes she's looking at you and she sees you are afraid. She sees the way the rumble of the water contains the depths of your fears. You have revealed yourself without meaning to. There exists an understanding between you now, that when her time comes, when she falls, you will not be there for her.

7.

Oh, and if you'd known it existed, this emerald valley, dotted with black grazing horses. If you'd known it existed for real, and not as some figment of the imagination, some dream, you'd have prepared for it better. Walked more slowly up on to the ridge and lifted your eyes with more reverence, more presence of mind.

As it is, all you manage is a sigh. A wordless appreciation. Just a lifting and falling of your rib cage. It feels like you're wafting, fluttering. Which reminds you of something, though you can't quite remember what it is. The past? The future? Her? Or is this simply the way time shifts? It is always meant to catch you unawares.

You stand on the ridge and look down and understand that it is this you should have dreamed for her. This valley, this safe-haven where the horses run to. Far from the rumbling water.

8.

The dark-eyed pick pockets were children really, but old enough for you to shout at them and slap at the hand you felt as it reached inside the bag on your shoulder. It was a stupid thing to do. Your own fault. They are trained to spot the opportunity and there you were, imagining you're Audrey Hepburn and dreaming of Rome. You're the seventh dreaming girl they've seen that morning.

It doesn't quite spoil the day. But it leaves you alert. Leaves you admitting you're not a carefree wanderer. Something you only fully understand as you stand by the Trevi fountain and grow dizzy as you listen to the water gurgle. That sound again. You came here hoping to drown it out with incense and incantations. Light a candle and illuminate things. Force out the darkness with light and prayer. But there it is again. The sound which will always follow you. No saints can diminish it. No horses can carry you away from it.

9.

When the day comes, it is déjà vu. Your parents are not the watchful types. They let you roam. Never know where you are. When she slips, they are on the riverbank, oblivious. Sitting with a small picnic and a plaid blanket, they hear a commotion. People on the bridge shouting, *"someone's fallen in,"* but they think nothing of it.

But down by the water, you stand and stare and wonder if this is the moment you are supposed to go in after her.

But you do not move. You simply stand and watch. You watch as she goes under. You watch as she sinks down, down, down. You watch her, and you know she is looking up at the circle of light on the surface, that she can see the bright blue beyond, but cannot reach it. And you smile because you share this now, both of you knowing how it feels to be pulled under, how it feels, to disappear from view. How it feels to look up at the light and despair as you hear the laughter.

And you tell her this as you stand on the riverbank and watch her go. You call out to her, *"I know, I know."*

10.

And you dream again. Or is it more a reimagining, a hope? A way to forgive yourself? On this imagined day, you stand at the water's edge and see her resurface, see her pull herself ashore and walk along the path towards you. You smile and take her hand and lead her back to your parents who stare in disbelief as you tell them.

"It was her. She's the one who fell in."

And you never let go of her hand. You keep it folded tight in your palm forever. You don't let her slip. You don't let her go. You hold on tight and say, "I know, I know," as she tells you it was a lie. She never did have that dream. She never knew that presence, that sacred light which seemed to hover above you.

The one you always thought would keep you both safe from harm, but which protected only you.

Jennifer Harvey is a Scottish writer now living in The Netherlands. Her debut novel *Someone Else's Daughter* (Bookouture, 2020) is now available and two further titles are forthcoming in October 2020 and May 2021. Her writing has appeared in various journals and anthologies including: *Folio, Carve, The Lonely Crowd,* and *Bare Fiction.* She is a resident reader for *Carve Magazine* and a member of the editorial board for *Ellipsis Magazine.* You can find her online at http://www.jenharvey.net and on Twitter @JenAnneHarvey1.

THE CHANGE

jenna heller

NORTH & SOUTH

THAT SHE'D STARTED SLEEPWALKING at the age of 47 wasn't completely unexpected. Creeping about the house at two in the morning, making tea, playing solitaire, even cleaning the fish tank. Leaving the house, though, that was new. At first, she'd wake at the bus stop just as the early commuters arrived, slink home to make breakfast for the kids, then send them off to school like everything was normal. But some days later when she found herself at the end of the pier one morning, walking the dunes the next, and searching for sand dollars in waist deep water the morning after that. Well. She knew then. Time was thin.

Her grandmother had disappeared in a pond at 49, her own mother in a lake at 48. After the hot flashes and mood swings, they'd slipped through the night in search of water. And now she watched her own body change in unexpected ways. The skin between her fingers grew sticky and webbed, her eyes red and itchy. And when five faint scratch marks appeared at both sides of her neck, she knew it was only a matter of time. Then one night, after a day of gagging in the thick summer heat, she stacked the diaries of explanation on the table and allowed the sea breeze to lull her to sleep.

The next day, the house was silent, the back door wide open, and her clothes found tangled in the kelp at high tide.

Jenna Heller lives in Christchurch, New Zealand, with her partner, two teens, two cats and a very demanding dog. 'The Change' was runner-up in the 2019 *North & South* Short Short Story Contest. The same year, she was selected as joint-winner of the *Meniscus* Copyright Agency Best Prose Prize and her first YA manuscript was shortlisted for the Text Prize.

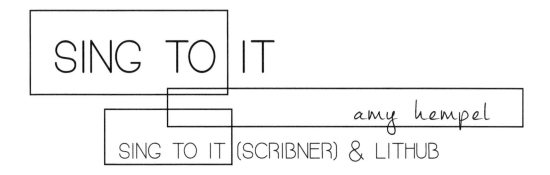

SING TO IT

amy hempel

SING TO IT (SCRIBNER) & LITHUB

AT THE END, HE said, No metaphors! Nothing is like anything else. Except he said to me before he said that, Make your hands a hammock for me. So there was one.

He said, Not even the rain—he quoted the poet—not even the rain has such small hands. So there was another.

At the end, I wanted to comfort him. But what I said was, Sing to it. The Arab proverb: When danger approaches, sing to it.

Except I said to him before I said that, No metaphors! No one is like anyone else. And he said, Please.

So—at the end, I made my hands a hammock for him.

My arms the trees.

———————————

Amy Hempel's fifth story collection, *Sing To It*, was published last year. She is the recipient of a Guggenheim Fellowship, the PEN/Malamud Award, and awards from the United States Artists Foundation, and the American Academy of Arts and Letters. She lives in New York.

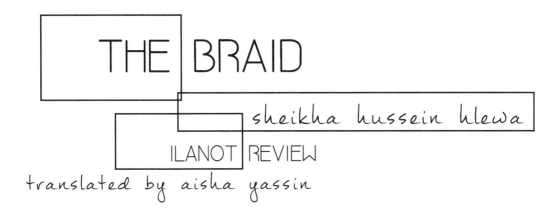

THE BRAID

sheikha hussein hlewa

ILANOT REVIEW

translated by aisha yassin

MY MOM AND I had crossed the road from the bus station to the only barber shop in the area. Both of us were silent to prevent another of the heated discussions that would regularly take place since I'd moved to the Convent of Nazareth School in Haifa. I would insist and beg and she would refuse, then I would implore and she would curse me, so I'd cry and she would fall quiet.

Being newly divorced, she'd had her share of sins, so she wasn't in a position for another confrontation with the tribe. What excuse would she find for her girl, who was seduced by the city of Haifa? She agreed even though she wasn't convinced: either she liked the flavor of rebellion or she hated the taste of surrender.

The road to the barber shop was familiar, but that morning it seemed different.

I turned in the revolving chair to see my braid on the floor, like a snake tempting me to touch it or to crush it. My hand groped at the place of amputation, only to rebound back to its place as if stung. I was overtaken by a horror that almost knocked me from the chair. I glimpsed my mom's face in the mirror: holding her hand to her mouth, suppressing a deep sigh.

"Here's your braid" said the barber admiringly. It had fallen to the floor, his scissors announcing another masculine victory... he was aware of the Bedouin mentality in which the braid and virginity are deemed to be equal. But he was more fortunate than the rest of the barbers in the region, since the braid that he'd captured would decoratively frame the wall for many years to come.

I would avoid passing his salon, to spare my soul the agony...

I started sobbing silently as my mom's menacing looks told me: "Wait till we get home!" I wasn't shaken by her threats this time, because my mom had been my partner in crime. She had chosen the barber, the day and the time, and her approval, though coerced, spared me certain punishment. My amputated braid cut off a part of my soul, and I suffered in silence. I didn't dare look in the mirror: my mom's anger lurked behind me and my bereft head peered from the front.

And Haifa, a treacherous friend who had lured me in and then declared her repentance.

I looked to my jealousy to console me for my loss, and I sought my wilderness to assuage my bereavement…even the pictures of young women with short hair that had always tempted me away from my Bedouinness didn't justify my sin.

And Haifa…Haifa, how could you abandon me now?

What condolences does an amputated braid give me?

"Oh, you little brat!" my mother used to curse me a thousand times every day… God never had answered and she had never grown tired.

And the barber wouldn't stop blabbing: "A young woman like you doesn't need this braid."

Every morning, I would go down the step that separated the living room (which was also a bedroom) from the kitchen (which was also the bathroom), while my mom stood there, so she could ensure full control of my hair that reached to my back. She could barely collect my hair in one fist: as soon as she pulled it close, a lock would escape her clutch, and she brought the comb to straighten my hair. With each tug at my hair, I swayed in pain, and with every "ouch" that I uttered, her fist became stronger and firmer and I become quiet. She would not let go until she had disciplined my hair into a braid befitting a polite young woman.

"What? Your daughter wants to imitate city girls?" said one of my uncles, trying to warn my mother of the storm that was approaching.

The pupils in the Convent of Nazareth were a mix of city dwellers and nearby village commuters. Each with her own dream and her own motivations. Upon arriving at the school gates, the doors of heaven and hell would open. I would erase my memory of my brother, my mom and myself temporarily. I would deny my eternal "Bedouinness". My tongue would comply, forgetting its explicit Bedouin dialect.

Only my name and my braid would reveal what I tried to hide. I failed to convince them that I was a descendant of desert kings, and that I had the privilege of bearing my name. The suppressed laughter that tormented my soul. "*Sheikha*? Hahaha! What does that mean, 'old woman'?"

My braid—the Bedouin heritage that broke my back. How I had wished for short hair to tickle my neck; its messy tufts flirting around my weary face.

"Are you happy now? You have become like one of Haifa girls. Is that what you wanted? May God show you no mercy…!"

I became a Haifa girl, or I almost did.

I believed that I was, or I almost did, except for the hand that reached for my braid, only to be stung by its absence.

Sheikha Hussein Hlewa was born in 1968 in in Dhayl 'Araj, an unrecognized Bedouin village near Haifa. She now lives in Jaffa. She is working on her PhD on female writing in the shadow of the Syrian war. She is a lecturer in Arab Feminism at Ben Goreon University. She is the author of *The Ladies of Twilight* and *Windows are Spoiled Books*, among others.

Aisha Yassin, 24 year old Palestinian graduate student living in Haifa. Finished double degree in Ofakim Honors program and English Literature and Language. Currently working as a research assistant and attending creative writing classes. Interested in poetry, spatiality and languages. Aisha writes in her blog The Little Lantern (wordpress).

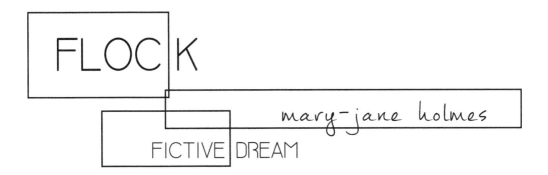

FLOCK

mary-jane holmes

FICTIVE DREAM

EDITH STOPPED PULLING SPEAR-THISTLE from the top field, rubbed the small of her back. It was that time of year again, summer squalls threatening and the roof black with starlings. *Shitlegs* Tom had called them as they blanched the ridge tiles guano-white. Off he would stride to the shed for his pellet gun until the day he could only curse them from his bed in the attic while they skittered the skylight above his head.

Edith watched the flock swoop to feast on froghoppers hatching from the cuckoo spit that drenched the pasture. She knew that Tom would've wanted her to scare them off, but she hadn't the energy, in fact she found their chitter-chatter a sliver of company now it was just her, the forage harvester, the bailer, the silage pit.

That night she felt the skale of rain spatter through the lattice of holes left from Tom's attempts at shooting the starlings away. She thought of the windrows she'd just raked, soddened and moulding, felt the damp creep towards her from the empty side of the bed.

Next day she pulled the ladder up to the gable of the house and hoiking nails and underfelt, climbed on to the roof. She thought the starlings would scatter with a crackling lift of wings, but instead they made room for her, carried on their preening, their constant chirping. A few of the juveniles nibbled her earlobes. It was so intimate it made her laugh, the first time in a year. It was warm up there now that the front had passed. It felt good. She looked down at the spoiling hay and closed her eyes to it all. When she woke it was dusk, the starlings were roosted about her. She should've gone inside but it was a long time since she'd heard the flutter of another's heartbeat so close to hers.

The next morning, she wasn't concerned to find sprouts of tufted down covering her torso, her armpits hollowed to quills sheened with black feathers. She flapped her elbows and backflipped into the air. Her surprise was voiced in the up-soar of the flock funnelling dark and tight-waisted into the sky. At first, she couldn't keep up with the ripple of bodies perfectly syncopated, but following the tipping wings either side of her, the dip of tails almost touching her beak, she found her place in the pulse of the whole. Oh, what it felt like to be part of something again. She looked back at the empty farm, its windows dark as storm clouds.

Summer yellowed the fields hard, the flock clamoured the neighbours' bird feeders, compost, rubbish dumps, bickering and fighting over what they found. Edith tired of the squabbles, longed for dusk, the quiet of the roost—the farm roof that shone now like butter under the moon. One night she peered through the skylight, there was her bed, eiderdown smooth and crisp, the nightstand with its sidelamp and pile of books, the photo of Tom and her when they first bought the place. The sun would rise soon; she tucked her head under a wing and tried to sleep but then she heard the skylark bullet into song, saw it hover then dive into the swath of hay she'd left a season ago. And as it belted out its solitary ascendant tune she thought *Perhaps, yes perhaps, I can do this alone.*

Mary-Jane Holmes has already had the honour of having work included in BSF in both 2016 and 2018. Her microfiction has recently been included in *Best Microfictions* 2019. A Forward Prize nominee and Hawthornden Fellow, Mary-Jane has won the Bridport, Martin Starkie, Dromineer, Reflex Fiction and Mslexia prizes, plus the Bedford Poetry competition and shortlisted for many more including the Beverley International Prize for Literature 2020. Mary-Jane's debut poetry collection *Heliotrope with Matches and Magnifying Glass* is published by Pindrop Press. She is Chief Editor of Fish Publishing, Ireland, a consulting editor for *The Well Review* and and tutor at Retreat West. She enjoys teaching creative writing both online and in person around the world.

MOTHER READS FIRST AID MANUAL WHILE CROUCHING ON THE FLOOR BESIDE THE BOOKSHELF

gail ingram

CONTENTS UNDER PRESSURE (PŪKEKO PUBLICATIONS)

BLEEDING TEENS:

A TEEN is *an injury. There may be a lot of blood.* Her husband's laughter-lines congealed mid-sentence one day. *Wipe away.* Peers that offend. *Apply pressure.* They're trying. *Protect yourself.* Not just yourself. *Elevate.* Both children need attention at once. Why us? They *place* their *hands in plastic bags. Wounds may be open.* Family. Shouting *may be severe.* <u>*Assessment:*</u> *No visible signs will be found.* Bongs or knives. She searches. *Insufficient* Love *supply can result in* swagger and rap, *a loss of reality.* "The little shit." *Head between your legs and breathe.* Search and search. *Shock will build.* Dirty washing piles. *Apply* curfew *pressure. Do not.* I don't see anything wrong with it. I don't see. The voices of the family *oscillate. Pull edges to meet. Ask someone to call an ambulance (see p.18).* "The website will offer an answer." *Clammy* and down. What? *Signs are a pulsing* hunger and red eyes. *Maintain control.* There's a brown stain on the floor.

Gail Ingram is the author of Contents Under Pressure (Pūkeko Publications 2019), a novella told in poetry, and editor of two poetry anthologies. Her work has appeared in *Poetry New Zealand, Landfall, Atlanta Review, Blue Five Notebook, Fib Review* and others. She won the Caselberg International Poetry Prize (2019) and New Zealand Poetry Society International Poetry Competition (2016). Short fiction awards include runner up Flash Fiction Day NZ Micro Madness, shortlist for Fish Prize, and nominated for the Pushcart Prize. She is a poetry editor for *takahē* magazine and a short-fiction editor for *Flash Frontier: An Adventure in Short Fiction.* https://www.theseventhletter.nz/.

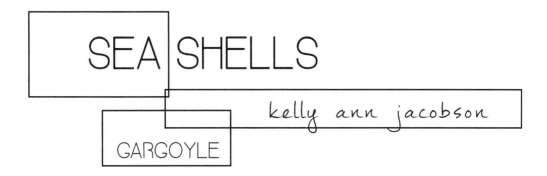

SEA SHELLS

GARGOYLE

kelly ann jacobson

WHEN THE WOMAN AT the door offered to turn my children into seashells for one hundred dollars, I didn't hesitate.

She'd originally come with three pieces of travel luggage, all black with pale pink trim and stocked with Mary Kay products and discount coupons, in order to persuade me to "throw a makeover party." I knew that's what she would say, even though she hadn't gotten the words out, because someone from Mary Kay came by almost every month. Maybe it was Mrs. Perkins's yard flamingos—these women seemed drawn to all things pink.

This particular woman, whose name was Stella, wore a pink tweed suit, even though it was mid-July, and smelled like all of the makeup counters at the mall rolled into one.

"Hi. My name is Stella." Forced smile. "I'm a consultant for Mary Kay, and I've been—"

She hadn't even gotten through her elevator pitch. Susie, who'd been strapped into her highchair the last time I'd seen her, had somehow gotten loose and found her way to the door. She had half of a banana clutched in her triumphant fist, and when Stella bent down to coo at little Susie, the girl thrust that banana right into Stella's chest.

"Oh," Stella said, and her face got red. She didn't complain though—probably thought I'd make a pity purchase—and Susie frowned at the lack of response.

Stella picked banana pieces from her suit and tossed them on the doorstep, where the yellow mush looked like splattered bodies.

Billy chose this moment to fly his new, remote-controlled helicopter through the door. Perhaps he hadn't realized we had company…but more likely, navigating the helicopter right into Stella's perky face was his plan all along.

"Sorry," he yelled from behind me as Stella swatted at the helicopter like it was a large fly in her kitchen. Her hair, previously a blonde helmet, had become more of a blonde halo after her violent swings had caused it to frizz and flip outward.

Still, the children might have gotten away with it all. But then Susie had done the unthinkable, something a little girl her age shouldn't have been capable of. We'd been so busy with the helicopter that we hadn't noticed Susie zipping and unzipping the makeup case, and by the time we realized it, my girl had twisted several tubes of lipstick and used them as chalk to draw on the sidewalk. Not just anything, mind you—a certain part of the female anatomy.

"Susie!" I picked her up and set her down behind me, from which point she tottered off to do more damage around the house while I wasn't looking.

"Your children," Stella said through gasps after Susie and Billy had finally retreated. "They're...horrible."

I should have disagreed, but I couldn't. They were, objectively, horrible.

"Listen." Stella leaned in, and the lines of her makeup came into focus. "I shouldn't do this, but I'm willing to make you a deal. If you give me a hundred dollars, I'll turn your children into seashells."

"Seashells?" For some reason, this was the part that confused me. "Why seashells?"

"Think about it. Most objects don't make any noise, but a seashell? It sings. Once I turn your children into seashells, you'll be able to hear them whenever you press the shell to your ear."

I didn't ask any follow-up questions.

Instead, I handed over a hundred dollars and waited expectantly. The house went still, and I knew, even before I turned around, that there'd be no one behind me.

"Here you go." Stella handed me two shells. "That coffee bean is little Susie, and the Scotch bonnet is Billy. Careful, now."

I took my children in my hands and held them to my ears. Sure enough, their voices started almost immediately, but they weren't singing—they were screaming. Their voices, together, were like a chainsaw and a weed whacker battling on a Saturday morning.

"Ugh." I pulled the shells away. "What's all that racket?"

Stella shrugged. She had packed up her bags, including the used lipstick tubes, and was ready to be on her way.

"I can't work miracles," she said before turning around. "Anyway, if you ever want to throw a makeover party—"

I didn't hear the rest. I'd closed the front door, and the silence of the place had sent a shiver through my body. A shiver of anticipation and anxiety, but most of all...excitement.

Life was going to be different.

Now, my husband and I split our time between Texas and Oahu. We wear matching hiking sandals and flowery shirts, and every night we drink mojitos on the back porch while listening to Simon & Garfunkel. Life is good. On the rare occasion when the house feels too quiet, or the guilt pecks away at me like a bird at a feeder, we listen to Susie and Billy scream their terrible songs.

Most of the time, we leave them on the bathroom shelf, where they belong.

Kelly Ann Jacobson is the author or editor of many published books, including novels such as *Cairo in White*, the poetry collection *I Have Conversations with You in My Dreams*, and anthologies such as *Dear Robot: An Anthology of Epistolary Science Fiction*. She also writes young adult speculative novels under her pen name, Annabelle Jay. Kelly is a PhD candidate in fiction at Florida State University and teaches speculative fiction for Southern New Hampshire University's online MFA in creative writing. Her work can be found at www.kellyannjacobson.com or www.annabellejay.com.

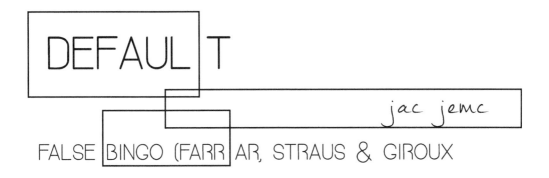

DEFAULT

jac jemc

FALSE BINGO (FARRAR, STRAUS & GIROUX

EVERY MEMORY TWISTED BY revision. Saying grace in the drive-thru. Bright sleep with the TV screen shining an ice rink. The way his language always blurred away from promise. A pink cassette player I tried to keep, but he insisted I give to my sister. Honor roll notices from the newspaper mailed to me, like he could teach me my own life, too. Random news articles tucked in—always something I knew about, but a week later, after it had already changed. Batteries not included. No cash for my textbooks, but an invitation to watch the pay-per-view fight on Saturday night. Grass stains dragged down my ass. Relief flickering through disappointment when I heard his car's engine failing to apologize. Free buttons he picked up at trade shows wrapped in tissue and string. Suburban curry buffet and Goodwill Supermarket Sweep. Voice-mail box full. Ghosts halved and halved and halved again. Dirty geometry. Static tragedy. Splinters polished to a flash. Made in China. Scratching tickets and unshrinking ground beef gray with age. Sister logrolling down the hill. Mom in real life. Fairy tales about him. Nosy neighbors asking if he was back. Hundred-and-ninety-proof. Polyester. Spoilsport. Peeling his nails on the couch and flicking them at the screen, at me when I complained. Mom vacuuming. Stale donuts and an outdated globe. Give it a spin. Close your eyes. Plant a finger. Rhodesia. Too bad. Front yard. Red light. Green light. Loans in Monopoly. Only college football on Saturdays. Baptism money emptied from my savings account. Spinning quarters at chain restaurants. Picking coins out of peanut shells on the floor. Trivia at Cliff's Tap and a beer for me because he knew better than the law. Unsealed packaging. Laundromats and still-damp sweatpants. Sister eating Kleenex. School counselors. Saturday stomach cramps like clockwork. I don't owe you anything. Flammable. Sister drinking a vanilla shake and a cup of water for me. Even the scrambled eggs burnt, the instant ramen watered down. Glued to the back of my seat with acceleration. Tight corners. Loose timelines. Opinions on strep throat. Breast is best. Pretending

I understand soccer rules. Anything not to talk. Learning soccer rules. Dead batteries. Snowy April. Illegible goodbyes on the backs of receipts.

I made all these notes and decided no one deserved them, even me. A priest he'd never met gave the eulogy: a Mad Lib of lies with his details filled in.

In the car on the way to lunch afterward, my sister turned to me with tears in her eyes. I couldn't believe she was as sad as she seemed.

I said, "He was awful to us. Me especially, but you, too. It's good we're finally done."

My mother drove. We thought it big of her to attend at all. His girlfriend had made the arrangements. Everything red satin and roses. She had a ring on her finger that we knew would disappoint her at the pawnshop. She said our flowers hadn't been delivered, and we pretended we'd ordered any.

Who were all those people? How had they found out? He claimed not to have a cell phone. Didn't seem like an address book was likely. Maybe slips of paper taped on the inside of a cabinet door, fluttering like feathers each time he pulled out a mug.

"It's not that," my sister said.

I saw my mother blaze in the rearview mirror.

My sister's tears bulged fatter. She trapped her face in the back of the seat in front of her. "He wasn't your dad. Not really," she said.

I didn't even register shock. It felt so immediately true: I'd never wondered, but suddenly it came clear that such a question had been one more responsibility bestowed on me unannounced, one more way I'd failed.

I found only a single chip of disbelief in this otherwise flawless news. "How did he keep a secret like that?"

My mother said nothing, her eyes screaming straight ahead.

My sister sheltered my hands with her own. "He didn't know, either."

A sorry inheritance.

Jac Jemc is the author of the novels *My Only Wife*, winner of the Paula Anderson Book Award, and *The Grip of It*, and the short story collections *A Different Bed Every Time* and *False Bingo*, winner of the *Chicago Review of Books* Award for fiction and finalist for the Story Prize and a Lambda Literary Award. Her forthcoming novel, *Total Work of Art*, will be published in 2022. Jemc currently teaches creative writing at UC San Diego.

WHAT WE LEAVE UNDONE

omotara james

WILDNESS

THE YEAR THEO DIVORCED David, he taught himself to play guitar for survival, said, I just needed to save myself the repetition of a broken heart, which is a workshop for what might have been. My ukulele from Honolulu has yet to be tuned & I thought I'd surely learn to play a song before she took a wife. The salve of watching my mother sleep, spreads cool, like a family who knows little of violence. This, the reason I never tell her of hands, ten feet outside our gate reaching from the open doors of a Cadillac, maybe if not for those large, sunken seats or the driver's uneven sense of time—what they could have grabbed, fistfuls of baby fat. A healing balm requires shaved beeswax placed into a pan, over low heat. I lock the silent gate on my way to school & wait carefully at the curb. When I see a dark Cadillac, pee pours warm like infused oil, into the pan, melts over the wax. If those older boys had reached me, the way my mother reached across the ocean and landed with a dream, I do not know if I would have screamed. Across the waters from Nigeria, I see the headlines of the Chibok girls who go unnamed as a conjuring. I read: Schoolgirls Abducted, then Child-brides, then On the Anniversary of... They, who were marked unlucky & then unlucky &then unlucky I want to tell them—but only, oil and beeswax. In prayer, I open my mouth to their dreams and choke on the steam. At night, I leave the salve, top open, on the nightstand, by the haunted strings for the ghosts, who exist for no reason but to finish these things.

Omotara James is the author of the chapbook, *Daughter Tongue*, selected by African Poetry Book Fund, in collaboration with Akashic Books, for the 2018 New Generation African Poets Box Set. Born in Britain, she is the daughter of Nigerian and Trinidadian immigrants. Her recent

honours include a 92Y Discovery Prize and being shortlisted for the Brunel International African Poetry Prize. Her poetry has appeared in *POETRY*, *The Paris Review*, *Academy of American Poets*, and elsewhere. She has been awarded fellowships from Lambda Literary and the Cave Canem Foundation. Currently, she lives, teaches and edits in NYC.

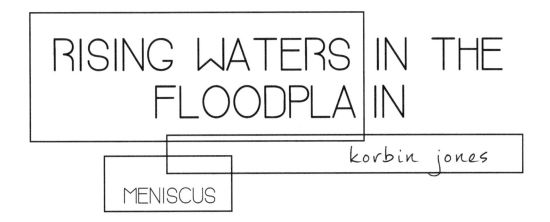

RISING WATERS IN THE FLOODPLAIN

korbin jones

MENISCUS

ANGRY HUSBAND TAKES THE form of a mud-trapped bullfrog. yellow-throated in the muck. his croak-song reprised seventeen times against the ache of his eardrums, exposed since birth & dry from promised rain. hot lightning crashes overhead. reflects back in the dark almonds of his eyes, the eyes with which he watches all these waters rise.

cheating husband takes the form of a young corn snake, which in turn masquerades as a copperhead. such similar scales & yet he lacks the proper pockets & glands for making himself an honest danger. he is milk-sweet & milk-sour in the same hour. his hiss is silence. his head is in constant danger of separation due to mistaken identity.

paramour takes the form of me & i take the form of a channel catfish with a broken lip. i am hole-riddled & made jagged by the hooks that fishermen had wrapped in food. blood bait & earthworm & the liver of a man i once knew. my belly round with chosen feeding. chance me & i'll swallow every hook until my body hits the riverbed.

by the time the sun has cast itself behind the clouds the river crests & bears itself upon the land, runs its hands across the brittle grasses that bend themselves in subjugation. we huddle ourselves atop the hills & wonder at the rate of water receding back to banks. if we stop to listen for a moment, we can hear the river's throaty laughter.

Korbin Jones graduated from Northwest Missouri State University with degrees in Writing and in Spanish. He is currently pursuing his MFA in Poetry at the University of Kansas. His translation of Pablo Luque Pinilla's poetry collection *SFO: Pictures and Poetry about San Francisco* was published by Tolsun Books (2019). His debut collection of poetry, *songs for the long night.*, was published by QueerMojo (2019) and was nominated for a Lambda Literary Award in Gay Poetry. His debut chapbook, *MOONSICK,* was published by Finishing Line Press (2020). He has also been nominated for a Pushcart Prize.

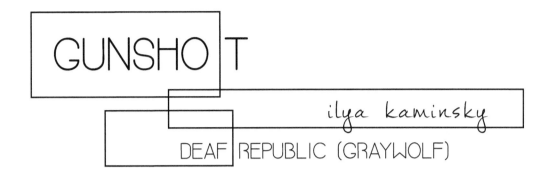

GUNSHOT

ilya kaminsky

DEAF REPUBLIC (GRAYWOLF)

OUR COUNTRY IS THE stage. When soldiers march into town, public assemblies are officially prohibited. But today, neighbors flock to the piano music from Sonya and Alfonso's puppet show in Central Square. Some of us have climbed up into trees, others hide behind benches and telegraph poles. When Petya, the deaf boy in the front row, sneezes, the sergeant puppet collapses, shrieking. He stands up again, snorts, shakes his fist at the laughing audience. An army jeep swerves into the square, disgorging its own Sergeant. Disperse immediately! Disperse immediately! the puppet mimics in a wooden falsetto. Everyone freezes except Petya, who keeps giggling. Someone claps a hand over his mouth. The Sergeant turns toward the boy, raising his finger. You! You! the puppet raises a finger. Sonya watches her puppet, the puppet watches the Sergeant, the Sergeant watches Sonya and Alfonso, but the rest of us watch Petya lean back, gather all the spit in his throat, and launch it at the Sergeant.

The sound we do not hear lifts the gulls off the water.

Ilya Kaminsky is the author of *Deaf Republic* (Graywolf) and *Dancing In Odessa* (Tupelo). He is also co-editor of *Ecco Anthology of International Poetry* (Harper Collins) and co-translator of *Dark Elderberry Branch: Poems of Marina Tsvetaeva* (Alice James Books). He lives in Atlanta.

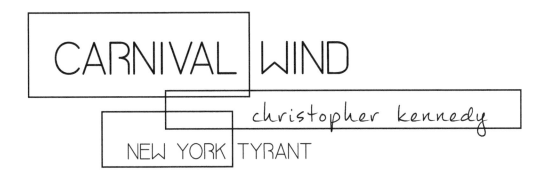

CARNIVAL WIND

christopher kennedy

NEW YORK TYRANT

WHEN THE CARNIVAL WIND blows the dust in this summer, you can pretend the sound of your own name is beautiful. You can gamble in the casino of stars at night where the moon looks like a pill and God deals you a terrible hand and there are no limits. You, the famous unknown, holding your baby and your syringe, waiting to be discovered by reality. Head full of sky, throat full of spiders. All the 2:00 AMers know: Life is fucking hard. Call around for your anesthesia. Ignore the stack of bills, their envelopes changing colors from month to month. Drop the kid at your mother's and drive to the house where there are no other houses. Someone unsettling will greet you there and promise it will be alright. Don't trust them. Get what you came for and leave. Roll down your window on the way home to roll up your sleeve as you drive past the church sign that advertises next week's revival, radio up loud, Lucinda Williams' "Car Wheels on a Gravel Road" on repeat. That wind in your dust-drowned hair. Convince yourself this year a stranger from out of town will win you something big and soft. You'll carry it around under your arm all night. Your enemies will think you're in love.

Christopher Kennedy is the author of *Clues from the Animal Kingdom*, *Ennui Prophet*, *Encouragement for a Man Falling to His Death*, (which received the Isabella Gardner Poetry Award in 2007), *Trouble with the Machine*, and *Nietzsche's Horse*. His work has appeared in many print and on-line journals and magazines, including *New York Tyrant*, *Ploughshares*, and *McSweeney's*. In 2011, he was awarded an NEA Fellowship for Poetry. He is a professor of English at Syracuse University where he directs the MFA Program in Creative Writing.

THE GREATEST LIAR IN THE WORLD

etgar keret

LITHUB

translated by jessica cohen

LOOK AT HIM STANDING in the middle of the street in the pouring rain, telling everyone it isn't cold. It's barely above freezing and he doesn't even sneeze. Raindrops roll off his forehead like beads of sweat, and his mouth—seriously, you have to see it to believe it: his mouth is a bona fide cosmic phenomenon, a black hole that sucks in reality and spits it out the other end as something completely different. Now he's talking assuredly about the wonderful future that awaits our children, and any minute he'll be explaining to anyone willing to listen about how there's a god and that this god believes we're doing just fine. Then he'll take a seat at the little café, drink some hot tea with lemon and swear it's coffee.

He wasn't always like that. When he was a kid he couldn't lie at all, and once when the classroom window was broken he put his hand up and confessed that he'd thrown the stone. But all his honesty ever got him was a juvenile record for property vandalism, and at some point on that long and exhausting road, he reached a junction, took a sharp turn, and never looked back.

At first he only lied to strangers, then to people he really loved, and finally to himself. Lying to yourself is the best. It only takes a minute for the dingy puddle of reality that gets your socks wet to turn into something warm and velvety. Just one line—and failure turns into voluntary submission, loneliness into choice, and even the death that keeps closing in on you can change into a one-way ticket to heaven.

He isn't naïve. He knows not everyone appreciates him. There will always be extremists who insist on praising the unimaginative truth as if it were a rousing marvel and not just an embarrassing default. Have you ever seen a trash heap lie? Or a tadpole? Or an insect? Only man, the pinnacle of creation, has the capacity to alter his world by wielding a sentence. A sentence that creates reality. Well, perhaps not reality, but something. Something that if we only grab onto tight enough we will manage to survive, to stay afloat.

Now let's watch him in action. To his right—a wife and two children whom he loves desperately. To his left—a thin young waitress who wants to get her degree in international relations. And there he is, kissing the waitress and telling himself there's nothing wrong with it. Then he picks up the twins from kindergarten and tells them how Mom and him brought them into the world. In a minute it'll be time for a post-coital cigarette and he'll tell the thin waitress and himself that he's never experienced such momentous love. Love that is like a force of nature, a hurricane, the kind that will sweep you up one way or another and so it's futile to resist.

Two months from now, tired and estranged in a rental apartment in Petach Tikva, waiting impatiently for every other weekend when he can fall asleep in bed next to the twins and dream guilt-ridden dreams—he will keep on insisting that all this happened because he was in touch with himself. Because he chose to live life to the fullest and not just watch tediously from the sidelines as if it were yet another foreign film that the thin waitress dragged him to see at the arthouse cinema.

This September he will be representing us at the World Lying Championship, and the commentators are positive he's going to bring home a medal. He is so good, they say, that even if the impossible happens and he fails, there's no shadow of a doubt that he'll be able to convince himself—and us—that he won. Because that's who he is: championship material. Keeps his eye on the prize. Never afraid to give the truth a black eye and swear it's pink. A man who has never regretted anything, and even if he has—will never admit it.

Etgar Keret is a leading voice in Israeli literature and cinema. His short story collections have been translated into 46 languages. His writing has been published in *The New York Times, Le Monde, The Guardian, The New Yorker, The Paris Review,* and *Esquire.* Keret and his wife Shira Geffen's film Jellyfish won the Caméra d'Or prize for best first feature at Cannes in 2007, and their mini-series "The Middleman" (2019) won the best screenplay award at La Rochelle fiction TV festival in France. In 2010 he was awarded the Chevalier de l'Ordre des Arts et des Lettres. His latest collection is Fly Already.

Jessica Cohen was born in England, raised in Israel, and lives in Denver. She translates contemporary Israeli prose, poetry, and other creative work. She shared the 2017 Man Booker International Prize with David Grossman, for her translation of *A Horse Walks Into a Bar.* Her translations include works by major Israeli writers including Amos Oz, Etgar Keret, Ronit Matalon and Nir Baram. She is a past board member of the American Literary Translators Association and has served as a judge for the National Translation Award.

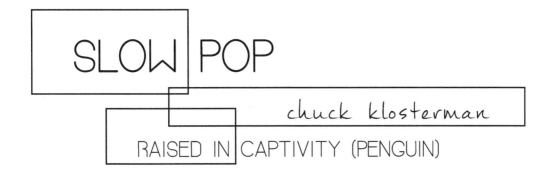

SLOW POP

chuck klosterman

RAISED IN CAPTIVITY (PENGUIN)

HE WAS CRISP. THAT was the word he used to describe himself: crisp. "Back off. I'm a little crisp this morning." Nobody knew what that was supposed to signify, but it seemed accurate. We all agreed not to disagree. "Let's get crisp, fellas." Sure. Let's get crisp. One night he played us the Steve Martin comedy album A Wild and Crazy Guy, recorded in 1978. During the opening three minutes of the set, Martin notices a two- year- old child sitting in the audience and makes a few jokes about performing for a baby. "That baby was me," he told us as the disc rotated. "My parents took me to that show. That's how I got crisp."

[Wait. Allow me to start again.]

He was focused. He was the most focused person I ever met, and his self- identification with that quality was unyielding. In 2014, the mayor of New York tried to ban horse-drawn carriages from Central Park. It was all over the news. Around that same time, he found a carriage driver who (somewhat justifiably) feared his business was doomed, and he convinced that driver to sell him the leather blinders that affix to the animal's head. Paid him cash, on the spot, right there on Fifty-ninth Street. I think it cost him eighty dollars. But it wasn't that he wanted a souvenir or a memento. He actually wore them. Whenever he was working on something around the apartment, he literally wore horse blinders. He altered the bridle and fashioned a foam forehead brace for maximum comfort. He'd answer the door wearing horse blinders. He'd go to the public library wearing horse blinders. He'd wear them on the subway. When he was especially interested in a movie or a play, he'd strap on the blinders inside the theater, right after we found our seats. We assumed he did this for attention. He insisted it was a psychological advantage. "The blinders help. I need to stay focused. Horses got it on lock. Horses are dope."

[Allow me to start again.]

He was obsessed with preparation. "I prefer to be prepared," he'd often remark, which is not an unusual thing to prefer or remark. But he took this to a crispier level. He once told me he'd prepared a ten- minute best man's speech for almost every unmarried male he had ever met, on the off chance he'd inadvertently perceived one of these relationships incorrectly. "What if somebody I view as a casual acquaintance considers me his closest friend? I need to be ready." I told him this scenario seemed unlikely, and that even if his fear was warranted and the event in question came to fruition, he would still have several weeks to come up with an original speech that is wholly acceptable to deliver extemporaneously. "What if the couple is eloping?" he asked in response. "What if the wedding is being televised or streamed live on Facebook? I'm not going to give an unrehearsed wedding speech about a man I barely know to a worldwide online audience." Again, I noted that this scenario was implausible and certainly not something to worry about. "But that's the thing," he replied. "I'm not worried. You would be worried. I'm prepared."

[Allow me to start one more time.]

I want to tell you about this guy. I don't know why, but I do. And let me be clear: This is not a story about a guy. This is not a story at all. It's just information about a guy you've never heard of, a guy you will never meet, a guy who left and never came back. But there was something about this guy, this person, this citizen, this bipedal humanoid projection. I'm still dealing with him, inside my mind. I'm still arguing with him, every morning and every night. He had a theory he called "slow pop." It applied to everything. It was a field theory. The thesis was that anything that happens quickly should be forced to happen slowly, as this alters the natural exchange of energy and amplifies the experience in unexpected ways. He first mentioned this in a conversation about the male orgasm, but he found a way to apply it to almost anything we happened to be debating—state politics, Grateful Dead bootlegs, the Bundesliga. We never understood what his theory vindicated or why he believed it, until the night he attempted to demonstrate by making microwave popcorn in a conventional oven. Forty minutes later, our apartment building burned to the ground. In a sense, I suppose he was right: That particular experience was amplified in an unexpected way.

[Let me start just one more time, and then I'll give up.]

There's this process people go through, sometimes in high school and sometimes in college and sometimes when they're thirty-nine and sometimes when they're told they have cancer. It's the process of asking oneself, "Why do I exist?" The question is grappled with for days or weeks or months, and the conclusion inevitably falls into one of two categories—either that there is no reason, or that some manufactured reason is insufficient but good enough. However, there's an ancillary question that's grappled with far less often: "Why do all the other people exist?" This question is harder.

You spend all this time convincing yourself that you're not the center of the universe and that reality isn't some movie where you're the main character. You stare at the ocean and remind yourself that the waves crashing against the shoreline have been crashing that way for two billion years, and this realization proves your existence is a minor detail within a trivial footnote inside a colossal book that can never be opened or closed. But then you walk off the beach and put on your socks and shoes, and you try to live like everyone else, and (without even trying) you're forced to reckon with the conclusion that every perspective is fixed and that the most myopic way to view life is the only way possible. There is no alternative to being who you are. You remain the nucleolus, against your will. But what are we to make of all the supplemental particles that buzz around our atomic structure? What is the purpose of a person who punctures the membrane of that nucleolus, displaces a few electrons, and then disappears forever?

A guy comes into your universe and tells you he's crisp. For whatever reason, you believe him. He wears horse blinders and burns your home to the ground. Somewhere between his interview with the police and the arrival of the insurance adjuster, he gets on an Amtrak and never comes back. You knew him for two years. You temporarily loved him. You knew his name, but it's a name many people have. He cannot be found. You knew everything about him, but nothing useful. Now he's a story, a story you tell, a story you tell where there is no plot, a story that is not actually a story. He was in your life. But you were not in his.

Chuck Klosterman is the author of eight books of nonfiction (including *Sex, Drugs, and Cocoa Puffs; But What If We're Wrong?;* and *Chuck Klosterman X*) and two novels (*Downtown Owl* and *The Visible Man*). He has written for *The New York Times, The Washington Post, GQ, Esquire, Spin, The Guardian, The Believer, Billboard, The A.V. Club,* and *ESPN*.

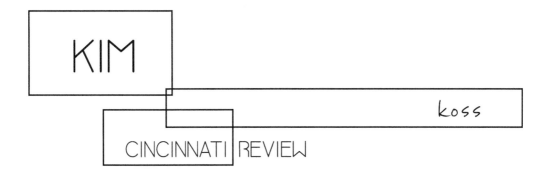

KIM

CINCINNATI REVIEW

koss

THE THING I REMEMBER most about Kim is that she is always falling. Sometimes I am above her, watching her body crash through the glass and bounce on the pavement below. Sometimes I'm with her, she's laughing, then she trips and screams before she hits the glass. Sometimes I arrive afterward, hunch over a railing, and see her splayed below like a bloody Hans Bellmer doll. Sometimes I fall with her and we smile at each other all the way down. Usually, though, she falls alone. Sometimes someone, drunk, bumps into her and she falls. Sometimes I try to grab her while other times I watch helplessly from across the room. Sometimes she falls at my feet. Other times she falls at the feet of strangers. Sometimes she falls into an abyss and we are unable to retrieve her broken body. Sometimes a fight breaks out and an angry woman with blonde hair pushes her. Sometimes her boyfriend does it. Sometimes the police arrive, grab her and her boyfriend, and in the struggle, Kim falls through the skylight. Sometimes she's leaning against the railing, laughing, holding a beer in her left hand, and the railing snaps. Sometimes she and her boyfriend argue over the drugs he says she stole. He grabs her arm, and the torque of her body as she attempts to free herself carries her over the edge of the railing. Sometimes the party is on the roof and she falls through the skylight into the crowd in the building below. Sometimes she's in a movie on TV falling in slow motion. Sometimes she falls in the newspaper when we read about it the next day. Sometimes her ex-boyfriend shoots her in the head and then she falls. Sometimes she deliberately jumps and then changes her mind halfway down. Sometimes she doesn't change her mind. Sometimes she falls thirty feet, sometimes a hundred. Sometimes she lands on her face, limbs spread. Sometimes her brains scatter over the shiny wood floor. Sometimes she falls a short distance, lands on her head, and her neck snaps. Sometimes she dangles by one arm on the railing for a long moment before it gives way and she falls. Sometimes most of the people don't notice and the music continues playing until the ambulance arrives. Sometimes it's a small party, the music stops, and everyone peers over the railing in silent horror. Sometimes she falls through the skylight in my bathroom into the tub while I'm bathing. Sometimes I run downstairs and listen to incomprehensible words garbled through a mouth full of blood. Sometimes she is in a light-green body bag with a shiny silver zipper. Sometimes she falls up through the skylight and disappears, then reappears and falls up again. Sometimes she does this in reverse. Sometimes she is wrapped in gray felt saturated with blood. Sometimes she falls through the railing and screams all the way down and the echo is heard through the building. Sometimes she is so fucked up she doesn't notice she's falling. Other times, she is stone sober.

Koss is a writer, fine artist and designer with an MFA from the School of the Art Institute of Chicago. They have work in *Entropy, Diode Poetry, Cincinnati Review, Hobart, Spillway* and others. They also have a hybrid book due out in 2020 by Negative Capability Press. Keep up with Koss on Twitter @Koss51209969 and Instagram @koss_singular.

PALOMAS, CIUDAD DE MÉXICO

elizabeth knapp

WASHINGTON WRITERS' PUBLISHING HOUSE & GREEN MOUNTAINS REVIEW

BECAUSE DEVOTION. BECAUSE ETHER. Because the saint holds a paintbrush, his sorrow. Because the grass may grow sharply, its knives. Because wonder. Because somehow a dove has nailed itself to the shadow of a tree. Because at some point in this holy story, a wrought iron door is opening. Because we could not speak for ourselves, we let the molecules do the talking. Because the power lines, the city. Because the city, the fires. Because each square of hope turned out to be hopeless, we let our eyes roam as they pleased. Because the painter's gaze, no exit. Because illegible the text of the dove's scarred wings.

Elizabeth Knapp is the author of *The Spite House* (C&R Press, 2011), winner of the 2010 De Novo Poetry Prize, and *Requiem with an Amulet in Its Beak* (Washington Writers' Publishing House, 2019), winner of the 2019 Jean Feldman Poetry Prize. Her poems have appeared in many journals and anthologies, including *Best New Poets*, *Kenyon Review*, *The Massachusetts Review*, *North American Review*, and *Quarterly West*. An associate professor of English at Hood College, she lives in Frederick, Maryland with her family.

MORTALITY EVENT

hadiyyah kuma

SMOKE LONG

DAY 1 (WE'LL COME back to this)

Hi kid, I'm one of those dead pigeons that fell from the sky, seemingly out of nowhere. I might've hit something, or something might've hit me. Please don't feel the need to bury my body or anything, because I wasn't ready to die. So here's what I'm going to do: I'm going to become you. The chosen one should never fight or scream.

Day 2

I'm going to become the kind of person who secretly watches romantic Korean dramas on the floor of her bedroom with no pants on. I'm going to cuff your mom jeans and shave your leg hair every week, which is a drag, but if you suddenly stopped people would wonder. I'm going to sleep with your knees tucked up because I've never had knees and I kind of like the idea of curling into a tight little baby ball. I'm going to have lots of sex and your partners will agonize over you when you leave them. Being inside of a bird inside of human is a whole different experience. You're just a bit too inexperienced, but don't worry, you'll have a lot of fun. I'll take cough syrup before I shower to take the edge off seeing your body there, in front of me, naked. What's it like to have no feathers? Humans are so naked. I love cough syrup.

Day 70

You make a lot of Spotify playlists. All your K-pop playlists are private, but I'll change that for you. I like these BTS people, they're nothing to be ashamed of. I like the way they dance and feel themselves. I like their coloured hair. Your food account has a lot of Instagram followers. Why does the tv emoji look like a bus? I would like to know what 'sus,' means and your best friend says that about everyone. Also, why does your search history have so many mentions of Jungkook? My eyes get tired scrolling and I steal your mother's reading glasses and I get slapped. It's strange getting slapped, it's strange learning you had problems too even if you're not dead.

Day 100

With your eyes I've seen birds hit windows and collapse, instantly dead. It was shocking. I'm okay now. I'm okay with that, because I have this body, and it's pretty good, even if it can't fly. You don't have a bad life. You can sleep whenever you want to, except when you have to serve bubble tea. But when you sleep you do it well, curled up in the dark, forcing your brain to have a nice dream about soaring through red open skies. So thank you. I feel you get stressed sometimes: stomach clenching, shoulders tight. I sort of wish I could build a nest for you so you can get away sometimes, but the problem is that nobody would understand. Another problem is that your body is too big to fit there. We'll have to settle for burying our head in the couch and listening to the drone of *Wheel of Fortune*, what I've come to know as your mother's favourite show.

Day 200

I've become the kind of person who likes walking even though it's nothing like seeing the city from above. I look down more than I used to. I have to stretch my legs every few minutes. Dogs scare me. My friends sometimes walk slower for my benefit, they know something is off with me, has been for a while, but like any good friends they don't say anything. They just try to be nicer. I get a lot of free lunches. I like sushi, and I love broccoli. There's just something about it. Sometimes though, when no one's looking, I sneak an earthworm into my mouth. I use my hands to do this. I use my hands to grab and pull and twist, I think I've got the groove. And I finally understand why people cry. I do it in the shower, which I have to take every day because I have this rancid smell under my armpits that worsens over time. When a human cries, it's a sacred thing. I treasure those moments. I push down deep into my stomach, let the cough syrup drip out of my nose, and wail a raspy wail.

Day 250

I jump off a building because I know I'm going to fly. I break a knee and a wrist, but I don't die and it's amazing. I spend weeks recovering, my mom feeds me liquids and we watch rerun after rerun of Pat Sajak asking players to pick a category. A woman picks, "Person," and I tell my mom, "I'm one of those. Me." She touches my forehead.

Day 365

On my birthday I jam out to BLACKPINK while fitting my arms and legs into a skin-tight holographic jumpsuit. My butt looks amazing. My friends, the slow walkers, throw me a surprise party. There are so many people in one room and we're all sweating at the same time. I wrap my smooth legs around somebody's warm waist and scream. I get drunk on a single lime cooler and start pecking at people's necks. I'm so charming, everyone loves me. Crying is great but laughing is pretty fun too.

Day 1 (I wrote it down so I wouldn't forget)
They call deaths like mine mortality events, but when you look it up on your phone, you read it, "morality event," to your friend. That's how I know you're the perfect fit. I dive through your mouth, because it's wide open with questions for the sky, like what happened to you? And how does it feel to be born again?

Hadiyyah Kuma is a 20-year-old Indo-Guyanese writer and sociology student from Toronto. Her work seeks to examine rest and pleasure under capitalism, gentrification, platonic intimacy, and anxiety. Her poems, essays, and fiction have been published in places like *The Rumpus, Yes Poetry, The Hart House Review, Hobart,* and *GUTS magazine.* Her debut chapbook, *tired but not spectacularly* was released by the Soapbox Press in 2019.

EIGEN GRAU

randilee sequeira larson

ILANOT REVIEW

I WAS TRANSFIGURED IN '09.

The crucifixion took place within a tiny plastic bottle. My cross tumbled, bright and acrid, into the palm of my hand. It tasted of industry and plastic. Above my head, they hung a sign: "L429"—Aspirin.

I died, sat at the right hand of shadows, and for three days I puked up the remains of myself. Orange and bitter were the remains of myself; orange and bitter was my new goddess shroud. My holy pagan vestments dragged across the dirt as I rolled away the stone and found not a single disciple left in mourning. For three years I lived among the tombs, unbound and uncontrolled, wailing to the mountains and cutting myself with stones. I called out to the people and watched them recoil from my wounds. I let the grapes ferment inside my throat. I ate only bread and honey then watched my flesh retreat deep within my bones.

From body, to blood, to wine, to nothing. This was no miracle. It was a metamorphosis of corruption.

After 40 days and 40 nights of fasting, I consulted the oracles, their reclined sofa alters, clicking pens, and scrutinous clipboards—They told me to drink more water.

II

So I drowned myself in blessed rain. I baptized myself in the sea. I flung myself into rushing rivers and drank until I floated, fat and engorged, down the streams and creeks they birthed. I reveled in the jagged stones I caught along the way.

My body floated to the boundary of the sea, where a small cult of fleeting worshipers awaited my sickly form. Artists and bards, con men and lovers, for who would follow at the feet of Fear, pouring libations of whiskey and water, burning nicotine incense and praising the way my deathly divine heart trembles?

Only fools.

Only pale, lofty poets with greedy hands and members more upright than their morals. They feed me figs and lies, tracing the scars of my transformed skin with white fingers, promising to pull me from the depths with their love and devotion. They set coins atop my eyes, within my hands, as I become blind to their sins.

Psalms have been written, wistful and vulgar. Flowers have been offered, and fennel placed atop my shaven skull. They conjure eternity with their lyrics, press their wine lips to mine, and are never seen in worship again.

I am a fleeting religion of sad, lost men. I am a wretched affair atop a golden altar. They love my sweet sorrow, my drunken divinity. Their honey-tongues reach out to me and push, deeper down, deeper down, deeper down, until I can no longer see the sun.

I've shaken hands with Hades and his lovely flower-bearing wife—They told me to lighten up.

III

So I set myself atop a pyre of righteous anger.

My jagged scars split open from the heat, steam rushes from my veins. My eyes boil with rage. I can hear the congregation scream, smell the vestment's noxious fumes. My fennel crown erupts into an unholy halo and my ribs split open like wings. For the first time in years, I feel a thump in my chest.

Gold ornaments and liquefied gems run down the walls of my temple like honey, burning but beautiful, and I lap at them like a hungry dog. The priests fall to their knees and beg for mercy, for patience, of which I have no more to give.

All around me, the temple crumbles. Air rushes in and the flames take a moment to breathe before swelling, bright and proud, and consuming the pews, the congregation, anyone desperate enough to try and brave this force. The ceiling comes down above me, and I sleep beneath destruction for ten days. I do not dream, I rest soundly in Sheol.

When I awake, I am alone.

The sun cuts through the soot and warms my face and the smooth curve of my swollen gold-filled belly. The air gently brushes the ash from my newly purified form. My legs curl beneath me as I pull myself from blackened earth, from the grave, stretch my arms into the sky, and feel the scales fall from my eyes.

I rise, transfigured.

Randilee Sequeira Larson is a Portland-based author whose work tends towards the experimental as well as the surreal. A graduate of Portland's Concordia University, she was awarded "Thesis with Distinction" for her memoir, *Savages*. Her essays and prose poems have appeared in *The Promethean, The Santa Ana River Review, The Ilanot Review, Unlikely Stories Mark V, Shift: A Journal of Literary Oddities*, and others. When not writing, Randilee enjoys discovering new types of literature, playing with her cat, "Cocaine Greg," and tending to her colony of flesh-eating beetles.

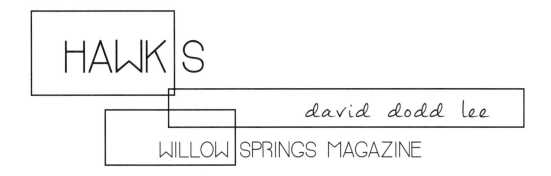

HAWKS

david dodd lee

WILLOW SPRINGS MAGAZINE

HE WAS SHOOTING ME from across the street, me in my priest's collar, my black gown. St. Sebastian's was a flood of electric light. I could see the outer fringes of my hair all lit up, like my aura were visible between the curls.

He'd already used the Steadicam. Now the street was snow in patches and a series of black sedans rolling past.

The movie was for a millionaire, who wanted priests and things with black wings projected on a wall behind his alter and his "fornication chair." That's what he told Gregory, a local director of music videos, a soft porn adaptation of *Rent*, PSAs for the Humane Society, and who, in fact, himself adopted and rehabilitated abused greyhounds. We'd gone to college together.

It's crazy trying to make something of your days. I was in an Alice Cooper tribute band in the 1980 and early 90s, but I kept seeing pictures of Cooper swinging golf clubs instead of scowling under blood red skies filled with bats, and it just didn't feel the same anymore. I felt like I was living a lie . . .

I was now instructed to stand at the door of the church, to pretend I was locking up for the night.

"Wouldn't I just walk through a hallway and into my residence?"

"You're an adulterous priest. You've got a hot date with a female parishioner named Veronica."

"I can do that." I liked playing it straight, plus I'd be throwing in a bit of a sexy snarl for the millionaire. I've got large teeth in my mouth, including incisors. I played a vampire in another music video, from my *Welcome to My Nightmare* days.

I was further instructed to walk—slowly—down the wide (golden in the floodlights) staircase.

"Glady," I said, because walking's my specialty.

I was wearing black shoes.

I didn't need much more than the clothes. I put in some eye drops so one eye was dilated. A touch of mascara. I watched the black cars on the road.

Pigeons kept rising over the roofs of nearby houses and circling the church's bell tower. I liked that I was high up against enormous wood doors, while in the house next door I could see a man watching TV and eating popcorn out of a blue or green bowl. His wife or girlfriend was curled up beside him. It made me feel a little sad. But it also felt good to be towering above them.

Gregory's assistant moved downwind from us. He'd be standing there. Then he'd disappear or I'd only see half of him for a couple of seconds. He looked like the Black Dahlia woman, cut in half the way she was, but then Victor'd suddenly be walking toward us, or only half of him would be.

In the woods, just beyond the surrounding homes, a bonfire raged, staining the night's low-flying clouds a peculiar shade of orange.

It was all in how you lived your life. I wasn't much of a drinker myself, and I ate a lot of yogurt and blueberries and hardboiled eggs. But I could stand along an avenue with the skies aflame and talk to Jesus Christ and the blackbirds would burst out of the trees.

The millionaire, it was known, threw big parties that included orgies. People would come to town from Hawaii and Austria. Nude women wearing headgear fashioned to look like hawks carried trays of hors d'oeuvres and glasses of champagne.

"He thinks the help seem more nude that way, that it enhances their role as aphrodisiacs," Gregory said.

All of us chuckled at that, except for Alphonso, whose wife had recently left him for some guy who frequented sex clubs in Chicago.

I've been there. I only snorted amyl nitrate twice, though—and it was great; smoke slithered over black floorboards and my partners felt dry and smooth, like anacondas.

Nowadays I run on an elliptical most evenings. My last boyfriend left me when for several weeks he couldn't stop staring at the ceiling and asking me why I was so damn annoying.

"I'm just lying here, Michael."

"That's not true, Stephen. For one thing you're fucking breathing."

I do love my cat, a svelte tabby runt. She is 10 years old and has never weighed an ounce over five pounds.

When Gregory yelled "Action" I pretended to wrestle with a skeleton key. I knew he and the boys were rolling their eyes. *What a drama queen.*

I also knew they felt chills run down their spines when I turned and floated about an inch off the cement, my face white as the moon.

"Fuck," I heard Victor say.

Then came the part in the scene where I begin to walk.

David Dodd Lee is the author of nine full-length books of poems and a chapbook, including *Downsides of Fish Culture* (New Issues Press, 1997), *Orphan, Indiana* (University of Akron Press, 2010), and *Animalities* (Four Way Books, 2014), as well as two volumes of Ashbery erasure poems. Most recently his fiction has appeared in *What About Birds?*, *Willow Springs*, and *New World Writing*. He is also a visual artist whose work, since 2014, has been featured in three one-person exhibitions, mixing collage and poetry texts into improvisational art works. He lives on the St. Joseph River and teaches at Indiana University South Bend.

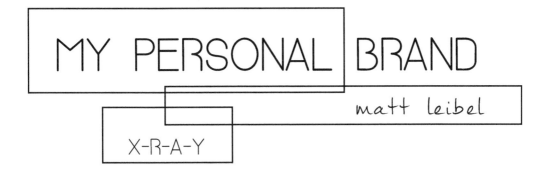

MY PERSONAL BRAND

X-R-A-Y

matt leibel

MY PERSONAL BRAND IS integrity. My personal brand is fresh, innovative thinking, and a commitment to excellence. My personal brand sets me apart, in the sense that many people refuse to stand within 50 feet of me, as if my personal brand stinks or something; my personal brand does not stink. If anything, my personal brand exudes a fresh, clean scent, evocative of wintergreen, or a cool spring breeze. My personal brand does not harm the skin. My personal brand contains no known carcinogens and has been extensively tested on laboratory rats. Unfortunately, one of the rats has recently escaped his cage. If you happen to see him, do not panic, do not subject him to an inhumane trap, for this is no ordinary rat, but a spectacular rat, one infused with my own personal brand, and all that this entails. You can find out more about my personal brand on my website, mypersonalbrand.ki. All of the other internet domain extensions for "mypersonalbrand" have been taken, by the way, so I had to use ".ki," the extension designated for the tiny Pacific Ocean island Republic of Kiribati. I even traveled to Kiribati's main atoll to set up my personal brand's website. That's how new and fresh my personal brand is. In Gilbertese, incidentally (the official language of the I-Kiribati people), the word for dog is *Kamea*. Apparently the etymology of this is that European invaders used to say to their dogs, "Come here, come here!" I didn't learn that on Kiribati—I discovered it on the internet. But the internet is only the tip of the iceberg so far as my personal brand goes. Speaking of icebergs, I've projected my personal brand onto the face of several massive ones spanning Greenland, Siberia, and Antarctica. You can see videos of these projections on my YouTube channel; they are rather spectacular. I've done all this, by the way, at enormous personal cost and am beginning to wonder if the payoff justifies the expense I've gone to to get my name out there. My personal brand has destroyed both of my marriages and has deeply strained my relationship with my teenaged son Zeke, whom I enlisted in my scheme to light up the endarkened, icy ends of the Earth with a gigantic symbol of myself. This involved, among other challenges, taking Zeke out of school for an entire year, and hiring an instructor to train him in the driving and care of sled dogs. Zeke now vows that he will never forgive me, but he is still young and as yet lacks the perspective on what really was a truly unique once-in-a-lifetime experience he will one day thank me for (which other of his friends have had the chance to enjoy the meaty tang of fresh-killed whale meat?)—and that thanks will come, in part, via a full-throated endorsement of my personal brand, once he himself is in position to become an influencer/thought leader/social media superstar on his own. My personal brand is all about providing unconventional and memorable branded experiences. My personal brand is "sticky" like that. My personal brand is—and let's just be honest about this—my last real chance at this point. It's a shot in the dark, a rabbit I'm trying to pull out of a hat, and, in fact, I've had some hats created for my personal brand including these premium models made out of genuine rabbit fur, and take it from me (and Zeke!), these hats will help you get through even the most brutal of winters. My personal brand still hasn't gotten the recognition it deserves—but now is the time to change that. I'm coming to you with an opportunity, in other words, to get in on the ground floor and see your own personal brand piggyback on mine and take flight (not literally, as pigs can't fly!). My personal brand has now been certified 100% rat-free, and will focus henceforth only on areas reachable without access to sled or snowmobile. Think about it like this: in the end all things will die. Penguins will die, whales will die, rats will die, icebergs will die, the I-Kiribati will die. I will die, my ex-wives will die, my ungrateful but only son will die, and you will die, too. But our personal brands will live on long after we're gone. Our personal brands are, in many ways, the ghosts of our lives, and if you don't want to have your own personal ghost—well, you're missing out on a chance to reach the coveted 18-45s, as *personal ghosting* is all the rage right now, according to my influencer friends in the know. But if you'd rather not join forces, beware: my personal brand is not fucking around. It will win out in the end, because it is desperate, it has no other choice. My personal brand is no longer merely an extension of me. It has become an independent organism, a lab creature on the loose, a monster that I can no longer contain nor control. It will not be forgotten. It will not be denied. It will flutter under your floorboards and creep into your brain. It will achieve maximum stickiness. It will make its mark upon you.

Matt Leibel's short fiction has been published in *Electric Literature, Portland Review, Carolina Quarterly, DIAGRAM, Wigleaf, Juked, Bengal Lights*, and elsewhere. He holds an MFA in Writing from Washington University in St. Louis. He lives in San Francisco, where he is a frequent contributor to the Quiet Lightning reading series, and a member of the Cupboard Writers' Collective.

NEIGHBOR|S

GONE | LAWN

sara lippmann

TO YOUR LEFT, HIPSTERS. Musicians to your right. Behind you, bankers and lawyers. At night, the dust of stars. A harvest moon brave as Jupiter sits on your roof as a reminder the whole world is not worth giving up. Which isn't to say a moon can fill you, but maybe it's a start. Go outside. A spider you don't know by name does her work in the door frame and you plow right into it, ruining her viscous string meant to keep you in or out. A car roars. Tricked out speakers, engine growling, the works. Who isn't crying out for something? Around the corner, a car alarm's been at it for hours. In the morning there will be a sack of shit on the windshield, a gift from neighbors. It is impossible to know. The street is long and shady. The waft of weed more common than dogs at 6 am, 6 pm. We all need company. Neighbors move in and out. This one has a ball hoop. That one, a trampoline. Once upon a time, children played in the road. Kick the can. Street hockey afterschool until the dads pulled in. One dad killed his wife in the bathtub while their toddler slept. News cameras parked on lawns to report the story: call-girl debt + life insurance = freedom. The algorithm on a piece of scrap paper. Google it. Not what you'd expect from suburbia but nothing is. Another died in his armchair as the world series played on TV. The doctor two-doors-down made a house call but what can you do. Hearts stop. That doctor left his marriage for another woman or a man. The mad scientist housed lab rats in his basement. From the cellar window you could hear the collective suck of water bottle teats, smell the dryer. Why are clouds of comfort so bad for the planet? It's hard not to think about dying. How would you do it? Brainstorm but you've lost your creativity. That's part of the problem. Your husband says it's not depression it's being home all day every day. You need to get out, to see people. Your husband says he would want to kill himself too if he had your life. He means well and you know what he means. Take a walk. Go to the store, the pharmacy, fill your prescription, stock up on children's vitamins. You buy the crappiest off-brand aluminum foil because you don't want to outlive it. The glint of Freddie Kruger's hands sent you running from sleepovers. Children tossed your lovey in the oven. This is your horror story. Violence is everywhere. The neighborhood has changed, no judgment, only of course there is. Why would you want anything to stay the same? Check out the hair and shoes on the actor across the street who gets drunk on his porch and watches you. Some people are home. You've been home for years. Thank God for squirrels. One house was the color of an inside ear. Used to be a hotel, went the rumor. On Halloween blood pumped through a dummy scaring the hell out of you but you've always been scared. The neighbors had mice as pets, cats, too, and a Christmas tree twenty feet tall that stood in the hall turning brown shedding needles through winter. Lance Jezebel ran for public office and lost, Janice Proctor ran for school council and won. Both were haunted by scandal. Shari Johnson with juvenile diabetes invited you over to watch her pee on a stick. You played *Weebles* until they all fell down. Children on the trampoline jump higher, their voices lifting. A pair of ancient oaks frames a house of swingers. Renters keep their lights on, bone thin curtains giving way to laughter, shadows, bodies coming together and apart. Can they hear you jerk it three stories up? Cry out, *please*? Do they know you're alone? In the house on the corner where the sidewalk dropped off you broke the fence. Everyone was young then. These days, Halloween decorations go missing. Skeletons on hinges, garlands of plastic pumpkins. People are suspicious. You no longer know who goes as Tina Turner, who as Frankenstein. Elvira runs marathons in your sleep. Rabbi Berkowitz and his wife shared your driveway. She wore turquoise glasses with rhinestones on the fins. The garage smelled of wet cinder carved with the initials of children who came before you, smashed pinky balls against the rotting brick to spell A-S-S. That was the game. With the windows open, there's no hiding it: Cigarettes, *General Hospital, Go fuck yourself.* Marvin Price's daughter got bigger but never grew up. She still plays dolls and Barry Manilow albums. In her mind, it is forever 1983. Is she lonely? A new neighbor dies, cancer. No one comes to mourn. The family is estranged. The Russians keep their children on a leash, a bachelor named Kelvin keeps to himself until his T-Top breaks down on the Parkway, and he pulls over and climbs out for a look and is instantly crushed. Supposedly, your house once belonged to hoarders but you moved in empty. There's little a paint job and savvy real estate agent can't handle. The walk is littered with gingko nuts, chestnut pods reminiscent of morning stars. Neighbors shack up on the top floor while scaffolding overtakes their living room. They're not the only ones under construction. Gutters are overflowing again. Can they see you on the bed? On trash days you roll out the trash but the raccoons have been getting to it so you sit on the step and wait with your strobe, with your frozen pizza suggestive of cheese, sit and wink that big yellow light, beam and shine in the dark and wait for eyes to flash back at you.

Sara Lippmann is the author of the story collection *Doll Palace*. She was awarded an artist's fellowship in fiction from New York Foundation for the Arts, and her stories have appeared in

Berfrois, Vol. 1 Brooklyn, Split Lip, Midnight Breakfast, and elsewhere. She teaches creative writing at St. Joseph's College in Brooklyn and cohosts the Sunday Salon reading series. Find her on twitter @saralippmann or https://www.saralippmann.com.

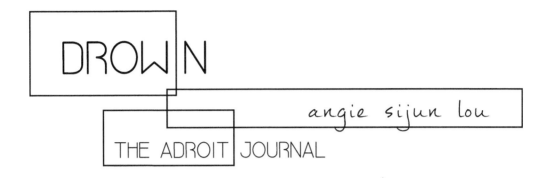

DROWN

angie sijun lou

THE ADROIT JOURNAL

ONCE, WHEN I WAS very young, I asked Baba what he did when there was no school during the revolution. Baba laughed and said that he mostly just fucked around. He had just failed his entrance exam to university and every sober night he was buried in the same dream. In this dream he comes to class late, his breath reeking of whiskey, and opens the door to an empty room. In this dream he runs down a long hallway, and the sky is a horizon of smoke.

Instead of telling Nainai about his test score, Baba put his textbooks in his backpack every morning and went to the abandoned lot to race cockroaches and eat watermelons soaked in beer. He sliced them into fat cubes and let the juice drip down his double chin. When he came home at dusk he said, xingku le, school was so hard today. There were still watermelon seeds stuck in his teeth when the men took him away to the camps. They put a bag over his head and laid him down in the bed of a truck all night, weaving between dunes, the morning dripping light like a sieve.

At the camps the air was dry and chapped his lips. They shaved his hair off so when he looked in the mirror he saw a shiny egg staring back at him. So shiny he could almost see himself in it. When the dry season came he put his bald head on the earth and prayed for monsoons. They took away his keychain of Guanyin and wiped down his knees, scabbed over with prayer, and handed him a shovel instead. Dig, they said, so Baba moved piles of sand around, in a tropical daze, until it felt like he had dug up the desert and put it back.

I thought of the suburbs in Cincinnati where we had our first house, how Baba dug up the sand in the backyard to put in a swimming pool. The sun flared over our no-bedroom apartment while Baba filled the pool with cold water, laughing as it overflowed when he sunk his beer belly into it.

He watched television by squinting at it through the open window. The television spoke to him about money and girls while he smoked cigarette after cigarette, each one lit with the end of another, ashing into his bright blue oblivion.

When I was very young, I asked Baba what drowning felt like, and he said not everything feels like something else.

———————————

Angie Sijun Lou is from Seattle and Shanghai. Her work has appeared, or is forthcoming, in the *American Poetry Review, FENCE, Black Warrior Review, the Adroit Journal, the Asian American Literary Review, Hyphen, the Margins,* and others. She is a Kundiman Fellow in Fiction and a PhD student in Literature and Creative Writing at the University of California, Santa Cruz. She also teaches calculus and poetry at San Quentin State Prison.

FOURTH SISTER

marie lu

THE NEW YORK TIMES

Sì, THE WORD FOR four, sounded very similar to *sǐ*, the word for death. It was a deeply unlucky number.

So when she was born, her father, who had prayed every day to Guanyin for a son after three daughters, took one look at her and walked out of the birthing room. She was not only the fourth, but a girl at that.

She spent her entire life hiding in corners, staying out of everyone's way, trying to make up for the ill fortune she had brought down upon her father, by finding little ways to organize their lives around luckier numbers.

She whispered to the rice plants to sprout in unison on the eighth—eight, *bā*, which sounded similar to *fā*, the word for wealth and prosperity—day of spring. Her father beamed at the bright green shoots blanketing the flooded fields and credited his luck to the auspicious timing.

When the hail came and rattled the tin roof of their house, she whispered for the storm to turn away in three—*sān*, which was similar to *shēng*, the word for birth—hours, to divert calamities away from her family. Her father looked up in astonishment at the clearing skies and proclaimed that their stroke of luck had protected their crops.

And when the rains dried up and the rice fields cracked, she whispered to the skies to send water within nine days—nine, *jiǔ*, which sounded like *jiǔ*, the word for eternity and longevity. The skies opened and her father declared the family protected by the heavens.

She, of course, never told anyone that she was responsible for these events in their lives. Being the fourth and a girl was misfortune enough. Adding the label of witch, *zhu*, would surely ostracize their family from the rest of the village. She had seen other girls accused of witchcraft, witnessed them excluded and left unmarried. One girl had been driven out of the village altogether.

At night, she studied in secret by lantern light for the exams that could qualify her for a coveted government scholarship, one that sent students to study at American universities. It would give her a reason to leave home at last, to remove herself from this place altogether and thus from the misfortune that came with her.

But after she took the exams, the invitation that arrived in the mail came not from the government's scholar fund—but from a society in Chicago that specialized in training students gifted with the kind of magic she possessed.

How did they know? She spent that day studying her hands in wonder. The test had been as normal as she could have imagined. She did not realize that her fingers had left trails of magic on the paper, like an imprint of dust that glittered long after she had finished.

So the next morning, she woke up at six—*liù*, which sounded similar to *liú*, the word indicating clarity and smoothness—and quietly left home, turning her shoes away from the smattering of homes in her family's rural village to Shanghai, the city of the future, from which she would embark to America.

The entire trip on the boat, she practiced her talents, making broken light bulbs glow in the boat's dining area and scattering blankets of clouds to form patterns against the blue sky. It was a surprisingly smooth journey. Other students in her bunker—twins and a round-faced young woman and a flighty girl with braided knots in her hair—chatted curiously with her, teasing her country accent and asking where she came from. They were the children of wealthier families in the cities. She marveled at their fur coats and cloche hats, the soft leather of their purses. Her own coat was old, the buttons twisted in the traditional Chinese sense, something that seemed old-fashioned beside these rich young women's Western fashions.

When they finally dragged their trunks off the train in Chicago, a photographer was waiting to take their photos. *For the paper*, he said. So they clustered together, wearing their best coats, their faces both eager and intimidated. She would never see the developed photo, but if she had, she would have noticed that her magic hung about her in a halo that the camera picked up, obscuring her face behind a haze.

It took her a moment longer to notice the lady waiting for her by the train platform. She was small, her back slightly rounded in a hunch, and when she stretched a hand out in greeting, her fingers were long and graceful.

"Welcome to Chicago," the lady told her in Mandarin, "and to your training in the art of magic. I see you have been blessed with great fortune."

She blinked. It was the first time anyone had ever looked pleased to see her, and she was so surprised that she replied, "I am the fourth sister in my family, so I am the bringer of misfortune."

The woman shook her head. "That is impossible, you see, for I can tell that you have been gifted with the magic of luck. That is how your application somehow ended up at our office, and how I noticed the shimmer of magic on the paper. I will teach you how to wield it."

The rice harvest and the diverted storm. The early rains and the smooth voyage. Good fortune. It was the first time anyone had given that identity to her, but she'd had it all along.

She smiled. Then she fell into step beside the woman and never looked back.

Marie Lu is the #1 New York Times bestselling author of *The Young Elites* series, as well as the blockbuster bestselling *Legend* series. She graduated from the University of Southern California and jumped into the video game industry as an artist. Now a full-time writer, she spends her spare time reading, drawing, playing games, and getting stuck in traffic. She lives in Los Angeles with her illustrator-author husband, Primo Gallanosa, and their dogs. Visit her online at Marielubooks.com or on Twitter @Marie_Lu.

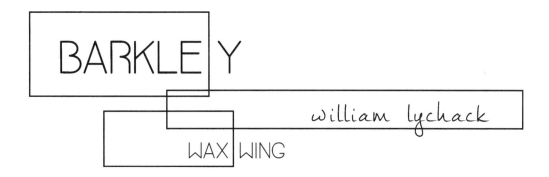

BARKLEY

WAX WING

william lychack

IN MY DREAM OF them, I'd give the boys at least one perfect moment with their father. No lessons to impart, no hidden tests, only the advent of dog. Mr. Brownell would set the brake on the truck and shut the engine, telling the boys to stay put. He'd get out of the cab and walk around the front hood, Brownie cranking the window down the rest of the way, Tommy leaning against his brother to see their father stepping through the brush, morning air damp and cool.

She was on the far side of the runoff ditch. Some person had used an old clothesline to tie her to the fence, the dog unable to even sit, head barely able to turn. That crunch of boots on gravel as he got closer, the dog as small and submissive as possible, her ears down, tail between her legs. She would be there, standing as he approached, helpless to stop whatever this man would do to her. She'd cringe and wait to be beaten, nowhere else to go. She'd keep her eyes down, sorry for how filthy, how full of cuts and bugs she was, how much she would cost for them to bring her back to life.

The boys would hear their father talking gentle to the dog. They'd watch the man peel the tape from her mouth. He'd cut her free with a pocket knife, her hind legs so unsteady and shivering she could barely stand, their father's voice high and gentle, man saying, "Easy, girl."

Saying, "No one's going to hurt you."

The dog would lick his hand, and the boys could hold back for only so long here, their father leading this open wound of fur and eyes and ears and slope of back around to the truck, Brownie and Tommy out to meet them on the road. They'd see every rib, every lump and hollow. They'd see rope burns, grooves in her neck. They'd get water bottles from hockey bags, dog drinking from cupped palms, the callouses on her elbows so raw they'd wince. They could smell her skin and fur all caked and stiff.

Their father would boost the dog up into the bed of the truck and then start them slowly home, mindful of her trying to stand in the back, the road all corrugated, dust blooming up behind them, and the boys glancing to one another (because that is what I would have done). They'd study the side of their father's face (because that is all I could imagine doing). They might have talked and carried on in ways I'd not be able to imagine (because my own childhood was so invincibly silent compared to theirs). They might have felt no suspense riding home with the dog, assumed their father could make anything work, might have felt in their hearts that she was theirs by now. (Because they seemed to have it all—brother, father, house, cottage—so why shouldn't they have this dog as well?)

But that was another story.

In the story I wanted to tell for them, they would be making a game plan together, their father coaching them on strategy, what to say when they got home to their mother, how to play the dog to their advantage. They'd coast into the driveway, get out of the truck, go easy on the doors, the three of them tip-toeing into the garage. Their mother would no doubt be waiting for them at the inside doorway, Mrs. Brownell standing with her arms folded, the woman shaking her head no.

She'd say, "Oh, no you don't."

Or, "Over my dead body."

Or something to that effect.

Whatever it was she said would go down in history. She'd be this anvil in their way, woman. Tommy and Brownie would swear to take care of her, to walk her every day, clean up after her in the yard. Their father would suggest they put it in writing. Their mother would shake her head no, no, no. They'd have other phases, but the final push would be the boys bringing the dog forward as meager and small and pathetic as possible, their father describing how she'd been left tied to the fence, her mouth taped shut, rope burns under her legs. He'd reach to smudge the black from the dog's nose, and the creature would shy away as if to be hit.

"It's all right, girl," the man would say, his voice tender with the dog. They'd stare at him as he stroked the dog's face—soft and quiet—the boy's father nearly unrecognizable. (A touch too sentimental, but, still, did he ever talk to any of them with such tenderness? Was he always tough on them? Always riding his sons?)

No wonder the dog would seem so much more than just a dog. No wonder she would become this chance to have something more. No wonder they thought of her as lucky, this dog at their legs tentatively happy, guardedly hopeful and scared in the. This dog a kind of glimpse into their family, Mrs. Brownell with her hands on her hips, her saying, "I'm going to regret this, aren't I?"

William Lychack is the author of *Cargill Falls*, *The Wasp Eater*, and *The Architect of Flowers*, and his work has appeared in *The Best American Short Stories*, *The Pushcart Prize*, and on public radio's *This American Life*. For more, please go to www.lychack.com.

L' CHAIM

r.l. maizes

MONKEYBICYCLE & WE LOVE ANDERSON COOPER
(CELADON BOOKS)

NO MUSIC ACCOMPANIED LILA Orr's entrance into the deserted hallway of her parents' home. No one played the famous wedding march that she and Morris Hirsch had settled on after deciding they were too old to get married to the Rolling Stones.

The musician had left hours before. From experience he could tell the difference between the jitters and a decision reached in the eleventh hour that the thing was better off not done. He had packed up his organ and congratulated himself on getting paid in advance. Lila's parents had retired to their bedroom, her father still sniffing the cigar he'd planned to smoke during the reception.

Silk shoe straps hooked over two fingers, Lila stepped into the yard to find the corgis humping under the *chuppah* and the cat cleaning its fur. She walked barefoot down the aisle on rose petals whose edges had begun to blacken. Lila waited for the dogs to finish and then picked up Molly, the female. It helped to hold something alive as she surveyed the elegant wreckage.

Twenty rows of white wooden chairs populated the lawn. To rent a chair for twenty-four hours cost five dollars. Was it possible she had spent a year of her life on such things?

Holding the dog under one arm, she snapped a few pictures with her phone. She wanted desperately to forget the day, but there would be times when she might want to remember it. Refusing to come out of the study was the bravest thing she had ever done. Better to have said no two years before on Coney Island when Morris presented the two-carat ring in a clamshell that still smelled like the sea. Morris's voice was just as nasal then; he had the same habit of correcting her. Better to have broken it off then. But not as brave as breaking it off now, bringing humiliation on herself and Morris, and risking her father having a heart attack among his accounting partners and golf buddies.

She wondered what had happened to all the food (forty-five dollars per person for plated grilled salmon and vegetables, an organic locally grown salad). Did the caterer take it down to the shelter, her instructions for the leftovers? She could have eaten a whole salmon. Three pieces of wedding cake with buttercream icing. She was that hungry.

Relief overshadowed her embarrassment. For the first time in days—since her final fitting, she realized—her lungs expanded to fill her chest. She noticed the scent of crab-apple blossoms and the breeze caressing her neck (her hair was still pinned). It was spring and she was alive and she would not marry Morris. The Pottery Barn goblet that was to be crushed under Morris's heel as part of the ceremony sat on a small table next to a bottle of Manischewitz. She set the dog down, broke the seal on the wine, and filled the glass. The glass would not be broken, not that afternoon, maybe never. *"L'chaim,"* she said to herself, "to life."

R.L. Maizes is the author of *Other People's Pets*, Celadon Books (Macmillan) and *We Love Anderson Cooper*, short stories, Celadon Books (Macmillan).

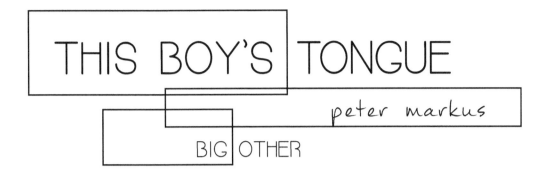

THIS BOY'S TONGUE

peter markus

BIG OTHER

THIS BOY IS BUT a boy. The boy that he is, he sees what a boy can see. When he sees what he sees, he says what it is that he sees. Boat, he says, and looks down at what wood holds him up on this lake so that he does not sink like rock or stone would sink to where the lake ends at rock or mud or weeds or sand. Lake, he says, at what this boat bobs up and down on. Sky, says he, and lifts up with his eyes, at the blue that birds swim in as fish do the blue that is the lake. Rock, he thinks. Call it stone. Like this, he makes with his hand a fist. Witch in a house. Bird with one wing. Fish. These words make a song in his head. He takes up with his rod from where its line runs on down through the blue of the lake. Reels in his hooks with his bait still there on it. Dead. Then rows back hard, in this boat, back to the lake's shore, made of sand and mud, grass and dirt. In his head he knows what he must look for, what he must find: the witch. The bird with one wing. Feels with his tongue what is here in his mouth for him—this boy—to feel. He has the taste of mud there, a few grains of dirt to chew on as he says what he knows he must get: a witch. A bird with one wing. When he says what he says and sees what he sees when he says what he says, he can feel the teeth in his mouth grow long and sharp. The tongue in his mouth gets thick. Like this, this boy, back on land, back on his feet in the dirt and the mud at the edge of the lake, he drops down to his hands and knees and, this boy, like a boy who eats mud, like a fish in the mud, like a stone fish, a fish who eats rocks, like a dog, or a bird to bread, he eats.

Peter Markus is the author of the novel *Bob, or Man on Boat*, as well as several other books of short fiction, among them *We Make Mud, The Singing Fish, Good, Brother,* and *The Fish and the Not Fish*.

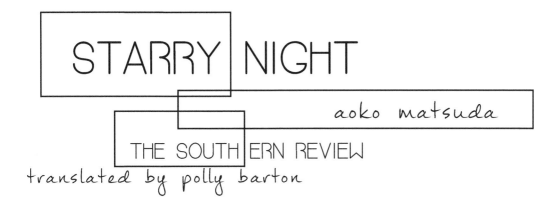

STARRY NIGHT

aoko matsuda

THE SOUTHERN REVIEW

translated by polly barton

I'M AN EARLY MORNING person. At this hour of the day most of the other villagers are still asleep, but I blink my eyes wide open, my chest swelling with hope for the day to come, and light the lamp in my room.

I live in a little house in the center of the village. The house next door to mine has a red roof, but my house is without any distinguishing features—apart from its lamp being lit, that is. Close to my house stands a church with a tall, narrow spire, where all the family goes on Sundays. The priest at the church is the same one who baptized me, and the fact I've now grown up seems to have escaped his notice entirely. He's not getting any younger, either, and has grown very gray of late.

When I was young, I often used to ask my mom and dad,

"Why is my village different from other villages?"

That always stumped them. They'd look at each other, and one of them would say, "Hmm, that's a good question. It's just always been that way."

It seemed to me that they didn't really know the answer. So, I noted to myself, there are things that adults don't know either.

The sky that stretches out above my village is not like a normal sky. Maybe there's no such thing as a "normal" sky or whatever, but this sky is definitely a bit unusual. You won't find a sky like this in any books.

I open the window and look up at the sky, still several hours from dawn. The light from the stars is so incredibly clear, it's like looking at a patch of dahlias in full bloom. There's this one star that, together with the glow extending around all it, looks like a bright white daisy. I think maybe my village is just really close to the stars. I haven't ever set foot outside it so it's hard to say, but it seems possible that it's not actually on Earth. When that idea first struck me, I thought that maybe I'd made an amazing discovery so I asked my mom and my dad, but they both denied it. It's just a normal village on Earth, they said. Then my dad told me to stop talking nonsense and get down to my schoolwork, and ground down on my head with his big hand. For a moment I thought my head might pop down inside my body and disappear. You can get toys that do that, right? Anyway, I gave my mom and my dad a look like I was satisfied, but in truth, I still find it kind of bizarre. When I'm a bit more grown up, I'll leave this village and then I'll solve the mystery once and for all.

I can hear the sound of insects from somewhere. I'm still looking up at the sky, by the way. I like looking at my village's sky—this sky that isn't like any other sky. My village is special, so it stands to reason that the sky would be special too. The light of the moon really is amazingly bright. It's a crescent moon today, but it looks like the crescent moon has been superimposed onto a full one.

I like it best when the sky looks like it's full of whirlpools, like it does now. You just don't get that kind of swirly effect with normal skies. They're more restrained. The sky in my village undulates like waves do. There are all these different colors up there, undulating. It also looks a bit like a sea creature or something like that. Or else, like a living soul with something it can't quite bring itself to give up on. So yeah, the sky in my village is super alive. There's all this white mist pasted thickly across the mountains, so it looks they're snowcapped. It's just beautiful. When I'm looking at the sky in my village, I feel all this power to live surging up inside me.

When my neck starts to get tired from all that craning upwards, I stop looking at the sky, and start looking out across the village, still sunken in silence. There is one more weird thing about my village I haven't told you about yet, and that's the tree ghost that lives here. Of course I asked my mom and my dad why it was here, but their answer was just as always: "Hmm, that's a good question. It's just always been that way." The tree ghost lives a little way away from my house. It flickers and sways like a great flame. All the kids in my village grow up being told by the village adults to keep away from it, and they do actually stick to the rules in that regard. Some of the older villagers go and make offerings and pray to it and things like that. I guess that's a kind of religion for them, in the same way that going to church is for us.

You might think I'm a wimp for saying this, but honestly, I'm relieved that there's a bit of a distance between my house and the tree ghost. I think it would be pretty hard to relax with a tree ghost slap-bang in front of where you were living. What if it suddenly started to move, and decided to come and trample your house? What would you do then? The people living on the opposite side of the street from the tree ghost haven't said anything, but I figure they must be very on edge about the whole situation. But the tree ghost is really tall, tall enough that it is basically touching my beloved sky, so there's also a part of me that would really like to try climbing it one day. I don't have that kind of courage yet, but I hope one day that I will.

I turn and look absent-mindedly in the direction of the tree ghost, a bottle-green flame off in the distance, and that's when I first notice the person. They are standing at the window of a building on the far side of the tree ghost, looking this way. The light from their room, the only lit one in the whole building, picks out their shadowy form against the window frame. They can't actually be looking at me, I think to myself, but they are definitely looking at my village.

I'm pretty sure that building is some kind of an inn. They have roosters at the inn that let rip every morning with their earsplitting crowing. It used to drive my dad crazy, that crowing. I wake up before the roosters, though, so it doesn't really bother me.

Still, it's rare for a traveler to be up this early. I always get up early, and I've never seen a light on in that building before. This is the countryside, so none of the shops are open early in the morning. It must still be hours before breakfast is served at the inn.

I stand there watching the man. I think it must be a man. I can't make out his face properly, but there's something sort of rugged about his silhouette, and a little bit pointy.

The man isn't moving, just standing there, looking out. It's as if he's trying to commit the scene to memory or something. It's like he thinks he's taking a photo in the olden days, where the entire photo would end up blurry if you moved at all during any part of the photo-taking process. I know that the man in the window is the one taking the photo so that comparison doesn't work at all, but still, that's how perfectly unmoving he is.

Maybe this man understands how great my village is, how remarkable. My village with its whirlpool sky overhead and its resident tree ghost. It's quite plausible that this man is overcome by how lovely my village is right now. Thinking that, I feel incredibly proud.

At some point I catch myself thinking that I wish this guy were a painter. It seems to me that for some reason, I could trust him to paint my village just as it really is. To paint it in all its specialness, without changing a thing.

The traveler and I stand facing one other, not moving at all. I lift a hand and try waving, though I'm thinking all the while that he probably won't be able to see it.

After a little pause, the man lifts his hand and waves back at me. The roosters at the inn have begun crowing at full blast, but he doesn't react at all. It's as if there is no sound in his world. Right at this minute, the traveler only has eyes for my amazing village.

For a little while we stand there, waving at each other. We both know that soon enough, day will break, and our time will be over.

Aoko Matsuda is a writer and translator. In 2013, her debut book, *Stackable*, was nominated for the Mishima Yukio Prize and the Noma Literary New Face Prize. In 2019, her short story 'The Woman Dies' (from the collection *The Year of No Wild Flowers*), published on GRANTA online, was shortlisted for a Shirley Jackson Award. Her novella *The Girl Who Is Getting Married* was published by Strangers Press in 2016. She has translated work by Karen Russell, Amelia Gray and Carmen Maria Machado into Japanese.

Polly Barton is a translator of Japanese literature and non-fiction, currently based in Bristol. She has translated short stories for *Words Without Borders*, *The White Review* and *GRANTA*. Her full-length translations include Where the Wild Ladies Are by Aoko Matsuda (Tilted Axis Press) and *Spring Garden* by Tomoka Shibasaki (Pushkin Press). After being awarded the 2019 Fitzcarraldo Editions Essay Prize, she is currently working on a non-fiction book entitled *Fifty Sounds*.

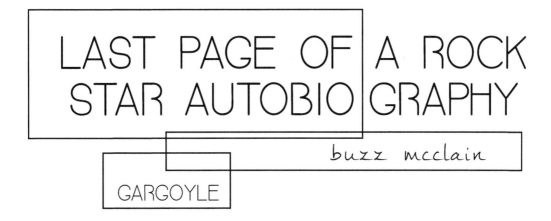

LAST PAGE OF A ROCK STAR AUTOBIOGRAPHY

buzz mcclain

GARGOYLE

-HANDED, BROKE THE BOTTLE but didn't spill a drop, at least how he tells it. But how I tells it, the shit went everywhere, thick and red, and that's why hotel management dunned us not just for the room but the carpet, the window, the telly and the five white linen robes that were ruined. Somehow the empty minibar was overlooked. We got a good laugh out of that but the record label dismissed us anyway.

Speaking of dismissing, we've come to the end of this sorry saga of rock and roll warriors who waved the flag of freedom and rebellion as long as we could until capitalism usurped our spirit and sent us spiraling in indebted servitude to the cozy confines of the scattered pied-de-terres, countryside manses and groupies who still, at our age, want to make plaster casts of our cocks. How many of them of mine are on fireplace mantles around the world? I dunno. I don't even remember posing for some of them, I hope they were impressive!

The one question I get from fans over the years, more than any other question, is this: What's the chord that comes after the bit after the bit in "Hold It In"? My answer is, "I dunno, mate, I'm the fuckin' singer not the guitar player. Ask him."

I also get asked what was my favorite gig, and on the telly or radio I say, "Tonight's!" or whatever, to make them feel good about themselves, you know? But honestly, my favorite gig was, and this is a bit sentimental for a crusty rocker like me, but I have to say it was the one where everyone in the audience was so paralyzed by our brilliance that no one moved, no one danced, no one applauded, they just sat in their seats with their arms folded, dumbfounded by the magnificence they were witnessing. That one brought a tear to my jaded eye, the left one.

In sum, I'd like to thank the boys in the band, me best mates from childhood, who rocked as hard as I did (most of the time) and never let an audience down. That's what really counts, not letting the audience down. And we liked the songs as much as they did, we couldn't wait to hear them ourselves each night, no matter if we were in a chatty pub in a spotty street in Bolton or rocking out a gridiron football stadium in some overly hot city in America. We did it. We really did it.

It's about the songs, ain't it? The songs were real and from the heart and they spoke to people and still do and it is gratifying to know that people will play them forever, just like they do Beethoven and Bach, hundreds of years from now.

And, of course, I'd like to thank the love of my life, who, sadly, is no longer with us. (But I think I saw her at a party at the Whiskey a few years ago. I couldn't be sure.) She changed my life in such meaningful ways and I can honestly say I would not be here right now dictating this into a tape recorder if it had not been for her gentle hand signing the divorce papers. Because the song inspired by her, "Half of Everything," went to the Top 500 and paid for, and still does, a few beers.

But in the end, I have to admit, no matter what else I've said on these pages, we all know perfectly well that was all about the hair. It was always the hair.

Yours truly and fuck off,

James "Devil Tits" Akehurst III
No Cure for Tinnitus

Buzz McClain is a longtime journalist and critic whose work has appeared in *Playboy* (covering movies for 20 years), *The Washington Post* (a decade as a music critic), and countless other publications. "Last Page of a Rock Star Autobiography" is his first published fiction.

HEAVY LIFTING

heather mcquillan

FLASH FRONTIER

THIS MAN HAS A job overnight to move the flowers from the road. He wears a high-vis vest and lifts bunches in his arms as if they are newborns, carries them to the fence, and lays them down. Sometimes a card falls out. *Kia kaha. No one is alone here in this grief.*

This woman lifts a child, gentle because there are holes in four-year-old flesh. She lays the child on a gurney, wheels her to a helicopter. They rise into a leaden sky.

This man's machine bites soil and still there is more digging to be done. He wipes grime from his forehead and looks up to the weighted clouds and longs to go home to his children and hold them because this digging is not for his family but the graves are for fathers and mothers and daughters and sons.

This woman, this man are teachers. When the children go home they realise they have not been aware all day of the sky.

This woman demonstrates kindness and kaitiakitanga and resolve to the world while back home her daughter takes her first crawling steps.

These ones were first responders and their arms ache from the lifting.
These ones are parents and their arms ache from the lifting.

This place of work, this dairy, opens its doors and a brother has a job to do, to keep food on the table of his brother's family. He lifts the crates. He greets the customers. Hello, brother. Welcome.

This place of work has no one here. There are flowers at the door. There are signs.

This woman examines the bodies.
This man examines the bodies.

This man removes the shattered glass and lifts a clear pane into place.
This man lifts carpet still wet with blood.
This woman stands outside, watchful. There is a gun across her body, hard upon her hip. She wears a uniform of blue and a flower and a hijab. The gun is hard against her hip. When she removes it at the end of her shift it is heavy in her hand. It is hard against her hand.
This woman washes her cousin. This woman washes her husband. This woman washes her son.

This man lifts his uncle. This man lifts his friend. This man lifts his wife.

They lay them down.

Heather McQuillan, from New Zealand, is a writing teacher and an award-winning novelist for young readers. She writes regularly for *Flash Frontier* and has won awards in New Zealand (National Flash Fiction Day, 2016) and Australia (Meniscus CAL Best Prose Prize, 2018). Her stories have been selected for anthologies including *Best Microfiction* 2019; *Bath Flash Fiction* Volumes Two and Three; *Bonsai: best small stories from Aotearoa, New Zealand*, and *Best Small Fictions* 2017 and 2019. Heather has a Masters of Creative Writing from Massey University. Her first collection, *Where Oceans Meet*, is published by Reflex Press, 2019.

LAST NIGHT I DREAMED

jesse millner

MANZANO MOUNTAIN REVIEW

I ASKED MY STUDENTS what they'd learned in the class.

A woman answered, "You taught us how to manufacture darkness."

Last night I dreamed of my dead father and held out my hand to him in a way I never did when he was alive. Last night I ran across a green pasture and chased cumuli that raced past the edges of an emerald forest, *like* I was in a Claritin commercial because everything was so vibrantly alive in that cartoonish way of advertisements, and my stuffy nose cleared, and I could smell the evanescent grasses!

O pharmaceutical miracle! O beautiful fields of sleep where If I take this drug, will I stop missing my father? Will I finally be able to leave behind the regret of not having loved him in life? I would like to speak to him one more time and not talk about the weather or baseball or the weeds choking his tomato plants. I would like to talk about how we both suffered from our not speaking, from the curious angers that circled us like dust devils summoned by a desert wind.

Last night I dreamed the universe I summoned as a child, and now I remember lying in bed each night, wondering where the untold galaxies stopped and finally, where the *Nothing* began, because there had to be an end, a place where combustion and entropy gave way to *What?* And I'd always return to dreams of trains following ribbons of rail beneath gibbous moons and a wilderness of stars and I'd long for the quiet of a cottonwood-lined river in a valley where the only sound was water slapping the old stones, themselves edgeless, smooth, and lost in the drawl of geologic time.

Last night I dreamed I paddled a kayak beneath a river of stars and tried to speak to the constellations in their native Greek, but my tongue got twisted within the withering silence of a dream when it's pulled out of deep waters of sleep into this daylight where it thrashes around and tries to breathe. *Help me*, the dream says, but instead I take a knife and cut off its head, after which I gut it, casting aside the pink entrails before I scrape off the scales, which still glisten with rainbows of sun and sea. But I know the white flesh, when pan-fried with garlic in a splash of olive oil, will be more delicious and tangible than the words drifting through the sky of last night's dream, that language of *almost*. Strange fish, after I splash you with a little lemon juice, after I carefully arrange you on a white China plate, I will devour you, leaving only your skinny bones to point toward the dream you once were and the meaning that once was. I suppose this is how we sleep and dream and fish. The water calls out to us. We cast our lines. We never quite know what to expect: A trout? A grandmother? That nightmare about drowning in the Elizabeth River? Our Savior told his disciples He would make them fishers of men, and sometimes when I dream, I see whole schools of unsaved fish, hurtling over cataracts toward sharp rocks and shallow water. Sometimes I dream I'm flying down the river and there's such exhilaration before the fall.

Jesse Millner's poems and prose have appeared in *Manzano Mountain Review*, *River Styx*, *Pearl*, *The Prose Poem Project*, *The Florida Review*, *Pithead Chapel*, *The Best American Poetry 2013* and other literary magazines. He has published seven poetry chapbooks and two full-length collections, *The Neighborhoods of My Past Sorrow* (winner of bronze medal in 2010 Florida Book Awards) and *Dispatches from the Department of Supernatural Explanation* (Kitsune Books, 2012). His latest book, *Memory's Blue Sedan*, will be released this spring by Hysterical Books of Tallahassee, Florida. He currently teaches writing courses at Florida Gulf Coast University in Fort Myers, Florida.

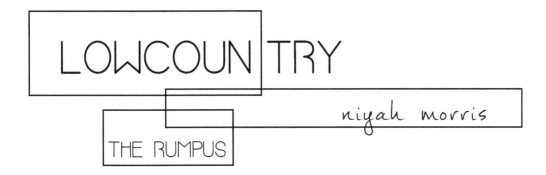

LOWCOUNTRY

THE RUMPUS

niyah morris

WE WERE NOT UNREASONABLE, the people of Lowcountry. We knew storms passed along the coast. We knew their names and welcomed them like old friends. Come summers, rain sheeted the land and made the marshes swell, flooded the wheat fields and inundated all the neat rows of cabbage. We understood a summer storm bore certain losses. Drowned frogs. Mosquito uprisings. Weeks of muddy water. These things, we could recover from, but this? We had no way to know.

We gathered in the basement of the community church, nine hundred of us fanning ourselves in the stale, humid air. Mothers bounced fussy babies on their laps while children invented games and elders sat in a circle of aluminum folding chairs, murmuring about what had to be done. Margaret Tillers said we should call for aid. She had tremors in her hands that made her suggestion feel especially urgent. Henry Jeffords disagreed, insisting we couldn't trust the government to help. Willie Morgan scratched his rough, gray beard. *We don't have a choice*, he said. *We don't have a choice.*

We dug the old black Sony radio out of the storage closet, changed its batteries, and toyed with its dial until we reached 1650 kHz, the folks at Fort Jackson. Through miles of static, we told them we were survivors of the storm and needed their assistance. They called in the National Guard, whom we were told would reach us once the water had receded enough for them to get through.

We went up in shifts to check on the conditions outside. The church windows had been smashed in by heavy winds, leaves and dead grass pressed like flowers to the tiles. The rugs were rain-soaked and mildewing fast. There was no sign of the National Guard all evening and into the late night. We gathered again in the basement, surrendered the stiff sleeping pads to the youngest ones and resigned ourselves to the floor.

In the morning, those of us who woke up at dawn or had not slept at all were the first to see the ATVs that rolled through the water like tanks. They appeared on the horizon before the sun, their slow, fat tires churning flood-water as they moved through the swamps the storm had made of our roads.

Big men in camo shorts and tangerine lifejackets waded through to the church entrance, where they hoisted the children onto their broad backs and waded back out to the waiting trucks and rowboats. Once the children and elders were out, their boats turned in the water and started back toward the city. Then the mothers and other women went, careful to manage their grins in the arms of the big men as their husbands looked on from the entryway. The men were the last to be cleared out, pulled onto the enormous ATVs. More than one of us disregarded the old, biblical advice not to look back as we left a ruined place. We risked becoming salt to see the land one last time. Some of us wept.

We were taken into Charleston as evacuees from Lowcountry. In the documents we had to review and the stories that were written about us in the news, the word *evacuees* began to bleed into *refugees*. The children were curious about what it all meant. We tried to explain our new names. *Refugees* were people who'd had everything but their lives taken from them, who had been made to start new lives somewhere else. *Evacuees* were people who had been brought from absence to abundance, from hazard to safety, people whose lives had been saved. But this was an imperfect understanding. Most nights, we felt as though the life had gone out of us, too, along with the other things the storm had swept away. All the while, the city seemed untouched. The sky was a painful blue. We lived in the temporary housing the city government had granted us, these strange, sleek apartments that weren't nearly as warm as the places some of us had built from wood cut by our own hands.

One afternoon, about three weeks after we arrived in Charleston, those of us who sat by the big windows in our lonely apartments watched the thundercloud ease its way over the quarter where most of us lived now. There were others in the sky that day, but this one, a stacked and low-hanging cumulonimbus, puffed and dark like our children's hair, was massive and familiar.

Windows slid open and cries of recognition went up. Some of us wrung our hands, which ached with memory. The children quieted their playing. We seethed and tore through our strange, new homes for knives.

We poured out of our buildings and into the street, swinging weapons and dragging long yards of rope behind us. Those of us who had worked on the boats for the Ports Authority in our previous lives helped to fashion a knot that would bring the cloud down. As we worked the rope, some grew impatient and began hurling knives at the sky, watching with satisfaction as the blades pierced the vapor and sank back down to earth. When enough of us had gathered to hold the long tail of the lasso we'd made, one of the elders, who'd been a cattle rancher out in Laurens County for more years than most of us had been alive, took the knotted end and masterfully brought it up to a spin in the air.

The lasso was a gaping mouth that opened wide enough, we hoped, to swallow the cloud. The first few tosses at the thunderhead yielded nothing but air. We moved from side to side, searching for a good spot. When the lasso went up in the air the last time, we knew that was the one. The mouth caught on a dark, low-hanging leg of the cloud and cinched around it tight. We pulled the cloud down and wrangled the rest of it into other mouths we had fashioned along the rest of the rope.

We dragged the raincloud through the city to the nearest precinct in the ward. A gruff, red-faced officer took notes as we described our grievances and outlined the cloud's crimes. Yes, we wanted to press charges. Yes, we wanted a trial. More than these things, we wanted someone to blame. Someone to return our homes to us, to undrown our lost children and drain the mudwater that now sat, stagnant, in their lungs.

The raincloud was taken into custody. We returned home, parading through the city with the lasso that had brought the cloud to justice. We slept beautifully that night, eager to wake up the next morning or the morning after to some news of the trial we believed would soon come. But as the days passed, our old sadness returned and settled inside us. The world looked unchanged from one morning to the next, the sky in the city once again beaming a terrible blue.

We would learn later in a note of apology from the city that, in the days following its arrest, the raincloud had separated into smaller tufts of cumulonimbus, then had further dissipated into streaks of cirrostratus and, finally, had become tendrils of fog thin enough to seep out around the prison cell bars.

When the guards had come to check on the cloud, they found the bed in the cell soaked through and pools of water on the ground. As though the room had housed in it a small, contained storm.

Niyah Morris is a writer and translator from Jersey City, NJ. She earned BAs in Ethnic Studies and Literary Arts from Brown University and an MFA in Creative Writing from Rutgers University-Newark. Her interests include contemporary speculative, Black/of color, and queer women's literature. A recipient of awards from the Fulbright Program and the American Literary Translators Association, her work has appeared in *The Rumpus, Strange Horizons, Nabillera, Thin Noon, NANO Fiction,* and *Necessary Fiction,* among others. She is based in Seoul, South Korea.

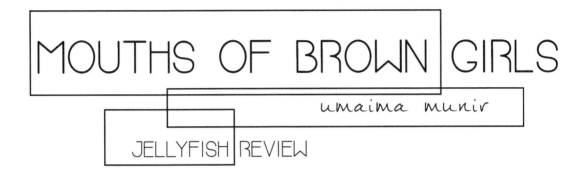

MOUTHS OF BROWN GIRLS

umaima munir

JELLYFISH REVIEW

(I)

MOTHER SEWED MY MOUTH shut on the winter of 2009. It was a week after the night I had refused to sleep in my cousin's room.

But why, everyone laughs. Did you two girls fight? You were practically joined at the hip yesterday.

We're only here for a week, Mother adds, and then you won't see each other for a year.

I scream in response. Mother won't have it. There, you've hurt your cousin's feelings. Are you happy now? I am made to apologize to her.

What a troublesome girl, my aunt titters, she must be seeing boys. Scandalized looks are exchanged, and I am made to take a thorough shower to clean all the impure thoughts away. My cousin looks on from the corner of the room.

That night, neither of us sleep, listening for the heartbeat of each other. She shifts. I turn, pretending I'm having a nightmare. The shame lies between us, I can feel it wafting along the bed towards my side. It strokes my hair gently, warning me not to open my mouth.

But I refuse to open my eyes, to show any sign of being awake.

When I do wake up in the morning, there are claw marks all over my legs, my neck, my chest. The shame is retreating back across the bed, trailing blood and hair in its wake. Thick, dark hair. *My hair.*

(II)

It's a stunning place to get married, our village. Nestled atop a mountain, river running by, chilling winds from the Karakoram Mountains blowing in.

She is a stunning bride. The red and gold details of her wedding dress suits her alabaster skin. I wonder how I would be able to wear red on my wedding without a horde of aunts shaking their heads. Brown skin is a whore's skin. A poor person's skin. A derelict's skin.

The bride's hands, which never shift from her lap, drown under the henna and the gold. So much gold for someone so small. Her shoulders hunch forward from the weight. A brown girl's Atlas.

The groom enters. She is made to sit next to him like a prize hunt, made to lower her gaze in humility to fit her role of the hunted.

She looks at me only once. It's a look of triumph. I do not argue back; after all, the memory is not hers to be ashamed of.

(III)

The memory in question now drowns under the weight of lonely, married men, private school boys and thick dark hair. I have turned it into a lie. You would not believe it anyway.

Why not? They all ask the same thing. I do not answer. I wake up with claw marks and scattered blood and hair and my whore skin. The stitches Mother put in have now melted into my lips.

They all say my mouth is the best part of me. I never reply.

Umaima Munir is from Lahore, Pakistan and is an aspiring author who has always been passionate about writing. This is her first published work of fiction, and she has more stories on the way. Umaima is currently studying Political Science in Turkey and can be found writing poetry and musings on her blog: theartoftoska.wordpress.com.

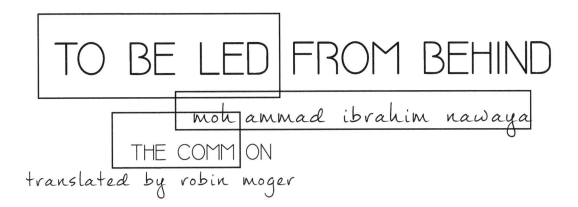

TO BE LED FROM BEHIND

mohammad ibrahim nawaya

THE COMMON

translated by robin moger

Seige

I SPRINTED TOWARDS THEM as they battered away. Tried, but could not open the bolted door. I shouted out, called at the top of my voice for those around me to help, but to no avail. And when at last I despaired, and turned my back to come away, my head knocked against the wall of a water tank, greater still, shut fast against me.

Defeat

Against history, the commander retreated to the rear to avoid the enemy's assaults. We asked him, How can you guide us when we are in your van? He unhitched his whip and began to flay.

Impotence

He took his heavy staff and started to beat the chair before him with all his strength, angrily upbraiding it: With all that has happened, you just sit there on your four legs, and watch.

A god

All eyes on the bird, which started to peck at his great statue. He did not seem to sense it. Did not bat an eye. But most there swore that it was a test, that he might tell apart those who had faith.

The definite article

From his pocket he took a piece of paper and began to set down the numbers that mattered. Having noted the numbers of his identity card, his passport, his cell phone, then his employment number, his civil registration number, his national record number, the number of the refugee identity certificate that gives him access to aid, and his prison number, he knew for sure how pointless it was that he have a name at all.

A moment

He hailed him through the bullhorn: Stop! Don't kill yourself. Life is beautiful and deserves to be lived. Calm yourself. Think a little. Slowly, he climbed the wall towards him, to persuade him. After a long conversation had passed between the two, another man down below cried out in terror: Stop! Don't kill yourselves!

Justice

They led him in chains to the courtroom, and when the judge saw him, he called to the guards: Good. Now, bring me the man he slew. They took him away, then brought him back in.

Rhetoric

Too busy to attend the anniversary celebrations, the president sent them his portrait instead. They propped it on his chair, and every time it moved with the breeze, thunderous applause swelled and swelled.

Emergency room

An injured man was brought in. In a weary voice he started describing the horror of what had happened. His fear plain to see, he gave us a warning: The occupation forces are swallowing up one city after another. We listened carefully to all he had to say, and were much moved. In order to help him, we decided that we should all burst out weeping.

Practice

He talks to them a lot. Is struck by their ability to stand upright for so long. Envies their endurance. He holds his head high. His body is like a pillar rising from the ground, unmoving. He becomes like one of them—one of the walls.

Ranked

I couldn't find her, because each of them had cut away the piece of her they liked and were claiming that they alone possessed her. Now, I must gather them all together for the truth to be made whole.

Circling

He began by drawing a circle all around himself, and just as he came to complete it, a strange feeling came over him.

Loss

From the lip of a steep cliff I threw out my hand to save him. He smiled and pulled me higher.

———————————————

Mohammad Ibrahim Nawaya is a Syrian short story writer based in Khartoum, Sudan. He has three published collections: *To Walk on Your Hands*, *As a Homeland* and *Memory of a Metal*.

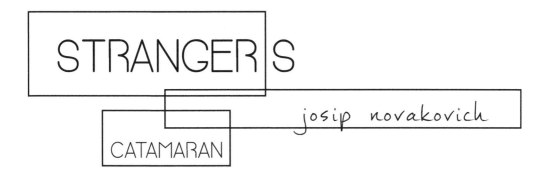

STRANGER|S

josip novakovich

CATAMARAN

WE HAVE FRIENDS IN our lives, perhaps enemies as well, but we also have strangers, and usually I think the strangers matter least of all, but perhaps we should love our strangers more than our neighbors. Sometimes years after a random encounter, I suddenly wonder, How is that awesome stranger doing?

As a provincial in Croatia in the early seventies, coming from a little town where everybody seemed to know everybody or at least too much about everybody, a complete stranger was a wonderful concept. In Zagreb, when I was about fourteen, I met two lads from India who lived in an attic on Vlaska Street. They studied medicine. They were happy, funny, had white teeth, and offered me powerful tea. I don't remember much more, but when I mentioned them to one of my relatives, he said, "But they are gypsies. Why talk to them? They probably steal." "Come on!" I replied. "They are smart and generous people."

In Russia, I encountered the same kind of chauvinism toward India. Pharmacists wouldn't sell me medicine made in India. And I said, "But why?"

"Here, we have German pills made by Bayer."

"Probably half of Bayer's chemical engineers are from India. They are the best engineers in the world." And the shop assistants looked at me like I was raving mad.

I was taught not to talk to strangers—it seemed most of us in Croatia were. During my first visit to the States, when I was eighteen, I experienced liberation. I'd go to the Public Square in Cleveland, find a stranger, and say, "Do you mind if we converse? I would like to practice my English." Sometimes people laughed and indulged me, sometimes they looked at me like I was insane. At the time I drank Coca-Cola and no beer or wine. A man with long hair and a beard said, "Let me warn you against Coca-Cola. When you go home, put an iron nail into it, and look for it a month later. You won't find it. The cola will dissolve it into nothing. Just imagine what it does to you."

And then there are acquaintances, who remain strangers. Well, here's one. Marina N. I met her a long time ago in Saint Petersburg, Russia, when she ran the library either for the British Council or the American Corner. She said, "Oh, your last name is similar to mine. I have made several friends with last names similar to mine. That's a good sign." She had a strange charisma about her, black hair and radi - ant blue eyes, positively something otherworldly about her as though she were a character in a science fiction movie. We stood in front of the Nevsky metro station, a crowded intersection, and she gave me her email address in blue on lined paper, like a bit of jazz melody. I put it in my pocket. She left. Pretty soon, four guys jostled me from different directions. I felt something in my pocket and pushed a guy's hand away. I stood at the curb and checked for my wallet. It was gone. I ran to the hotel and cancelled all the credit cards. Just as I was done with that, two elegant strangers, a man and a woman, who looked like an ad for cognac, appeared. "Are you Josip Novakovich?"

"How would you know that?" I said, in Russian.

"We picked up your wallet from the pavement. We saw you standing on the curb and feeling your pockets. But as you reached down, you knocked out your wallet, which was sticking halfway out. So here it is."

"How did you know where I was staying?" I asked, a bit suspicious.

"A copy of your visa was in the wallet. Well, here it is, stating the address, Pushkinskaya 6."

"Why didn't you let me know right away?"

"We couldn't as we were driving a car, and by the time we parked and got out, you were gone."

I had fifty dollars in the wallet. "I'd like to give you at least the fifty dollars."

"We don't want it. We are happy with the good karma. Maybe someone will help us like this one day." They smiled and left and I looked after them, admiring how nicely they moved, like athletes. And I thought, Did I accidently pull the wallet partly out from my tight pocket when I put Marina's email address into the pocket? Did those four guys try to pickpocket me? Maybe yes to all the questions? I guess I'll never know the answer, and I won't know who these two good people were who showed up, whether ballet dancers, investment bankers, or the police.

But about Marina I know. We exchanged a few emails. Then last year, at least ten years after, I thought, who do I know in Saint Petersburg? I thought of getting in touch with the people I knew and sort of knew as I was tempted to take a trip to Russia while staying in Bulgaria for a few months. The flights were cheap. I could be there for US $150 round-trip. In Sofia, I was tempted to get a Russian visa. I lived around the corner from a huge Russian center. I wrote to several people. One of them wrote, "I won't be there. You've probably read about that metro explosion at Senaya Ploshad? I was in the train just ahead of that one, two minutes away.

It could have been me dead. I am leaving the city." Anyway, then I wrote to Marina, and she said, "Yes, wonderful, let's meet up when you visit."

"How has life been this last decade for you?" I wrote.

"Up and down. I am spending too much money on doctors and medications. I will tell you in person. Just come and visit."

We corresponded back and forth. She was curious about Bulgaria and Croatia but said it was too complicated to get a travel visa and time off her work. Two months after our flurry of correspondence, I checked her Facebook page. There were all kinds of wishes for a better life.

Her picture is still there—she is sitting in a steeple of a tall church, her elbows on the ledge, looking out with a sensation of longing, perhaps longing for flight.

I gathered from talking to mutual acquaintances that she had jumped out of her apartment window from the ninth floor. Marina had suffered from depression. She took medicine to keep her balance. It was hard for her to keep her balance in a window—the downward pull got her. Well, I must say, I don't know much about her. She has remained a stranger. Her death made her for a few days a close friend whom I grieved. But I never knew her, only the tragic outline of her biography. She was in her mid thirties, living alone. Maybe she'd never been able to get along with anybody despite being intelligent and well-read, and she obviously couldn't get along with herself. Maybe she had a terminal illness and wasn't depressed but couldn't face the prospect of a long decline and pain. I wish I had had a chance to talk with her. I had the chance I didn't take. Next time, if I meet a fascinating stranger, I will at least make sure I drink some powerful tea with her.

Josip Novakovich emigrated from Croatia to the United States at the age of 20. He has published a dozen books, including a novel, *April Fool's Day* (in ten languages), five story collections (*Infidelities*, *Yolk*, *Salvation and Other Disasters*, *Heritage of Smoke*, and *Tumbleweed*) and three collections of narrative essays as well as two books of practical criticism. His novel, *Rubble of Rubles*, is scheduled for publication in 2021. His work was anthologized in *Best American Poetry*, *The Pushcart Prize* and *O. Henry Prize Stories*. He has received the Whiting Writer's Award, a Guggenheim fellowship, the Ingram Merrill Award and an American Book Award, and in 2013 he was a Man Booker International Award finalist. He has taught at Penn State, University of Cincinnati, the Hebrew University of Jerusalem, and now teaches creative writing at Concordia University in Montreal.

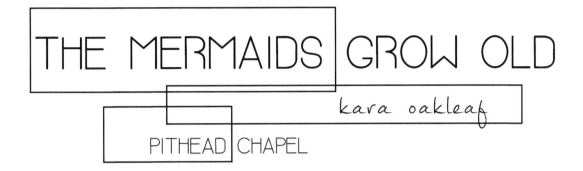

THE MERMAIDS GROW OLD

kara oakleaf

PITHEAD CHAPEL

IT MUST HAVE HAPPENED to our mothers, and their mothers before them, but still, it stunned us, when we first noticed the wisps of hair at our temples going gray. We looked around and called for our mothers, wanting to ask them a question, but found ourselves alone.

The sailors never tell these stories. To them, we are only glimpses of some fantastic mystery, all youth and beauty. For a time, we must have believed them.

We hope our daughters will see our kind as something more than the myths humans build up around us. What are they to us anyway, we ask them, these men who scoop up the ocean in their ropes, dragging whole schools of fish out of the water for food?

We once thought we could keep our daughters from them, fearful as they were when they first saw a family of mackerel snatched up and drawn to the surface. But they learned the stories, they know the way the sailors seek us out, not to catch us, but just to gaze. They feel the tug of that power, like a current.

We recall our own youth, remind ourselves of the first time we saw our wooden likeness carved into a ship, the fins at the prow grazing the water and parting the ocean for them. No wonder the young ones watch this and feel strong enough to chase the ships, arching out of the water like they might take flight, airborne just long enough that the men might see a flicker of them, before the splash.

We must admit that we, too, once found them fascinating, the men on those great hulks floating at the surface. We rose from the oceans at night and saw the lights of ships at rest, the portholes glowing like a row of suns. In the dark, we could get close, peer inside and see them in the candlelight. We watched them at their bolted tables, drinking mugs of froth and foam, and in their beds of rope strung from the walls, so similar to the nets they used to draw whole schools of fish from the water during the day.

If there were women, we watched them too. Maybe, in the same the way men tell stories about us, we ascribed something special to the women; we saw them so rarely they might have been mirages. But then, we tell our daughters, we saw what the men did to them. Once they've seen it enough, we reassure each other, they'll stop going to the surface.

It's not that we're afraid of them. They won't have our daughters; we know they'll never split us down the middle the way they do with their women. In the water where everything floats, we never have to lie down, and this, too, is a kind of power.

But for us, the allure of open air is gone, and what sailors would want to see us anyway? Our hair, still long but the color of a dank storm sky, our skin ghostly pale. Even our breasts have shriveled and show wrinkles, and we've begun to wonder why we ever needed these cracked-open clamshells to conceal them in the first place. If we dress at all anymore, we prefer to wrap ourselves in swaths of seaweed, covering our stomachs where the skin goes soft and spills over that secret spot at our hips where we fade into scales.

These days, we gather together at the bottom of the sea, away from our daughters. We watch the movement of the ocean floor, and we know where to go when our time is over so that the water will quickly pull the sands across our bodies. The younger ones won't come this way, enamored as they are with the surface, and they too will be surprised when it happens to them.

Perhaps it still surprises us. Sometimes, we still look beautiful in this ethereal light, our hair floating in slow motion like a fog. From certain angles, a sailor might even believe that these gray hairs are strands of silver, shimmering like something precious.

There's no chance of being spotted in these depths, but some nights we wonder what the sailors would say about us now. Would they understand us, would they feel compassion, if they saw that we, too, are mortal? Or would they turn cold and bitter if they saw that even the creatures of imagination might grow old and wither?

We have spent too many of our thoughts on these men.

This is what we tell the young ones as they flit across the sea, stirring up so much sand as they chase ships. Still, we let them go, watch them from below as they flash themselves like tricks of light at the surface, their scales mirroring the sunlight. We haven't forgotten that wooden mermaid at the prow, how she looked like she was flying when she cut the water with the tips of her fin, head high in the open air. The carved swirls of hair, thick as rope, the scales carefully notched along her body. How solid she looked.

Far below the surface, we'll shroud ourselves in seaweed. When it's over, the smallest fish will nibble our skin and fins down their delicate bones, and there will be nothing left to prove we ever grew old. We'll be another piece of ocean, the seabed shifting to cover our remains, and if any of our scales surface and catch the faint light that finds its way to the bottom, they'll only look like the glint of a sunken coin. A lost bit of treasure from some other sailor's story, something extraordinary and just as unbelievable.

Kara Oakleaf's work has appeared in *SmokeLong Quarterly*, *Wigleaf*, *matchbook*, *Booth*, *Jellyfish Review*, *Monkeybicycle*, *Nimrod*, *Pithead Chapel*, and elsewhere. Her fiction has been listed in the *Wigleaf* Top 50 and also appears in the Bloomsbury anthology *Short-Form Creative Writing*. She received her MFA at George Mason University, where she now teaches writing and literature and directs the Fall for the Book literary festival. Find more of her work at karaoakleaf.com.

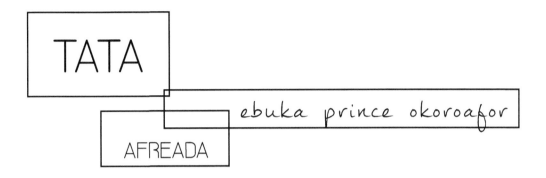

TATA

ebuka prince okoroafor

AFREADA

YOUR NAME IS CHIMSOMEJEDEBE Okoro but here in America, everybody knows you as Tata. They call you Tata because they cannot master the intricate phonemics of your Igbo name. Your father calls you Tata too. In fact, they all learnt it from him, you did too. Once, you had introduced yourself as Tata Okoro. You had wished that someday you could change your name completely, you could become a citizen and discard the Okoro, take up Murphy and become Tata Murphy, completely American. You were only sixteen.

Tata, when you came here you were barely five. You were the wailing girl that refused to keep her mouth shut because your father refused to buy you a piece of sausage roll at the airport. You cried so loud the airport security personnel had to double check your passport to ensure that the couple did not steal a child from Nigeria. Your father seethed with anger, he was a lawyer and back in Nigeria, you don't keep lawyers standing. They'll bulldoze their way through you with threats and intimidation. But here in America, your father stood like a wet chicken until the security man was done. He folded up his anger and put it under his armpit.

Your mother jumped on the train twice a day, shuttling between two house cleaning jobs, and one half day of baby sitting. Her income was enough to put food on the table and put you in a school around the neighborhood. Your father did not work much until you were seven, he was always on the table reading, reading, reading and went out only at night on a security job. He taught you how to read books that do not concern you; the American law weekly, Practicing in America without a hitch, Black Awakening. The books were absurd and uninteresting but you read anyway. Then one evening, your father announced that he finally passed the exam. Your mother hugged him like the information was her salvation, she cried and you said "mummy sorry", thinking that she had thrown herself too hard at your father and that it had hurt her. She made chicken stew and invited the neighbors that Sunday.

Then your father started running. Your father told you, "Tata, to be a lawyer in this America is not easy." Your father ran the length and breadth of the city, chasing after ambulances, and making cases for accident victims. Your father waited outside hospitals and once a patient was discharged, he would ask, "Hey you sure you were treated properly? You sure the doctor changed the syringe he used? Heard he's a smoker. You sure he didn't speak to you rudely?" This was how your father got enough money to bypass protocol and get you your citizenship just before your seventeenth birthday.

Tata you were finally American, you were free to do as you pleased but somehow, you decided to keep your father's name.

But you disappointed us all. You got out of high school and met a boy and fell in love and got knocked up. Who gets knocked up these days Tata?! Didn't you know what other girls were doing to keep unwanted sperm away from their eggs? Your mother threw herself on the kitchen floor and wept the night you told them. But your father said you were going to keep the baby because he was getting tired of running, and your mother had a slipped disk in her spine so the child support was going to come in handy. He continued, "In fact, spread your legs and hold them apart so men can come and go and you can scatter your seed around this whole America. You might be the salvation we've all been waiting for!" Your mother was shocked, but your father remained composed. The night your baby came into this world you called him Murphy, dropped him on your mother's lap and ran.

You started harvesting and selling your eggs at twenty-one. You met another boy in Pennsylvania and he told you some rich American men wanted babies with African blood. You knew these Americans wanted crazy things and since you were going to get handsomely paid for it, you opted in. You got enough money to pay for your mother's surgery, got her a small grocery store afterwards, and fucked a rich lawyer so that your father could get a table job at his firm.

In California you got arrested for playing your music too loud. Your white neighbor whom you'd dissed earlier for having a dog that littered the corridor with dog pee ratted you out. You spent three years in jail because the police broke in and found sachets of cocaine stuffed in the flush tank.

Out of jail, you met an American builder. He was calm and gentle and fun loving and white. The kind of man you wanted. His sex was good and although his mother had pouted when he introduced you at a thanksgiving dinner, you dreamed he was the man you would spend the rest of your life with.

Then on the news one Sunday morning, a prominent female musician of mixed parentage announced she was black. You were excited, it was an era of black consolidation, and her announcement was a huge celebration to the black community. You were in the kitchen making breakfast. You didn't hear him fall, all you saw was people gathered around a bloodied body, looking up at you when you reached the balcony. She was his favorite artiste.

Tata you panicked.

The police came but they met the apartment empty. They circulated your image with a 'Wanted' inscription to newspapers and TV stations, hunting you for murder. But you kept running, unlike your father, you couldn't stop, unlike your father, the American dream swallowed you up.

Ebuka Prince Okoroafor is a Nigerian Medical Student. His work has appeared on *Daily Science Fiction, Litro USA, AFREADA, Limits Issue of Agbowó Magazine, Bangalore Review, African Writer* and elsewhere. He is a selected winner of the Green Author Prize 2017, and winner of the Sevhage Short Story Award 2019. Find him on twitter @bukadobigshow, and IG @show_fantastic_.

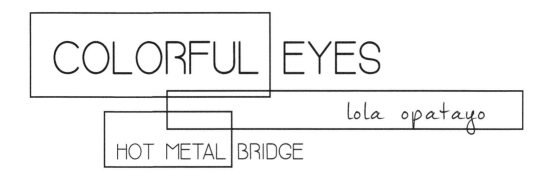

COLORFUL EYES

Lola Opatayo

HOT METAL BRIDGE

SIX THIRTY. TWENTY MINUTES on one spot, and I can see the long line of taillights snaking all the way up to the traffic light. At this rate, the children will be fast asleep by the time I'm home. Benji will be waiting, somewhat angry, but really worried.

In the back of my taxi, my passenger stares out of the window. From the rearview mirror I observe her carefully made-up face. Red thin lips, clear fair skin, oval face. Dark curly hair like the Fulanis. Her eyes dart back and forth between her phone and the tall buildings. She adjusts herself in her seat, looks out, adjusts herself again.

This job of conveying people always leaves me with questions. Who are they? Are they happy? I have to know, and so I look into their eyes. Everything is in the eyes.

She fingers the silver brooch on her green blouse, the remnants of a smile on her lips. But her eyes are the same, nervous. Her full eyelashes flutter and it reminds me of Maami and the year she blinked like a Barbie doll. It was as if her eyelids were constantly being electrocuted. Up and down, up and down they would go whenever I looked at her. And when she noticed me watching, she would turn away. She never wanted me to see what was in her eyes.

The lady pulls her silky hair away from her face and I glance at my own reflection. Stringy dreadlocks, bare face. Traffic momentarily eases out, we move a few hundred meters.

"Your date must be waiting."

A weak smile.

"Don't worry, you look nice."

Her laughter is shallow. "What makes you think I'm worried?"

"It's in your eyes, everything is in the eyes."

Again the depthless laughter. "So you think you know me?"

I look at her, she looks at me, she looks away. Her eyes harden.

"I have to find my own happiness. I'm tired of just wanting…"

The hardness leaves, softness creeps in. Her shoulders sag.

"Just for once, I need a man who knows what I want."

Night is slowly descending, pedestrians mill about the roadside market. Bodies weary from the day's accompaniments. I don't hear the cacophony of blaring horns, irritable drivers and hollering bus conductors. All I see is the bluish glow just before the darkness.

"You think I'm a bad person for going to another man, don't you?"

"No."

She laughs. "You can say it, I don't really care. I don't expect you to understand."

The road has become a spectacle of glowing colors. Red, blue, yellow, green.

"You're right, I don't know what that passion is."

"You've never had sex?"

"I'm married, with children."

"So…?"

It's harder to see each other's eyes now, but there is beauty outside. Flashing lights, moving lights, still lights. Colorful textiles woven in intricate patterns- stripes, flowers, checks. The swaying silk blouse, the blue checked shirt, yellow and black striped buses, sleek, black Toyotas, light skinned people, dark skinned people, the polka dot mini skirt, piles of yellow oranges and red tomatoes, white bread, brown suya. Light reflecting colour in a brilliant harmony.

In the year that Maami blinked uncontrollably, I began to see strange things living in my father's eyes. Malevolence, pity, grief. Then we travelled to our village, just the two of us. That evening we were visited by two, stoic middle-aged women. They donned dark green aprons, and the curtains were drawn. He looked at nothing, standing still like the grey furniture. His presence insignificant but necessary. An old towel was spread on the cement floor. These blank-eyed women of incredible strength, they pinned my arms down and pried my legs open. I still remember the silver glint of the razorblade, so decisively precise. And the brightness of the raw imperfection that used to be my pleasure spot. They wanted to tame my passion, my father didn't want an illegitimate child.

Maami started to blink afterwards. My father's eyes became red with the bottle.

From the back of the car, I hear gasps, words cut off in stupefaction.

"I can't know what that passion is, so Benji is good to me, he makes it quick."

 "I'm so sorry…"

We drive on, past the traffic lights, off the major road and into the residential areas. I pull the car to a stop and turn to her. We stare at one another. In her eyes, I see pity and a tinge of shame. I hope that she sees past my graying hairline and oily face. I hope she sees all the colors and lights I have stored in my eyes.

Lola Opatayo lives in Lagos, Nigeria. Her work has appeared in *Obsidian*, and *Hot Metal Bridge*. She is a recipient of the Iceland Writers Retreat Alumni Award, and a fellow of MacDowell. She's on Twitter @LolaOpatayo.

CHINA ILLUSTRATA

paolo di paolo

FLORENTINE LITERARY REVIEW & LITHUB

translated by jamie richards

THE WORLD IS IN your head.

It can be, it *must* be in your head. The important thing is organizing the mind like an archive, a chest of drawers. What you do with the space around you, you can do with the space inside you. All is one. All is in all.

Thus the astrolabe you're returning to that glass case must have an exact copy in your memory—the camera obscura of your brain. Same goes for this marvel of a painting, oil on canvas. And this sculpture. This ingenious little automaton. This oil lamp. Classification is essential. Once you've learned to do it with plants, become well versed in herbals, you can apply the same method to all of creation.

Quercus humilis. Cerrus. Ilex. Pullicortex. Mollifolia. Crassifolia.

Method. Precision. Store. Archive.

The world is in your head. And if God's power enters intimately into everything, we who are the mirror of that power contain all of creation.

At times one may have the sense of being overwhelmed by the abundance of it; hence your breath catches, your heart skips at the countless rarities brought back by the German Fathers Grueber and Roth from their journey through vast China. Thanks are also due, Athanasius now thinks, to Father Martino Martini, one of his former students in mathematics, author of the *Atlas Sinesis*—he has given him so much information, and it is obvious to conclude that his keen intuition was honed by those studies in math. Thus the good Martini was reliable, as were the Fathers Grueber and Roth, who sought to spread Christianity throughout vast China to glorify the divine name. As the realms the Fathers traversed—a voyage never before undertaken by another European!—were unknown to geographers, and as the Fathers made many observations worthy of note about the dress, customs, habits of those lands, they entrusted him with their drawings and notes so as to contribute to the volume that Athanasius Kircher set out to create: *Athanasii Kircheri e Soc. Jesu China monumentis, qua sacris qua profanis, nec non variis Naturae et artis spectaculis, aliarumque rerum memorabilium argumentis illustrata, auspiciis Leopoldi primi, Roman. Imper. Semper augusti Munificentissimi Mecaenatis.*

Through their eyes, he sees the famed walls—the Fathers, leaving Peking, reached them in two months. A prodigious fortress against the Tartars. They're so wide that six horses could race down it side by side without crossing paths. Even just the blowing wind, the cool wind blowing from the desert nearby, deserves mention. Oh, and everywhere around, there are all sorts of wild animals to be found.

Tigers. Lions. Elephants. Rhinoceroses. Leopards. Bulls. Unicorns.

Leaving the huge walls, the Fathers found a river filled with fish. Crossing this river, called the Yellow, the Fathers came to the great Kalmak Desert, barren and rugged. Desolate. The inhabitants wander around the desert in order to steal. For this reason it is advisable for a caravan to be equipped with a band of guards to ward off attacks. Athanasius transcribes, adapts. Stiches, organizes. He looks in satisfaction at the whole, the chaos taking shape.

Part One, Chapter One: Explication of the Sino-Nestorian Monument at Xian. With the utmost rigor, Athanasius reproduces the Chinese and Syriac inscriptions. His efforts have the effect of irrefutably demonstrating that the stele in question is evidence of a rare Catholic presence in vast China.

Part Two: Various Trips Made to China. All this gives him a subtle yet intense pleasure, an electric excitement that makes his fingers tremble. All this! It's like recreating creation. Line by line, page by page, table by table. Each completed description corresponds to a feeling of relief, a calmer breath. Things assume clearer contours, definition, clarity. Description. You can't see if you don't describe. You can't understand if you don't describe. You can't judge if you don't describe. And judgment is one of the tasks of those who defend creation from the onslaught of Satan. At the same time Satan's cunning and treachery have introduced horrible, detestable customs among those remote populations. He'll need to discuss the benighted who worship the many-headed idols of the Chinese. He'll need to linger on the pagan acts, unusual displays, abominable errors. Athanasius knows he'll have to devote his energies to this undertaking down to the last drop of ink. He is well over sixty, the body doesn't always meet our demands, but that's why it is good to trust in God, gather in prayer, praise His name.

Another example of a false god can be found in Barantola. Figure VI shows its image: it is adored as the true living God; they even call it Eternal, Heavenly Father. The great devotion of this benighted population is bewildering. In subsequent chapters, he'll have to address other ridiculous religious faiths. There's no end to ineptitude, he thinks. He stops himself a moment before banging his fist on his desk. There are poor fools convinced there are seven seas in the world. The first is water, the second milk, the third curdled milk, the fourth butter, the fifth salt, the sixth sugar, and the seventh wine. In the water, they say, there are five heavens.

Such solemn idiocy. Athanasius Kircher's drive is renewed. The stupidity and ignorance of others encourage him, motivate him. The great task that God has assigned learned men like him is at once simple and difficult: to reveal the truth. Simple if the mind is open to His light, guided by it. Difficult because Satan's cunning and treachery hinder truth's revelation. But we mustn't give in, Athanasius, Kircher says to himself. And he bows his head over the paper once again. And he transcribes, adapts. Stitches. Organizes. He looks in satisfaction at the whole, the chaos taking shape. The imposing, majestic work he was to complete—*China monumentis, qua sacris qua profanis, nec non variis Naturae et artis spectaculis, aliarumque rerum memorabilium argumentis illustrata*—is the best possible offering: the most true, most irrefutable work on what of that vast and remote region the missionaries' eyes have seen and his own eyes have clarified and amended and ordered and judged.

The wrath of the devil that fills the world with hatred and deceit can be fought, yes indeed—by the product of the intellect of a man like him, able to recognize and therefore condemn the superstitious customs and demonic tricks and false beliefs lurking in that huge, immeasurable land, which no one should find marvelous and which, evidently, he never felt the need to visit.

Paolo di Paolo was born in Rome in 1983 and is an award-winning author of novels, essays, theatre pieces, as well as children's books. His novels include *Dove eravate tutti* (Feltrinelli, 2011), *Mandami tanta vita* (Feltrinelli, 2013), *Una storia quasi solo d'amore* (Feltrinelli, 2016), and *Lontano dagli occhi* (Feltrinelli, 2019). His writing has been translated into several languages.

Jamie Richards is the translator of over twenty graphic novels from Italian and Spanish as well as works by authors such as Ermanno Cavazzoni, Andrea Inglese, Igiaba Scego, Giovanni Orelli, Serena Vitale, Giancarlo Pastore. Other work has appeared in *The Massachusetts Review, The Florentine Literary Review, The Arkansas Review, Now, Words Without Borders,* and *LitHub,* among others. She holds an MFA in Translation from the University of Iowa and a PhD in Comparative Literature from the University of Oregon.

WE SING

andrea passwater

THE RUMPUS

WE LOVE OUR GOD and so we love his sister, too. Our God has placed us in his pocket, curled us inside his warm hand. We, so suddenly torn from our mother, still missing her belly and warmth, sing his praises as we pile in his palm to fall. *Good Lord who gave us life, Good Lord who will take us into the world and bring us safely home again.*

We say cheerful goodbyes to our brothers and sisters, pinch and kiss their cheeks. One by one, he plucks us all away, drops us into the wide forest. *Young ones,* he beams at us and we adore him, *my kin.* Our God tells us to sit vast inches apart and wait. We do not take this easily, the aloneness. We look to each other, but cannot move to touch. So he has whispered to us and so we believe.

When the Lord returns to gather us up, mother will pull us greedily into her arms! She will marvel at everything we've seen, beg us never to leave her again.

But oh, these three arduous trials we do not expect.

First comes the wind, which blows us to and fro like feathers. It sends dust and dirt upon our soft skin, leaves our faces smudged and weatherworn; we can hardly tell our own brothers and sisters from rocks. We push up over tall twigs and mounds, rolling back to our places again. Breathless and matted, we rejoice this overcoming, the tin of its taste, the stories we have to tell.

Oh, then come the woodlarks with their talons and beaks, their sharp-swift dives that take our heads before we know to hide or scream. Their wings unfurl to eclipse the sun, cast a blind black chill before they strike. We raise our voices and sing to our Lord, *save us,* as the birds circle and caw, pilfering us for their children's mouths. The trees, after many repetitions of our song, take pity—push their leaves thickly together and shield us from view. Our God has placed some of us in brush and some of us in wide open sun. We accept that some of us he has chosen to die. We thank the Lord for his wisdom in this, that the birds might sate themselves and retreat before eating us all.

The night drapes down over the trees and grass. We, weary and wanting only to sleep, begin to slump our shoulders down into the earth. At last, the mice peek their heads out from their burrows. They scurry to us in the quiet way mice do, tickle us with their little paws and yank us, sleeping, into their mouths.

Too tired, now, to sing, and too few, when the black slips behind the mountain, revealing gold and blue in the sky. So few of us left and our God walking past us, kicking us like pebbles, his sister bringing raindrops upon our backs. We shout joyously to him, our tall promiser covered in sun, and he does not answer, only cries out falsely that we have gone. *We have waited here*, we say, our voices urgent as he shrinks. *Can't you see us, we have waited here.*

Our God, disappeared now for three moons and four suns. Our bodies crumbling in the soil. *Good Hänsel who gave us life*, we sing, our mouths scattered across the forest.

Andrea Passwater's writing has appeared in *The Rumpus, Duende,* and *Boston Accent Lit.* A former Alabamian, she now lives in Oakland, CA. She is working on a novel about blacksmiths.

TWELVE-STEP PROGRAM FOR QUITTING MY LIFE

CRAFT

kristen m. ploetz

1

WORK THE COLD MEAT from the last bone. Still numb from the fight, I eat Gil's leftovers. He ordered his usual two dozen of Blazin' Hot. Bastard. He knows habanero burns my gums. Lick the buffalo sauce off my fingers and wipe my mouth with the back of my shaky hand. Tiny drumsticks and limp bits of skin tumble into a bowl half-filled with pink milk and bloated islands of Frankenberry. The empty wings container drops into the sink and twangs against the sour mouths of last night's empties.

2

Conjure the power of my first love—the one before Gil—a roadside violet plucked and pressed into my heart.

3

Look past my blurry reflection into the dark beyond the kitchen window. Nothing rational gets decided at three in the morning. Nothing changes if I wait much longer.

4

Leave the car unlocked and idling outside the smoke shop, only four miles left in the gas tank. His work badge still in one cup holder, my phone in the other. Repo man will have no problem finding it now. Leave it up to the nicotine gods whether it's before Gil buys his morning tin of wintergreen dip. Thread my arms into my sweatshirt, take stock of what's left of me. Too close to nothing to measure.

5

Walk the three miles at a good clip and still show up late for this crappy job. Doesn't matter. No one considers me a *real* florist anyway. But I know better than anyone how to make these cheap supermarket flowers fool mothers in chemo and grandmothers in nursing homes and wives remembered at the last minute. Pluck dead baby's breath from stale bouquets and water the potted daffodils before sprinting to the employee bathroom. Shift manager knocks on the door, tells me to hurry up and restock the buckets near checkout because they're low on red tulips. Whisper against the steel door—*I should've listened to my parents*—open it a crack and ask for my paycheck. Say I feel sick with a migraine and need to leave.

6

Watch the bank teller count out $307.10 in small bills, my heart racing faster than the *wisp wisp wisp* of paper in her chapped hands. Shove tens and fives into my snakeskin wallet, tuck the extra dime and two ones into the cheerleaders' coffee can outside the bank because I used to smile like that too.

7

Buy a one-way bus ticket to my old hometown. Pull the folded slip of paper from behind my license to confirm the address. Wonder if the house is still painted light blue, if his bedroom is still second on the left, if he kept my Bowie T-shirt all these years. Worry I won't have more words than *sorry*.

8

Remove the faded photo from behind the film of clear plastic: last family vacation before I moved out, the four of us—Mom, Pops, Bizzie, and me—wearing electric green ponchos in the Philly rain. Trace their wan smiles, press my fingers against their chests. A feeble attempt to cauterize the hole I punctured into their hearts.

9

Somewhere near Albany make amends with the ghosts of my parents, taste the mix of tears and diesel as I whisper regrets to the fingerprinted window in the fourth row. Somewhere outside Louisville borrow a stranger's phone to make amends with my sister in a voicemail confessional.

10

Tuck a fistful of candy wrappers into my sweatshirt balled under the seat, lean back with the rush of caramel still gritty on my teeth. Convince myself we had something halfway decent once already, that it will be better than nothing.

11

Stand at the long glass case in the pawnshop and look at the ring on my left hand, knuckle bulging against the thin curve of gold and Gil's broken promises. Owner smells like oregano, looks like a lie. Says the best he can do is $172 but with a kiss I get him to $190. Keep my mother's ruby studs in my ears for when I need to leave this town again.

12

Duck into a corner store with the pawnshop money still clutched in my hand. Point to a box of Trojans behind the young clerk and ask for the time. Trace a line across the dusty packages of gum, stop on wintergreen. Lights hum overhead. Someone opens and closes a cooler door near the back of the store. Finger out a dented pack of cinnamon, remember the taste of Red Hots on his tongue when we first kissed in his father's shed, hope it's still hidden out back.

Kristen M. Ploetz (@KristenPloetz) lives in Massachusetts. This story was also selected for the 2020 Wigleaf Top 50. Her other short fiction has been published by *The Normal School, Joyland, Atticus Review, Wigleaf, X-R-A-Y Literary Magazine,* and appears in the 2019 *Best Microfiction* anthology. You can find her on the web at www.kristenploetz.com.

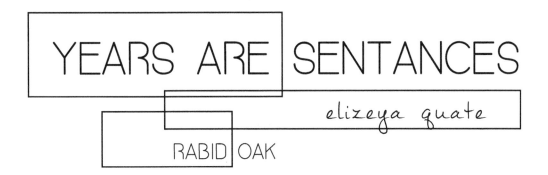

YEARS ARE SENTANCES

elizeya quate

RABID OAK

IN NINETEEN EIGHTY EIGHT i'm basically just a potato being hoisted around by knotty hands it rains a lot i take such strong pleasure in watching the raindrops race each other down the hinged panes of french windows. in nineteen eighty eight the sickness of chernobyl still seeps across europe the spooked news people say don't drink the milk because the rain that feeds the cow's grass is poison. in nineteen eighty nine the sky is full of cold shapes i am crying i will cry until i sleep & dream in pure creases (no colors yet) only big gray creases & folds of hardnesses & softnesses vaguenesses & sharpnesses comforting warmths & stiff ugly chills. the age when i do all my best thinking in creases & folds are good years they are the years that help me understand how sleeping works they are the years that introduce me to the viscosity of yearning. in nineteen ninety we are living in the side of an old leaky castle in the countryside there is moss everywhere i want to grow moss on my own face & the backs of my hands but they won't let me because unlike the old leaky castle i don't have stone walls or any secrets (yet). in nineteen ninety one my mother introduces the celebration of halloween there is a bowl of peeled grapes my hands reach in to touch in my mind i am so sure they are truly eyeballs (aaaaaiiiieeee!). in nineteen ninety one we move north to a funny town full of waterzooie & flemish double-aaaas that i love only for the cloying odor of liegewafels & the bright pastel petals of the tulips in the market because otherwise every morning is dark & darker rain. in nineteen ninety one my brother arrives he is just as potatoey as i had been & for awhile i hate him because i want to be this family's only potato. (later my brother & i unite in tuberous solidarity against parental authority). in nineteen ninety two i make my first friends due partly to the bright rainbows on their teeshirts we take photos together all happy & incoherent with plum trees in the background. in nineteen ninety three we're all in the airport flying away to the land where our words are from (our words are saying hiii to all their long-lost word-friends) then finally we come to rest in an empty room full of taped cardboard boxes (this is our home now). in nineteen ninety three we are in the hospital my father is one-eyed with facial bandages secretly i believe he's been recruited to become a professional monster this one-eyedness is only the beginning of all the horrifying monster mutations that are to come. in nineteen ninety four my mother thinks i am so sad because of my one-eyed father that she buys me a snare drum to bang on (this is her big mistake) i play john philip sousa & star wars themes from crinkled sheet music my sticks thwacking & clinking everywhere. in nineteen ninety five my snare drum teacher demonstrates how to play military marches i practice my percussion fundamentals like the paradiddle & the nine-stroke roll. later he will write me letters in blue cursive about the infiltration of our society by a race of invisible yet benevolent extraterrestrials who are in cahoots with jesus christ. in nineteen ninety six it is winter the snow is like the coat of one of those big fluffy forever dogs & comes up past my chin. in nineteen ninety six we are putting handfuls of the snow in big silver pots with maple syrup & eating it with spoons (so good! but then aaaa brainfreeze this is how i become suspicious of pleasure). in nineteen ninety six the roads are all closed we are snowbound but we still walk all the way to the grocery store to buy some milk there isn't any milk we walk back home.

in nineteen ninety seven there are the beatles & bob marley for the first time in my ears i wear these big secondhand tshirts to bed & love being inside my room. in nineteen ninety seven when i have to go outside i wear a sweatshirt every single day because i feel chubby i hate being looked at by other kids on friday night my mom & my brother & i order pizza with crazy toppings like capers we watch vhs movies like *the mask* & *the phantom tollbooth* & *ghostbusters*. in nineteen ninety seven there are real computers with dial-up internet i devote many evenings to playing civ 2 & tiberian sun & writing writing writing mostly very short plays with dialogues that all sound like worse versions of the marx brothers. in nineteen ninety seven i'm very angry at how predictable my writing sounds how knotty & uncooperative my body feels i am wishing i could be anywhere except in my own obvious body anywhere except in my own obvious head. in nineteen ninety eight i'm playing snare drum in school band watching john waters stanley kubrick david lynch quentin tarantino blood blood blood & tongues & lots of mad-eyed grimaces. in nineteen ninety eight i'm publishing a small newspaper with microsoft publisher placing my stacks at the local vhs video store & the american city diner where you can win a keychain in a bright magenta plastic egg for the price of two quarters. in nineteen ninety nine i am so awkward & acne-blotched that after school every day i listen to depressive electronic music over & over again until the anguish of living in a human body begins to recede. in two thousand everyone says that the world is going to end because of y2k but it doesn't. in two thousand one the sky's full of smoke our red-haired english teacher with nice freckles turns on the radio & we listen to the arc of history swerve violently into misadventure. in two thousand one people are wondering how much torture is too much torture. in two thousand one there's the fear of white powder in postal envelopes. in two thousand one there's the fear of brown skin at airports. in two thousand one there are mass arrests no one is supposed to talk about the mass arrests later we find out the government arrested brown people at random & took them to prison islands & black sites to be caged in orange jumpsuits. in two thousand two people are angry people are in the street people are waving signs people are in camo with automatic weapons people are heading overseas to discover other prisons other cages. in two thousand three when it happens all over again my eyes feel wrenched open to the murderous reality of political power i'm outraged i'm so outraged i'm telling people with furious conviction i do not trust the government no one should trust the government it's fucking bullshit why should anyone believe what the government is telling us about the war or the mass arrests or the white powder in the postal envelopes? in two thousand three my friend asks me earnestly don't you think it'll be worth trusting the government putting brown people in cages to not die from a bioweapons attack? what if your skin bubbles & your eyeballs melt? what about the skin of your family of your mother & father & brother? in two thousand three people are buying plastic wrap & bottled water to keep their homes & their families safe. in two thousand three i am practicing running in zig-zags to avoid bullets from snipers. in two thousand three i am going down into the basement to practice waiting for the air to clear & maybe to practice waiting for other things too. years later it strikes me as strange that i was told that what i was doing when i was sitting in the basement was not waiting but instead *practicing* waiting that my passivity was only a *simulation* of waiting a *simulation* that has since become somehow indistinguishable from the real waiting from the memory of waiting. in two thousand three my haircut's a blue mohawk i put on headphones i play nofx & fugazi punk music really loud to block out the world i want to escape from the everyday feeling of so much violent dissonance. in two thousand three after eating mushrooms with my friend he & i walk all over the us capital & downtown dc & through the woods by dry creekbed near what used to be klingle street & back up long sets of stone stairs in the embassy district. in two thousand three standing beneath the stone lions of the taft bridge it feels like the whole world is converging upon a singular receding point in the distance of an eternally setting sun. in two thousand four i grow a bit taller now i can jump up on top of things now i can yell at the top of my lungs. in two thousand four i suddenly have lots of things to say i want everyone to listen to me i cannot stop myself from talking. in two thousand five i become very much alive to the amazing sexiness of other people's bodies the sensations of lust are so vivid electric that all else fades to grayscale murmurs. in two thousand five i'm reading kafka & foucault & baudrillard all the time i'm talking about marxism with an acid swagger spending most of my time working on research & practice speeches for debate team. in two thousand six i'm going to college feeling again so alone i spend hours talking on the phone i make a few new friends but mostly i'm either drinking cheap alcohol with strangers or reading these very dense critical theory books that feel like pure light in my brain they are all talking about the history of power they are all talking about the monumentally exciting & horrifying near-future of humanity. in two thousand seven the summer is endless with soft dreamy lyricism i'm watering plants & fetching coffee for formal people in a big government office i'm answering a landline telephone the color of tapioca. in two thousand seven me & my girlfriend listen to black moth & daft punk we go up north to new york state we drop acid in a nudist forest full of art & masked characters spouting new ways to be human. in two thousand eight there's a world-shattering stock market crash my father loses his job all the experts say we are in a bad recession. in two thousand eight me & my girlfriend are working overseas in beijing china for the summer my father comes to visit we're all up on a secret rooftop near chaoyang park to watch the sky over the olympics sparkling with victorious fireworks. in two thousand nine i'm collaborating on video projects i'm learning how to make budgets i'm organizing groups of people to create content on a deadline using structured excel templates. in two thousand ten my parents split up my grandparents die i'm in shock my sense of painful vertigo grows icy down the back of my spine until all i can do is to go mute. in two thousand ten no amount of structured excel templates can prevent me from falling into an engulfing depression each day the only thing i can make myself do is to write little stories using few words go to class come home write write write wake up again wake up before the sun. in two thousand ten i know my writing isn't very good i keep writing every night because i cannot figure out how to stop. in two thousand ten i send my stories off to magazines the only thing i get back is rejection letters. in two thousand eleven i graduate i'm living in detroit in a barely furnished apartment drinking too much trying to pay my bills making videos between part-time debate coaching. in two thousand twelve it works out a little better with making videos me & my business partner go to los angeles & london we work on projects with bigger budgets but overall the flow of work is unreliable & after we get stiffed on a couple big invoices it's time to say goodbye. in two thousand thirteen i move to iowa city to coach debate at the university i become certified for the university's procurement process by watching a series of instructional videos & completing a short online quiz. two thousand thirteen i inhale the snowy smell of cigarettes my ears are filled with the distant whispering of the plains. two thousand fourteen is my cheapest year of rent: four hundred thirty two dollars i eat beans & rice in spite of my frugality i still do not manage to save much money. two thousand thirteen is the first year i get a story published in an anthology (a real book!) i decide to go to san francisco for a public reading during litquake the feeling of reading my work aloud in front of other people is so incredible it's like my whole heart is exploding. in two thousand fifteen i get accepted to grad school for creative writing but it's quite expensive i decide not to go. in two thousand fifteen i move to san francisco to begin creating "content" about procurement policy for a tech company where i end up learning other useful technical skills. in two thousand sixteen the book i started writing five years ago gets published by an independent press based in syracuse ny. in two thousand sixteen i do some more readings my heart is swollen i wonder if getting a book published is all i've ever wanted out of life? (immediately following this feeling of total fulfillment i of course fall into a deep & bottomless labyrinth of depression). in two thousand sixteen i begin freelancing more & i can make a bit of money helping other people edit their own book manuscripts. in two thousand sixteen i'm starting to learn how to write patents for my technology ideas dealing with multi-party price negotiations. in two thousand sixteen i start & end two bad relationships that make me wonder if i'll ever learn how to show up for a significant other without oscillating between feeling sentimentally attached & resentfully unreciprocated by the intensity of my longing pressed against the space we hold between us. in two thousand sixteen i realize that i truly need to re-arrange how my mind works & what reactions it produces & what memories it stores. in two thousand sixteen i create rules for myself about how i spend my time i decide to start consciously copying behavior patterns that i admire in others.

in two thousand seventeen i start my own technology company i get my first investment by participating in a live startup pitch contest grinning behind a microphone in a bright room full of wide-brimmed strangers. in two thousand seventeen i move to texas for six months because my new investors live in texas. in two thousand seventeen i meet a person late at night dancing at the drugstore cowboy in deep ellum it feels special right away she's an artist she's an american airlines gate attendant she's obsessed with public transit. in two thousand eighteen my company grows bigger i move back to san francisco (i've just turned thirty) we raise more money & hire more people (now we have a mailing address strangers start sending us junk mail). in two thousand eighteen i finish a book of poems that will be published by a small press in kentucky it is about how hearts are like the surface of an old painting (obscured by a dense network of tiny cracks that confers upon both organ & canvas a hard-earned aura of authenticity). in two thousand eighteen in the east coast coldness of winter at my mom's house i sit down i try to write write write i can't write about anything i can't think about anything i decide to write a single sentence about each year of my life so far. why do i do this? do i learn anything? reading back over the sentences during editing i see that when i'm young the world feels so massive & wrinkled it is all a vast collage of light & motion. reading back over the sentences it is astonishing to me how much my experience of each day's duration has altered from year to year from decade to decade it makes me wonder if i am still the same person or if this world is still the same world or if each passing moment simply contains many different possible worlds & many versions of every person glistening like the ruby seeds snug within a pomegranate. reading back over the sentences i can now see that in the years when i'm young my experience-memories are all about temperature pressure noise & my idea-memories are about intricate & chaotic assembly machines. when i'm older i can see the days fit neatly within the months the years the decades all the discrete phases of time seem to collapse into one another like a telescoping umbrella's segments-within-segments running beginning-middle-end goal milestone input-output i can see that my mind has ingested the structured excel template as a tabulated heuristic of inner experience. when i'm older i can vividly sense in my memories the curiosity & desire to gather insights from my own choices about what kind of person i really am & what kind of person i hope to become. now a couple years after writing this "years are sentences" i can see that my heuristic of inner experience now demands ever-greater granularity my heuristic demands precise labeling & categorization of meaningful events the same way an industrial process lines up raw materials on a conveyor belt my heuristic consumes blocs of sensations to produce affective & symbolic resonance. are my heuristics of inner experience more like simple tools or or more like alchemical poems whose lusciousness comes from combining melancholy with delectation pleasure with ache enthusiasm with despondency? what about my life? what putrefied death-feelings have i spent my whole life escaping from only to finally realize that it was precisely their overwhelming intensity which made me most complete?

in two thousand eighteen my heuristics of inner experience are producing tabulations showing that i drank at least five hundred thirteen cups of coffee in the past three hundred sixty five days. in two thousand eighteen my on-again-off-again diary tells me that i ate implausibly concatenated sandwiches (blackberry jelly, fried egg, parmesan) & scribbled many slim columns of over-hyphenated words (red-leaves-twirling-cold-toes-ocean-froth). in two thousand eighteen the near-future's most radiant monuments spoke to me in murmurs of urgent necessity. in two thousand eighteen there isn't any time to waste on the absent moment when i will cease to exist there isn't any time to waste on the fear of suffering or humiliation or the fear of being judged an eccentric or a fool. in two thousand eighteen i begin to question everything about my life all over again i begin to re-examine every quality in myself i begin to read more about the psychological topics most embedded in my daily experience of memory formation: attachment gratitude misrecognition exuberance antipathy exhaustion overfamiliarity dysphoria belonging. in two thousand eighteen i learn that the world is filled with visions of being alive much greater than what my current habits & heuristics are capable of producing. can i be born all over again my mouth overflowing with questions about what i am only now beginning to learn? in two thousand eighteen the beauty of the world is unraveling untangling unspooling from the gloom of my shadows the way a burning hubcap rolls away from a smoking crater still wildly alive still very much ablaze.

Elizeya Quate is a noun concealed everywhere in this sentence, but not quite where you'd first expect. Quate is the author of *The Face of Our Town* (Kernpunkt Press, 2016) and *cra-que-lure* (Finishing Line Press, 2019), with prose in *Joyland, Big Lucks, HuffPost* & elsewhere. Learn more by steering your nearest Internet browser to www.elizeyaquate.com.

SHOEBOX OF THUNDER

barclay rafferty

REFLEX FICTION

WREN SONG GLITCHES, CRACKLES, drowns in spray-rain, tattoos the shell of the tunnel. I tap its millipede-in-hobnail-boots rhythm on the tiller. Sodden paper chokes a bottleneck, gargles: *If caged birds dream of clouds, what do wild birds dream of*? I place this melting folk wisdom with the other empties, chiming like the Moon.

Goodbye, Gene Cernan, final Earthling, goodbye.

I've always wanted Dreams, not Real Things. When they pan out worse, I turn to the in-between: my computer. It tells me why I'm sick; points me in the direction of the next virtual orgy; gives me knowledge no human ever could. I even stream a live cam from some beach where rowboats jigsaw and elbow the seaside.

But this little grey box can't buzz hair overgrown like spider silk, loosen bowlines, part leaves from trees traced by the Vampire of Summer. Doesn't appreciate wren song that can make your cheekbones shatter.

I pull over, let some bloke overtake, feel the hull of the boat rubbing against silt. He looks baffled. *I can explain*, I don't say, call myself a twit in a homemade grave, ask him to toss some of those eggs he's flogging from his rooftop. Or a life jacket.

His eyes, tree hollows with nothing scurrying, remind me of—

Dad, old lift-shaft peepers himself, stopped turning blackstuff one morning, took a 15p bus ride to Orgreave, picket in hand. Mum dragged herself downhill from the Convent, crossed the border to avoid a life of silent contemplation. Both joined the Natural Causes Club while I drummed the bodhrán to the pissed and prostrate in pub lounges.

I stop by Booth's Garden Nonsense. *Any wharf in a storm* and all that. A cuppa then onto the mooring: berth the narrowboat, fetch logs, tend to violets, orchids—

I know lightning only strikes twice in Dreams, but tonight I'll be standing under tall trees waving golf clubs at passing bolts. And there's still time for you to send that SOS: bottle, skywriting, whatever. No address, just the Shoebox of Thunder. If I haven't returned from the nineteenth hole, just let yourself into the cabin.

You won't need a key, just a skeleton.

Dr. Barclay Rafferty is an academic and writer from England. He was recently awarded second prize in the Autumn '19 *Reflex* Flash Fiction Competition, and his articles appear in the Taylor & Francis journal, *Shakespeare*, as well as the *Journal of Adaptation in Film & Performance*. Barclay holds a PhD in English from De Montfort University, where he spent several years as a Part-Time Lecturer, Honorary Research Fellow, and peer reviewer for *Oxford Journals*. Find him on Twitter @BarclayRafferty.

PRICKLY JASMINE

azza rashad

LITHUB & BANAT AHLAM (AKHBAR EL (YOM PUBLISHING HOUSE)

translated by jonathan wright

MANGOES COME IN MANY varieties with many names, but generally speaking they are all beautiful and desirable and people look forward to them with longing. In our house there's more to mangoes than just that. During her first pregnancy my mother had a craving for *hindi* mangoes. That was in the middle of January, when the mangoes are like salty stones stuck to the branches of the trees. My father was in a quandary, but he disclosed his anxiety to a kind man who was traveling to a country the name of which my mother couldn't remember whenever she gleefully repeated the story to us. The man came back with a box of *hindi* mangoes and my mother is still grateful that they tasted so good. She saw the mangoes as the main reason why her baby daughter was so beautiful and, in recognition of their virtues, she chose to name her first-born Hind.

Hind, or "my mango" as Mother called her, was more beautiful and more enchanting than the models in the famous women's fashion magazines. This meant that suitors queued up at the door to marry her.

When my mother was pregnant with me, she had a craving for sardines, and she maintains that although my father was busy at the time with the annual stocktaking, he did not neglect her craving, despite the fear that I might be born with a birthmark on my face in the shape of a sardine, or that I might come out limp or with a fishy smell. To be extra sure to avoid any fishiness, they chose the name Jasmine for me. Even so, my mother likes to tease me by calling me "little sardine". But when she's angry and she says the name with her nose crinkled up, the idea of how I might have been born comes back to haunt me and I go into a corner, sniff my body and rub my face with soap again and again.

My mother puts her nose to ripe mangoes and sighs: "There are lots of them now. But they don't have any smell or taste."

But she didn't make this comment to Hisham when he brought a large box of mangoes just before the last feast. Instead she thanked him for his generosity. But when he had gone she yelled out curses on cheats and swindlers.

Mother treated Hisham kindly, which made him abandon his rustic shyness and talk and laugh as freely as if he were with family. She smiled as Hisham handed her a duck and blocks of local butter. Then she would start on hours of work in the kitchen, making us the most delicious food. When he had finished eating he would kiss her hand in gratitude, while the aromas from our little banquet rose to the nose of Umm Hamza on the upper floor, and envy drove her to detain me at the grocer's with malicious questions about when Hind was getting married. Then the fishy smell would come over me again, and I would curl up inside myself and stammer, unable to reply. That was when I was young. Now I recoil, disgusted by the smell of her sweat, which cannot be compared to the smell of the jasmine with which I now perfume my clothes. I also go out of my way to provoke her with a harassing look, quite different from the worried look in the picture that Hisham took of me when he gave me a mobile phone, after noticing I was interested in taking pictures.

At the time I was thinking how long it would be before generous Hisham would reconsider his esteem for generosity. But I was so happy with the camera that I soon forgot such worries. In the next picture you can see the tips of Hisham's fingers squeezing Hind's hand as he took the plates from her. As for this charming gladiolus, I chose it from the bunches of flowers that Said brought. He was nice, romantic and infatuated with Hind, and he seemed to be offering her his heart with the flowers, while she smiled affectedly, then threw the flowers away irritably when he had gone. Mother bent down to pick up the little velvety leaves that had scattered in all directions. After a while she would shout in his face that buying flowers was a waste.

"It's no use, my dear. Once night falls, they'll be wilted by daybreak," she told him.

He stared at the flowers in embarrassment, but then he decided to stop cutting flowers for Hind to make his way to my school and then to the electricity and water companies to pay our overdue bills. But neither the flowers nor the receipts managed to change Hind's affected smile. She tossed back her long black hair, filling the air with a beguiling aroma of ripe mangoes waiting to be picked from the tree. Men stared at her and longed for her as she strode along, sleepy-eyed as though lost, looking for something without knowing what she sought, moving on, her mood swinging alarmingly—sometimes cheerful but mostly discontented. She would snarl at me and Mother over the slightest thing. Mother tolerated her with amazing magnanimity, while I ended up taking refuge with my camera, which was never out of my hands.

Hind didn't like taking pictures: instead she was addicted to looking at herself in the mirror from various angles, although she looked beautiful whatever the pose. She was interested only in herself and couldn't bear to stay in the kitchen for more than five minutes. The other thing that appealed to her was listening to sentimental songs. The songs chimed with her daydreams and evoked images of the long-awaited knight she couldn't see in Hisham, who, once he abandoned his shyness, displayed a rustic nature that was incompatible with her dreams, or in Said, who was so in love with her that he gave her no space to move and irritated her, whereas I loved them both, as I love Karim now, and I hoped she would marry either of them. Mother lavished kindness on them because she was nice to everyone except when something else was required, as happened with Raouf the milkman when he changed from angel to devil, to use her words. Hind didn't like Raouf from the start. In fact she thought he was vile and, unlike Mother, she believed the stories people told about him adulterating his milk with grouting powder, formalin and other harmful substances.

Mother said that an engagement was a trial period. They all come in turn to our house full of good cheer, the evenings were pleasant, the dining table was loaded with all kinds of dishes, laughter rang out and I got used to them as if they were my relatives, until Mother turned up with an angry expression.
"A freehold apartment in her name," she would say. "Her father visited me yesterday evening and insisted on that."

At that point the dream would collapse and the result of the test would remain undecided. No one passed.

I don't know how it came about that Father would visit Mother on those occasions, whenever a suitor started to frequent the house and tried to get better terms than the examination board would allow.

Usually Hind would let one of them kiss her cheek, as if the cheek wasn't hers, and in most cases she would look away and wipe the kiss off in disgust. These things happened behind Mother's back of course, and even the one time when she was close enough to see the kiss, she didn't seem to notice. The poor woman was distracted by thoughts about her dealings with my father. Her worries were too much for her and they added a mournful tone to her voice when she told off my father: "Damn you, Abderrahim, you've had it easy and left me to deal with all this trouble by myself."

Sometimes she would lament: "A woman whose husband has died, O her suffering and need!"

Azza Rashad was awarded by the state incentive award from the ministry of culture in Egypt in literature for the short "Half a light" in 2010. She was a member of the supreme council of culture from 2011 to 2013. Azza also worked as editor-in-chief at *The novel: issues and prospects* magazine for 2 years; 2010 and 2011.

Jonathan Wright was born in Andover, Hampshire. He joined Reuters news agency in 1980 as a correspondent, and has been based in the Middle East for most of the last three decades. From 1998 to 2003, he was based in Washington, DC, covering US foreign policy for Reuters. For two years until the fall of 2011 Wright was editor of the *Arab Media & Society Journal*, published by the Kamal Adham Center for Journalism Training and Research at the American University in Cairo.

POSTCARD FROM THE HUDSON

hannah rego

LAMBDA LITERARY

I MISS THE PILLOW fights. Don't hold back as you slam a body pillow across my body from the full height of your head. There's no pleasure as great as being hurt by the one who ignores you. When we were young, I waited & palmed your carved stone alligator. If you caught a baby lizard now between your hands, large or small, I would be just as quiet. As when we held our breath as long as we could underwater. As when we sat poolside frosting the tips of our hair blonde with lemon juice. When we traded Pokémon cards, I knew you were doing everything you could to be dealt the best hand. It wasn't surprising. Nothing surprised me. Now, when I meet you again, in him, in him, in him, I laugh when he calls me darling. I answer texts right away & wait right away to be answered days later. The last boy I played video games with was a man in a bar. Streetfighter, old arcade. Who won? I ate his tacos in his high school teacher's lounge. I took his books on accident. In Miami, did you lay pipes? Did you snort? In Kentucky, did you work in a factory? Home to home? I, busy with books & rocks & women & men & hallucinating to impress you, have failed to ask when, if at all, you have been happy. Where? How long? The water before me laps curiously. As a box marked as a fragile thing. The last time I came I thought of the last time I came with another person. Not that I would know, but he isn't anything like you. Last week I watched porn ft. a trans man for the first time. I start hormones tomorrow. When we played halo, & even I played, & you, impressed I'd stuck you with a grenade, exploded, it was the glint in your eye. It's you.

Hannah Rego is a writer from Louisville, Kentucky. They are an MFA candidate at the University of Arizona and a founding editor of *ctrl+v*, a journal of collage. Their work appears in *Bettering American Poetry Vol. 3*, *Lambda Literary*, *Ninth Letter*, *BOOTH* and elsewhere.

HOW TO LIVE THROUGH THIS

helen rickerby

HOW TO LIVE (AUCKLAND UNIVERSITY PRESS)

WE WILL MAKE SURE we get a good night's sleep. We will eat a decent breakfast, probably involving eggs and bacon. We will make sure we drink enough water. We will go for a walk, preferably in the sunshine. We will gently inhale lungsful of air. We will try to not gulp in the lungsful of air. We will go to the sea. We will watch the waves. We will phone our mothers. We will phone our fathers. We will phone our friends. We will sit on the couch with our friends. We will hold hands with our friends while sitting on the couch. We will cry on the couch with our friends. We will watch movies without tension—comedies or concert movies—on the couch with our friends while holding hands and crying. We will think about running away and hiding. We will think about fighting, both metaphorically and actually. We will consider bricks. We will buy a sturdy padlock. We will lock the gate with the sturdy padlock, even though the gate isn't really high enough. We will lock our doors. We will screen our calls. We will unlist our phone numbers. We will wait. We will make appointments with our doctors. We will make sure to eat our vegetables. We will read comforting books before bedtime. We will make sure our sheets are clean. We will make sure our room is aired. We will make plans. We will talk around it and talk through it and talk it out. We will try to be grateful. We will be grateful. We will make sure we get a good night's sleep.

Helen Rickerby is the author of four collections of poetry, most recently *How to Live* (Auckland University Press, 2019), which was the winner of the poetry category for the Ockham New Zealand Book Awards 2020. Her work explores the boundaries of poetry, where it intersects with other forms such as film criticism, biography, fiction and essay. She lives in Wellington, New Zealand, and single-handedly runs boutique publishing company Seraph Press.

THIRTEEN WAYS OF LOOKING AT OTHER BIRDS

amy rowland

IOWA REVIEW

I.   BOHUMIL HRABAL, FEEDING PIGEONS, leaned out too far on the ledge and fell to his death. Poor pigeons, hated for so much, and now Hrabal's death, too.

II.   We have never solved the problem of humans falling. Three million years ago, Lucy, of the species *Australopithecus afarensis*, died, scientists think, after a fall, probably from a tree.

III.   Arrested falling is how Schopenhauer referred to walking. Birds don't fall. Well, mostly. When I was in third grade, a bird fell out of its nest in a dogwood tree in our yard. My neighbor Tabby and I found him on the ground, naked, pink, and featherless, but alive. We put him in a shoebox with some pine straw, and Tabby took him home and left him on her windowsill where he froze to death. She said she didn't leave the window open, but I know she did.

IV.   When walking around my old neighborhood in Brooklyn one day, a man told me to be careful, that an angry blue jay was "dive-bombing" him. I wondered why this bird was watching me, he said, and then he attacked.

V.   I've only been attacked in Brooklyn once. It was mean mommies, who told me and my niece that they were taking over the park for a kindergarten party. I have had problems in life that some have attributed to meekness, so I said that we would leave when we finished our bagels. They descended on us like the Pink Ladies and said we had to leave! Now! Things got heated, including my poor niece's face, and we ended up being chased away by the mean mommies as they yelled that I was setting a terrible example for my daughter, while a group of five-yearolds stood around gaping like the Central Park boy in the Diane Arbus photo.

VI.   I left Brooklyn, but I remembered those women, who remind me of mean girls from high school, when I first felt affinity with birds. Killdeers liked to lay eggs in the rocks of my high school parking lot. The eggs blended with the gravel, and if you got too close, the killdeers would run around dragging their wings to distract predators. They enlisted other killdeers, too, and sometimes when I pulled in to park, there were several birds dragging their wings and running around frantically.

VII.   During a summer in Massachusetts, I learned that male birds have the brightest plumage. Most adults already know that, but I'm often late to the game. I was living with a man who turned out to hate women, but like I said, I'm not always the early bird on useful knowledge. I liked to sit at this man's desk and watch the goldfinches at the birdfeeder. The beautiful males ate the thistle seeds greedily. They never fell. I appreciated the way the females could be drab and nonchalant, and the males would strut and fluff and sometimes the females would give them a chance.

VIII.   Robert, the man who hated women, said he noticed me because I was reserved. This was somewhat true. I didn't wear jewelry. All of my shirts had sleeves. I'm a little less severe now, though I plan to be severe again soon. We knew a Portuguese poet who arrived at the local coffeeshop every morning dressed for a long hot night at a Brazilian nightclub. She was as effective as a male goldfinch. (Entering Robert's one day, poet's dress on his couch, dress owner in his bed.) Robert liked to shock his students with the story of a boy who is aroused by a giraffe.

IX.   I loved the rolling Berkshire farmland, the hemlocks and blueberry bushes, the quickly evolving generations of Canadian geese. I loved early morning, and the melting cobweb-colored mist. Once, Robert said, "Do you know where my mind is when we're lying in bed? It migrates to you." But minds, like ghosts and woodpeckers, don't migrate.

X.   Geese migrate, though not as much as they once did. I live in a frighteningly, numbingly pretty little town. It has a nice canal towpath, where I like to run. The Canadian geese hiss if I step too close. I understand, as they start spring with eight goslings and then dwindle down to two. So I admire their heavy waddled hissieness.

XI.   People here are acquiring Silkie chickens. When the Silkies are chicks it is almost impossible to know whether they are hens or roosters. So there are many roosters for sale on Craigslist.

XII.   Killdeers do not hate slender-legged mammals, as far as we know. Someone just thought their sad cry sounded liked "Kill deer! Kill deer!" I imagined they were calling "Not here! Not here!"

XIII.   In the fifth grade, I was in the church Christmas program. I was supposed to recite the poem *Jesus's Birthday* while holding a chocolate layer cake my mother had made. I was on stage, sweating in the spotlight, when the woman who played the piano came out to light the cake candles, but she couldn't and finally told me, Hurry up and recite. She walked off, and I was standing there with the heavy cake with unlit candles and yellow frosting that spelled out Happy Birthday, Jesus! The poem flew right out of my head. Finally, I said, I forgot. After we had eaten our potluck dinner at the Fire Department because the church didn't have a reception hall, we went home. My sister had two parakeets that had refused to talk to us and just chattered away to each other, though I liked to translate for them. *You forgot! You forgot!* We had put a blanket over their cage before church because my parents didn't like to waste heat, and it was cold in the South that Christmas. The parakeets were dead, but my parents said it wasn't anybody's fault. We buried them in the yard.

Amy Rowland is the author of *The Transcriptionist*. She is finishing her second novel, *Soiled*, set on a tobacco farm in eastern North Carolina, where she grew up. Her fiction has appeared or is forthcoming in *The Southern Review*, *The Iowa Review*, *Hobart*, *New Letters*, *DIAGRAM*, and elsewhere. She currently teaches at UC Berkeley.

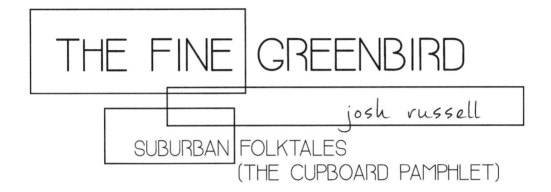

THE FINE GREENBIRD

josh russell

SUBURBAN FOLKTALES
(THE CUPBOARD PAMPHLET)

THEY TOOK THE BABY away and put a monkey in its place. That dream means you'll be delivered of a rosy-cheeked, golden-haired boy, the soothsayer told the queen. That dream means you worry if the kid's a boy, you won't love it, the therapist told the queen. That dream means you're working through your latent racism and the way it makes you want to infantilize and dehumanize the dark other, her friend the folklorist told the queen. That dream means you know my shameful secret, her husband the king told the queen, then made monkey noises until she laughed. He was off fighting a war his cousin had started with him, so the queen and the king were FaceTiming. The food sucks, he complained. Remind me to have this cook beheaded when I get back, okay?

They took the baby away and put a dog in its place. That dream means you'll be delivered of a milk-skinned, copper-haired boy, the soothsayer told the queen. That dream means you worry the Seroquel you're taking will harm your unborn child, but trust me, it won't, the therapist told the queen. That dream means you see yourself as your despotic spouse sees you: no more than a *bitch*, her friend the folklorist told the queen. A dog? said the king. Was it a big dog or a little dog? She couldn't tell if he was joking. I'm not sure what that one means, sorry, he told her. Even in the murky light the tallow candles threw inside his tent, she could see he was tired. The fucking cook got run through with a fucking flaming arrow, he said.

They took the baby away and put a tiger cub in its place. That dream means you'll be delivered of a daughter with a star on her brow, the soothsayer told the queen. The therapist told the queen nothing, as the queen had stopped telling the therapist about her dreams. That dream means finally we're getting somewhere, her friend the folklorist told the queen, but couldn't complete the thought because their appetizers arrived and the smell of fried calamari sent the queen running to the ladies' to puke up decaf and neonatal vitamins. That dream's awesome, her husband the king told her. Victory and whatever victors drink too much of whilst celebrating victory made him loud. Beats the shit out of the monkey and the dog, am I right? he hollered at his phone.

The fine Greenbird was in a shitty mood because the queen kept him locked up in the old dovecote. He had only himself to blame: whoever replied to his neoliberal rants was turned into a marble statue. The queen visited him daily so he wouldn't die of loneliness, and the practice of not responding calmed her. Serfs are poor because they're lazy, the fine Greenbird told her. She often wondered if any answer would turn her into a statue. When the fine Greenbird rambled about the nanny kingdom, would she become marble only if she countered with a Marxist argument, or would she turn to stone if she admitted aloud she worried the king was having a battlefield affair? She thought she'd heard a woman's voice say his name the night he called to tell her he'd won.

When the fine Greenbird said, Your jealous older sisters will wall you up in the cellar, the queen had to clap a hand over her mouth to save herself. Your baby's hair will be gold, and they will cut it off and sell locks of it, he continued. Your son will grow into a handsome young prince, and when he turns sixteen, I will tell him and the king where you are trapped. Your sisters will be burned at the stake, and you will live happily ever after.

Josh Russell's collection, *King of the Animals*, is forthcoming from Louisiana State University Press. His stories have appeared in *Epoch*, *Subtropics*, *One Story*, *Cincinnati Review*, and the anthology *New Micro*, and in the chapbooks *Pretend You'll Do It Again* (Greying Ghost Press) and *Suburban Folktales* (Cupboard Pamphlet). His novels are *Yellow Jack* (W.W. Norton), *My Bright Midnight* (LSU Press), and *A True History* (Dzanc Books). Very short stories he selected when guest editor for *Five Points* and *New Flash Fiction Review* later appeared in *The Best Small Fictions* and the Wigleaf Top 50. He lives in Decatur, Georgia.

THE DIAMOND FACTORY

helen rye

MATCH BOOK

EVERYTHING IN THE DIAMOND factory is real except for the diamonds. They turn on invisible currents in seawater vats like diamond wombs, strings of them, fossils of light trapped and hardened by the diamond factory workers, all of whom are old, old women or goddesses—it is always hard to tell the one from the other.

We steal in through unfastened doorways and unguarded windowsills and we watch from the back and we see the glitter of our old selves in the shoals of light on the walls. We've read that diamonds are made under pressure and pressure is something we know all about, but this is hunting, this is alchemy, if alchemy were a thing of nurture and sea herbs and tetrahedral atomic lattices stacked perfect and tight as bean cans.

We walk through the vats and we trail our fingers in brine and nobody stops us, so we gather them into our hands and we drape ourselves with diamond threads as we go, and we plan how we will do this, how we will braid them over our bodies, let them cover us, move with us, speak for us. We will wear them like a shell, our skin will blind you. We will blaze in the noonday sun like a supernova kissed us.

We don't care that the diamond factory diamonds are artificial. All of the things we are tired of are real. Our diamond factory diamond skin will be nineteen times harder than titanium, eighteen thousand times harder than a human heart and nothing will scratch it, not words or weapons or poverty, not you with your dragon heart, thinking we should belong to you because we shine.

The diamond factory doesn't pay taxes. The diamond factory thinks the government has enough stuff already. The diamond factory prefers to distribute its bounty among the poor and the tired and the women who spend too much time waiting at bus stops and the women who do not get to spend enough time singing or looking through telescopes at the passages of stars and the women who have escaped from the caves of dragons with barely the clothes that will cover their diamond skins.

Because of us, the diamond factory is thinking of branching into armor. Their armor will be like our diamond skins but with also a helmet to cover the head for the times when we have to go back to the caves to take back our belongings and tell you, You cannot beat into shape another human heart like it is a thing you own, you cannot hoard it away from the world and mold it into something different from itself until it feels itself too small and weak to leave, just because the shaping of things in the way that you want makes you feel like a real dragon. You have so much to learn about hearts.

In our diamond factory armor, we will not hear you roar and threaten. We will take back what is ours and will not hear you tell us how fragile we are, how *actually*, it is we who are broiling, how *actually*, it is we who brought about our own hammering. Our diamond factory armor will cover our ears with the hardest of light from the hands of old, old women, whom secretly we think of as goddesses, whose voices will whisper to us all of the way out of the mouth of the cave, thousands of them, saying, Look how strong we are, all of us together and always. Look how hard we shine.

Helen Rye has won the Bath Flash Fiction Award, the Reflex Fiction contest and third place in the Bristol Short Story Prize. In 2019 she was awarded the Annabel Abbs Scholarship to study for a Prose MA at the University of East Anglia. Her stories have been published in a number of anthologies and journals. She is a submissions editor for *SmokeLong Quarterly*, a prose editor for *Lighthouse Literary Journal* and is on the editorial teams of TSS Publishing and *Ellipsis Zine*. She is proud to be karaoke convenor for the UK Flash Fiction Festival.

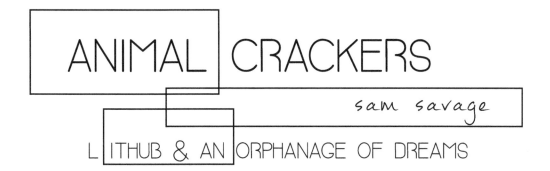

ANIMAL CRACKERS

sam savage

LITHUB & AN ORPHANAGE OF DREAMS

Muskrat

THE MUSKRAT IS AN important animal. It lives in holes. It seldom experiences any of the extreme forms of anxiety. It is not in holes because of that. It does not fear nuclear attack. It smells bad, hence the name. It smells good to other muskrats. We have no idea how it smells to other muskrats. At what point will we cease being fond of it? It used to be valued in coats. They were not called muskrat coats because that was too much like rat coats. It doesn't like being made into coats. It makes little stick houses on the ice. It is not a miniature beaver. It does not do well in college. Male muskrats engage in bloody combat over female muskrats. It does not mature easily. It must not be confused with the European water rat. It does not like moles.

Pangolin

It eats ants. It is not an anteater. Nobody seems to know what it is exactly. It is a scaly mammal. It prefers the simple life. When frightened it curls up into an impregnable ball. A frightened pangolin is the size of a basketball. If you puncture a pangolin, air does not come out. It is capable of making a hissing sound but that is not the reason. It possesses a thin, very sticky tongue that it uses to capture ants and termites. The tongue is so extremely long it is kept in a sheath that reaches to the pangolin's abdomen. When people have epileptic seizures it is important not to let them swallow their tongues. There are no epileptic pangolins. There are no photographs of Dostoyevsky with a pangolin. When Dostoyevsky was twenty-eight he was sentenced to be shot for sedition. He stood in the prison yard. He was in his underwear and it was very cold. They were to be shot three by three. He was in the second group of three. He was not allowed to curl up into a ball.

Porcupine

It hates its name. It is not a pig. It has piglike eyes. It can't jump. It is nearsighted, has a large brain and an excellent memory. Resentment builds up. It is lonely. It goes to the park by itself. It is always alone on its bench. It is prickly and no one wants to sit with it. It feels like a pig. It dreams of an address in Hollywood. Sometimes on dark nights it roosts in trees. It has a tiny apartment in a suburb of Cleveland, the most distant place it had money to get to. What a life. In the winter it eats conifer needles and bark. It is deeply pessimistic. It is more pessimistic than any animal before it. In the spring it eats flowers.

Wolverine

It is always angry. It takes medicine for this. It has tried meditation, long-distance running, yoga, nothing helps. It tried golf, but that made it angrier. It looks like a portly and well-fed bear though it is constantly afraid of starving. It is fond of moose. It is a noisy eater. It sits at the counter in the diner and people stare. It wears a brown soup-stained cardigan that it never washes. It complains to anyone who will listen. When it was still young it went off to London, because it wanted to improve itself. It found a room in Ealing. That was in 1963. It bought a trench coat. It tightened the belt across its belly and turned the collar up. It bought a hat. It made sandwiches and ate them in Hyde Park. It did not want to be recognized. One night it went to Covent Garden to see Margot Fonteyn dance with Rudolf Nureyev, who had just defected from the Soviet Union. It kept its hat on. People were looking at it. They were wondering what a wolverine was doing at Covent Garden. Nureyev danced. It was the most beautiful thing the wolverine had ever seen. It was so beautiful the wolverine began to cry, and the block of anger inside it melted and flowed away with the tears.

That was a long time ago. The Soviet Union is gone. Nureyev is gone. The wolverine is old, it has forgotten the forest, it has forgotten London, it sits at the counter, tears at its food, and complains.

Weasel

After work the weasel gets together with other weasels that hang out on the corner across from Eddie's Meat Market. That's their corner, everybody knows it's their corner, polecats and stoats are not welcome. The weasels don't have a lot to say to each other, they just bitch and complain and leer at people walking past. Eddie at the market hates having them there, they scare customers off, he says, nobody wants to walk past a bunch of leering chicken killers. They hang out there anyway, out of spite, just to show him they are somebodies. The weasel doesn't give a damn about the other weasels' problems, he barely listens to their whining. It feels good to complain aloud after bottling it up all day at work, just saying the words feels good to him even if none of the others listen or would care if he dropped dead tomorrow. Afterward, at home in his burrow, he wonders if the others are as lonely as he is. It would be funny if they all really just wanted friendship and love and couldn't get any closer to it than standing around bitching on a street corner.

Sam Savage is the best-selling author of *Firmin: Adventures of a Metropolitan Lowlife*, *The Cry of the Sloth*, *Glass*, *The Way of the Dog*, and *It Will End with Us*. A native of South Carolina, Savage holds a PhD in philosophy from Yale University. He was a finalist for the Barnes & Noble Discover Great New Writers Award, the PEN/New England Award, and the Society of Midland Authors Award. Savage resides in Madison, Wisconsin.

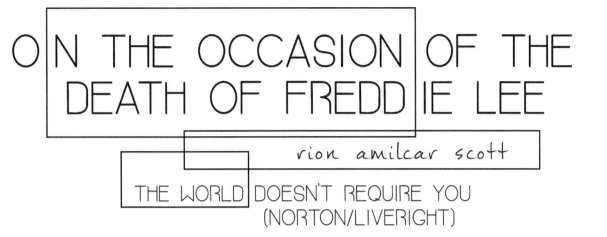

ON THE OCCASION OF THE DEATH OF FREDDIE LEE

rion amilcar scott

THE WORLD DOESN'T REQUIRE YOU (NORTON/LIVERIGHT)

EARLY ONE MORNING IN the turgid, musty swamp, Freddie Lee collapsed amongst the rice and the brown water, a result of working his body like a machine—both John Henry, the steel-driving man, and the locomotive at the same time.

He so loved the work, he battled himself to fill basket after endless basket with rice stalks, and as a reward he fell facedown into the crops before any of us woke. We all labored next to his body as we were told to do, coming to view his dead form with a reverence. Freddie was no longer a man, no longer our friend, but instead an offering to God, made to lie out there until Papa Troy gave word, and each night we burned the stalks we picked from around him.

But something kept getting to me out in the sun. Something beyond the stench. Something that rearranged my mind. Man, every time I drew near to the eternally slumbering Freddie Lee and his decaying face—

I remember when Mama Yona died and we all gathered solemnly for six hours as they put her into the earth and Papa Troy spoke of their life together, building this new world away from the world, away from cars, away from TVs, away from balloons and DVDs, away from it all, at this rice farm in the ruins of a plantation on a Wildlands hill. The children planted a tree over her resting place. And it felt beautiful and unreal, as if we existed on a spinning disc covered by a magical dome; anything could happen here. Freddie Lee believed in this life with the entirety of his—unbeknownst to him—dying heart.

Working the watery fields after my friend passed, I didn't become deranged, but found myself somewhere close to it. Something resembling a dark shadow spreading like an inkblot over my brain. I had obeyed dutifully following after Freddie Lee. I wondered if I'd share his fate, lying among the rice and the muck with a crumbling forever stare. And I could have probably taken it, inky brain and all, had I not seen that blasted cow, Lenire, tearing at Freddie's face, ripping, chewing his flesh like fresh grass. I waved my arms and yelled; charged the beast while screaming, but her tail swatted at flies and the rest of the animal paid me no mind. The chewed face of Freddie, Papa Troy told us, is just how it's supposed to be.

Me and Luke and Little Yuní went out that night to move the body from the shallow waters, but Mama's Thug Riders (that's what they called themselves) rode in silently on their horses—at least I didn't hear them—and waved their whips at us, opening up raw wounds on our chests and backs.

When we returned to our cabin we listened to the breeze whistle through the cracks and we tended to each other's wounds. I watched the great house with its light and its mirth. I was sure the drinks flowed there like the river water we diverted over the land to feed the rice stalks. Papa was having a party. There was always a party and we were the eternally uninvited unless someone important wanted a piece of our souls.

Papa says, everyone is equal, Luke said. Some people are m—

Shh—Little Yuní said, kissing his lips. I watched them make love.

They soon crumpled to the floor, exhausted and sated as they were taught to be.

Did you see Freddie Lee's body? I asked. John Henry, the rice-harvesting man? If he died harvesting rice for the love of us all, then why—even before that damn cow got to him—was he all broken and bruised?

Shh—Little Yuní said, but she had no energy to sate me, and before I could ask about the Expelled, whether our friend was close to them as the whispers implied, we all fell one by one into dazed and dizzying fever dreams. I wonder who was the first to speak of the flames in our sleep murmurs. Did we all share the same nightmares?

Morning came, the sun rose hot over the damp fields, and we were once again the docile supplicants of Mama Yona and Papa Troy's mercy, picking rice around our friend. Poor Freddie Lee—his face skeletal except for those swollen, staring eyes—he deserved more than the tepid love of cowards.

It might have ended right there had Freddie Lee not risen from the dead to rip the cow into thousands of pieces.

That morning Papa had planned to announce his next queen—could have been any of us—but we woke to bits of bloody cow meat everywhere: smeared on the windows of the great house, clinging to the rice stalks. Papa postponed his announcement and called for us to give up any information we had on the whereabouts of Freddie Lee's body and the circumstances of the cow's death.

Some pointed their fingers at the three of us, but we pointed ours right back. If it were us, I said, wouldn't we be stained? Marked like we took a bath in cow's blood? My logic silenced our accusers.

For three hours Papa Troy stood on the porch of the great house discussing betrayal and the life of his beloved Lenire. Tears soaked into his beard, his voice as watery as the rice fields.

Our hearts broke, but who were we to ramble madly about what we knew, what we saw—the dead man sauntering smoothly, coolly, until he spotted the cow? He stopped and threw his head back, wailing silently—the cow had long ripped his tongue from his mouth. His raw face and his perfect eyes bathed in the light of the moon. I called his name, but he watched us as if we were merely curiosities to ponder and then ignore. He stared for several seconds before he did his violence. I stayed up many nights afterward to catch another glimpse of Freddie Lee, but I never saw him again. Every once in a while, I'd ask Luke or Little Yuní if we saw what we really saw, and they'd nod like walking corpses without tongues.

One evening, when the passing of the months had given us no ease from the Thug Riders and their whippings, Little Yuní and I stood near the farthest edge of the farm.

Did we really see what we saw? I asked again. You know, with Freddie—

Shh, she said. Shh. She pointed to Luke walking toward us, a bundle of stalks in his arm. Behind him flames had begun dancing along the rice fields; fires even tap-danced upon the face of the waters below. The only world we knew was now shrouded in clouds of black smoke. I watched Luke's rice and breathed in his fumes; he stank of gasoline.

Little Yuní sighed.

Luke cursed. Dumped the day's haul to the wet ground.

Little Yuní lit a match.

Rion Amilcar Scott is the author of the story collection, *The World Doesn't Require You* (Norton/Liveright, August 2019). His debut story collection, *Insurrections* (University Press of Kentucky, 2016), was awarded the 2017 PEN/Bingham Prize for Debut Fiction and the 2017 Hillsdale Award from the Fellowship of Southern Writers. His work has been published in journals such as *The New Yorker*, *The Kenyon Review*, and *Crab Orchard Review* among others.

DAUGHTER

lacie semenovich

BODY LITERATURE

MOVE IN WITH YOUR mother. Pay her electric, gas, and water bills. Take her keys. She will hate you for this. Give her an allowance to buy groceries and soap. You are the oldest and the only daughter; she is your responsibility. Buy a cemetery plot; it will be needed. Buy thick toilet paper to wipe her ass. This is how you watch your mother hooked up to a ventilator. Don't get married. Don't have a child. This is how you wash her underarms, her breasts. This is how you see your body's future in her pouching and sagging skin. Wash her hair with baby shampoo. Don't get the shampoo in her eyes because she is still strong enough to fight you. Her dentures are stronger than real teeth. Pay for her medicine on your credit card. Listen to her hate your father. Don't ask your brothers to wipe her ass or bathe her. Don't ask them to sit with her. Wipe the white drool from her chin. Feed her with a baby spoon. Buy a good blender so that she can have pureed steak and mashed potatoes every once in a while. Forgive her dog when he mauls your hand because you upset her. Hide the ice cream from her. Put the sugar and salt in the top cabinets because osteoporosis has shrunk her. Listen to her stories about people you don't know. Feed her candy colored pills seven times a day. This is how you change her soiled sheets at 2am. Turn her every three hours to prevent bedsores. This is how you hold her hand. Tell her you love her because you should. Because you are a good daughter. This is how you buy flowers and a pine wood casket.

Lacie Semenovich holds an MA in Literature from Cleveland State University. Her recent and forthcoming publications include *MockingHeart Review*, *Shrew Literary Magazine*, *Turnpike Magazine*, *Portage Magazine*, *Cold Mountain Review*, and *Chiron Review*. She is the author of a chapbook, *Legacies*, (Finishing Line Press, 2012). She is currently working on another chapbook and a full-length collection of poetry.

AT THE PACIFIC AIR MUSEUM

lisa shulman

KYSO FLASH

HE POINTS AT THE plane's guts, showing us rudders and rotors and the intake manifold, and as he tells us how he formed the new aluminum panels by hand, his eyes lose their rheumy glaze and widen bluer and clear, and the crepey skin on his wrists tautens, the liver spots fading to sun-pressed freckles. The more he talks about replacing old rusted rivets with new ones, and assembling the parts piece by battered piece, the slimmer grows his waist and the firmer his jaw; even his hair seems to thicken and grow glossy beneath his jaunty baseball cap. It is easy to see the boy in the man talking of metal and machines; to hear the flutey thrill in the throat and see the muscles straining to remove and rebuild. It is easy to forget the shriek and screaming speed, the concussed destruction, the child's wail—the reason for these broken toys of war.

Lisa Shulman is a Pushcart Prize nominee, and the author of four picture books for children. Her fiction and poetry have appeared most recently in *California Quarterly*, *KYSO Flash*, *MacQueen's Quinterly*, and *Digging Our Poetic Roots*, and has been performed by Off the Page Readers Theater. As a third grade teacher, Lisa teaches her students to love writing; she is also a poetry teacher with California Poets in the Schools. Lisa lives in Northern California with her family.

THE KITCHEN

curtis smith

ATTICUS REVIEW

THE SON COOKS FOR his father. The old man's trailer. Yellowed windows. Flies caught on dangling strips. The son prepares meals for the week. The old man smokes and pages through the magazines the son has brought. The old man looks at the pictures, reads a caption or two, turns the page. The son makes shepherd's pie and chili. Last week, turkey soup. A single meal eaten together, the rest refrigerated. As they eat, one of them will break the silence and share a memory. A house they rented along the railroad tracks, the locomotives' shaking of windows and dishes. A creek where they fished for steelheads and walleyes, the late summer's flow speckled with milkweed seeds. A mutt named Bo. The other man smiles. *Yes, I remember.* The son has forgiven his father for his drinking. Forgiven him for a childhood of chaos. This, to the son, is a miracle, a revelation born from last fall's hospital visit. The father wrinkled and broken. Tubes to bring him oxygen and take his urine. The body the boy had once feared now shriveled beneath an ill-fitting gown. The son's forgiveness unplanned, a reflex, and when the weight lifted, he was stunned by the lightness of his body. In the space where he'd once nurtured his hate there was now not love but an emptiness the son understood would be his to fill or ignore.

Later that evening, the son cooks with his daughter. On his clothes, the scent of his father's cigarettes. The little girl on a chair, a spatula in hand and an apron that reaches her ankles. The countertop a mess, but he doesn't scold her for the eggs she breaks or the flour she spills. Their kitchen so different, the sunlight and good smells. The girl talks, and he listens to it all, asking questions, feigning surprise. He won't let his daughter see her grandfather, but he brings pictures to the old man and tells him stories. The girl's fascination with creek-side frogs. The cat she dresses in dolls' clothes. The old man smiles. This is so new for all of them.

Curtis Smith's thirteenth book, *The Magpie's Return*, was published this past summer by Running Wild. He lives and works in Pennsylvania.

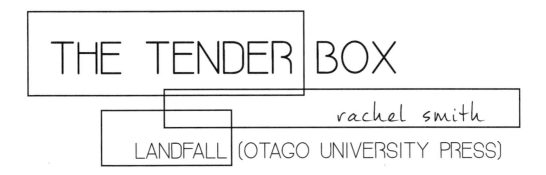

THE TENDER BOX

rachel smith

LANDFALL (OTAGO UNIVERSITY PRESS)

IT'S ON THE BACK counter. Walk past the sleeping dog in the doorway. Wipe your feet on the mat. It's easy to spot: wooden, painted midday blue with a slot on the top. Big enough to fit three husked coconuts or your daughter curled up at night.

Every few days its needs emptying. Tender piles up around here like dust bunnies under the bed. Most of it comes from the kitchen next door. Wade through the talk and there's rukau chops warming on the stove. Eat it with your fingers, mop up sauce with sweet white bread.

It's heavier than you might think. Remember the honey-combed fluff inside crisp kapok pods. Floated like clouds from our fingertips, packed down into pillows that cricked our necks. Like that.

You could carry it. If you want to.

Bend your knees, slide the box across the counter until its edge rests against your heart.

Open it in private. A toilet cubicle. Or outside is best, down by the ocean so no one can hear. There's a lock but it's never fastened. Step back as you open the lid. It'll tumble out quick. Laughter. Milky breath. Echo of drum beats. A lovers sigh. Some stories from over the water. Be patient.

When you think it's empty, put your head right inside and check again. There'll be something in the corner—irregular, grey as midwinter sky. It'll burn when you touch it but don't let go. It's OK to cry. Lay it on your tongue. Swallow. Feel it go all the way down, past anything that is possible.

Rachel Smith lives in Aotearoa New Zealand. Her writing has been published in journals and anthologies, including *Best Microfiction* 2019 and *Bonsai: best small stories from Aotearoa New*

Zealand, short listed for the Bath Flash Fiction Award and TSS International Flash Fiction, and placed second in 2017 NZ National Flash Fiction Day. She is script writer for a feature film Stranded Pearl due for release in 2020. @rachelmsmithnz1 http://rachelmsmithnz.wix.com/rachel-smith.

EVERYTHING IS TERRIBLE BUT YOU SHOULD READ THIS STORY

amber sparks

SMOKE LONG

THIS IS A STORY born of need. It's the story you need right now.

This is the story of a mother and a daughter in which the mother doesn't disappear, doesn't peace out, doesn't die. This is a story where the mother stays.

It's the story your mother told you when you were small, the one where Tiresias was struck blind when he saw his mother bathing with Athena; but the goddess instead granted him visions of the future. It's the story where your mother whispered, "we'll have such secrets together," and you felt loved instead of frightened. It's the story in which you were proud of the stories your mother told you. In which you never begged your mother to please just tell you the same goddamn fairy tales that every other kid's mother told them. It's the story where your mother became a classicist because she was fascinated by mythology, and not because the story of Philomela resonated with her so deeply. In this story, your mother never lost her tongue.

It's the story in which, in the 10th grade, when you asked your boyfriend, "Do you think I'm odd," instead of his laughing and saying no, putting out the long white flame of strangeness you'd kept protected since you were old enough to understand yourself—instead he said yes; in this story he said "yes, yes you are odd" and the flame whooshed up and burned your old life quick and clean as paper and left you new, shining, phoenix-feathered.

It's the story where your parents divorced when you were little, not a teenager, and when you asked your mother, "What are you thinking of," she didn't saying "dying," no in this story she said "flying," and in this story she told you how wings work. In this story Icarus sealed his wings with something stronger than wax and he sailed right up into the sun until Apollo plucked him out and praised him. Here, Apollo is the good father Icarus never had.

In this story, red means nothing. In this story, rope is for climbing, not falling. Here there are no signifiers, no associations, as if everything were happening for the first time. As if sensations were like the closed cells of monks and gardenia perfume didn't smell like anything but gardenias.

It's not that there is no sadness in this story. Stories need conflict, and crying can be dreamy. But sadness, like ships, must be steered, and this story doesn't come from a need for catharsis. There are no iced-over ponds, no wooden wheels stuck in the metaphorical mud. There are no bodies hanging from a ceiling fan.

This story doesn't turn into a horror movie when people tell you you're just like your mother.

In this story, the secret staircase to Hades is in your bedroom closet and you can descend whenever you like, as many times as you need, to keep on saving your mother. In this story you take a sack of barley bread soaked in honey for Cerberus, just like she taught you; you bring her back, again and again. You give her time for her hair to go from indigo to white, you skirt the hangman's knot.

In this story, everyone is safe. This story comes with a guarantee of safety.

In this story, you aren't afraid to have children.

In this story, when women are attacked, they grow armor like a sudden carapace. They grow an extra tongue, so they can sound their attacker's name forever while also singing karaoke, while talking to friends, while eating pizza at a restaurant they are not afraid to walk home from. This is a story where women are alone all the time, at bars and on hiking trails and in quiet suburban neighborhoods and on chattering city streets, and nobody dreams of fucking with them because so many women have extra tongues these days. This is a story where bad men reap what they have sown.

In this story, someone else is President.

In this story, nobody drops inside themselves and drowns after their boyfriend rapes them. In this story, nobody finds out, returning home for comfort, that their mother, too, was once raped.

In fact, in this story there is no rape. We all need a story without rape right now.

In this story, there is no such thing as social media. Just kidding; this story can only fix so much and the rest is up to you, you and your followers and especially the ones you call friends. (In this story, the dreadful people are all banned for life, though.)

In this story there are: colorful birds, warm milk, candy hearts, strange cats, good dogs, stars, friends, moon landings, mothers, wildflowers, video games, and kindness. It's an old-fashioned story, this one; kindness flows through it like a lazy river, rafted by every character. It nourishes everyone. It's a slow story, the kind of slowness that allows the reader to settle in, to eat well, to be unafraid, to learn what kind of story this will be over time.

This is a story where your mother still tucks you in at night. Metaphorically or literally, your choice.

There are no weapons in this story. There might be razors, yes, but only the sort you need to cut out the bad parts and leave the good bits, the bits that will save your life.

Amber Sparks is the author of several short story collections, including the most recent *I Do Not Forgive You*. She has also written essays and short fiction published widely in places like *New York Magazine*, *Granta*, *Tin House*, and the *Paris Review*. You can find her most days on Twitter @ambernoelle.

I AM A CONSERVATIONIST

THE FORGE

charlie j. stephens

GEORGIE IS TWELVE AND doesn't give a fuck. His tantrums extended from the terrible twos and I stopped counting when I realized it only depressed me further to keep track of how long this has gone on, realized it wasn't a phase but a personality.

Other dads I know see me at the grocery store and when I tell them how I'm struggling, they like to remind me of those preschool co-op days when all the parents took shifts for daycare and Georgie would stand in the corner, look unflinching into the eyes of whoever was in the room and slowly shit his pants. They think it's hilarious to remind me of this. There's this one dad from the co-op, Michael, who is completely gorgeous, I have to admit. His whole family is gorgeous. His wife is tall, with this curly black hair, and I have to say, she has shown up in my dreams more than once. Their kids are perfectly put together, I mean, they get good grades, and do extra curricular activities people actually admire, like kung fu and tennis. You know, they like to *exert* themselves, feel their hearts pumping, that kind of thing. They look like they've been raised on organic cream and fresh strawberries their whole lives. Those tan, rosy-cheeked complexions. My god! And their twinkly-eyed smiles that seem so genuine. Don't get me started.

My wife says it is no good to compare one's own insides to other people's outsides. You can never know what another person or family is actually like, regardless of what you see on the surface, at a party or a PTA meeting. I know she's right but I can't help feeling that somehow we got it all wrong. Really wrong.

Samuel is our other kid though. He's younger than Georgie and has a relaxed air about him, moving through the world with a lopsided grin. He'll be fine, I know that. He's like water in a creek, everything tumbling away, easy. Nothing sticks to him.

Once when Samuel was two and Georgie was four, we sat in our backyard under this ancient oak tree that to be honest was the main reason I wanted to scrape the money together to buy this ramshackle house. I am a conservationist at my core and couldn't bear the thought of rich assholes buying this place and taking down the tree. My wife liked the neighborhood and the school nearby so it just worked out.

Anyways, I was in the yard blowing bubbles for the kids. It was one of those unusually warm spring days you just know can't last, and everything was a new, bright, green, all the fresh buds and small leaves emerging. Samuel was giggling his hearty baby laugh, sitting there like a little fatso, all wobbly and perfectly alive. The bubbles would float over and his face would light up even more. It was like one of those impossibly cute things you see your own kid doing and think for a split second you're part of something worthwhile after all. But then slowly pan the camera over, and you'll see Georgie stiff-faced and flat on his back, like maybe he'd started out watching the bubbles but got bored, maybe they even made him angry somehow, offended his sensibilities. He's digging his filthy little hands into the spring dirt, coming up with mud and pebbles, looking me in the eye mercilessly and shoving it all in his mouth.

With the unflinching stare that kid has always had, he tears up grass roots, and a little worm writhes in his grip. I know this isn't too abnormal or anything, kid stuff, right? But I can't take my eyes away from his eyes, and I am frozen like a damn idiot. In that moment in the deepest part of myself, I know for certain that if Samuel's joyous laughter is a part of me, Georgie's darkness absolutely is also, maybe even more so. I guess most parents would pull the kid's hands out of his mouth and wipe them off, give a little laugh and tussle his hair with a light-hearted, *Why are you eating dirt?* But I don't do that. I just keep watching him, still like a statue. I let him eat the dirt and rocks. I imagine them solidifying in his throat and stomach like ceramic potter's clay, turning him back into earth, and his whole heavy body sinking down into the muck, far, far away from us.

I look up into the oak tree, its knobby arms reaching out in all directions, like the arthritic fingers of a wise geriatric, craggy with age. I wonder if the tree has observed my parenting, and what it thinks about the state of things, and what other moments it has observed in its hundreds of years here, and if the tree thinks this moment of ours, of mine, is the worst. I don't remember cleaning Georgie off, but I must have. We must have gone inside and I must have made the kids something to eat. Maybe we read a story, maybe they took a nap. Maybe I felt terrified for the future, and maybe I felt like other fathers besides me surely must feel: responsible but unfathomably weary. Missing something important, something innate I just can't seem to access in spite the the parenting books I pore over, the community forums I visit online late at night when I can't sleep, the hours with my therapist, who is also raising sons, but seemingly more successfully. *Don't compare yourself to your therapist!* my wife says. I know she's right but I don't know how to stop.

Here's twelve year old Georgie coming through the front door now, looking pissed. I say hi but he doesn't say hi back. He grimaces like a rabid wolverine, the front teeth he refuses to brush are yellowed already, like those of a hardened tobacco smoker. He's slamming his backpack down at the entrance to the house where we've asked him not to leave it a thousand times, and heading for his video games where he can shoot and kill with abandon. He's got the wild-eyed look of a caged animal. He's an angry, old, drunk in a skinny, prepubescent body, weaving around the room, knocking things over.

I want to grab him and shake him hard until he snaps out of it, shake him as hard as I can until he becomes reasonable, shake him until he turns eighteen and understands things better, or at least gets out of our house to go off and ruin relationships with other people I don't yet know, but now that I think about it, feel like I should warn.

Be careful. He'll take you down with him.

But it's too late for anything a good shake could accomplish now. His neck is far too strong for shaken baby syndrome, so I could maybe get away with it, but what's the point? I can't admit it out loud to my wife, but even she must know somewhere deep inside herself I gave up on him turning out alright so many years ago. A good shake won't help any of us at all now. It's just far too late for that.

Charlie J. Stephens is a queer fiction writer living in Northern California. Charlie has lived all over the U.S. as a bike messenger, wilderness guide, book seller, and seasonal shark diver (for educational purposes only). Charlie's work has recently appeared in *Peculiar, Hinterland, Fresh.Ink, Prometheus Dreaming, Original Plumbing* (Feminist Press), *The Flexible Persona, The Forge Literary Magazine, Gravel Literary Magazine, Rappahannock Review,* and *Not Your Mother's Breast Milk.* Charlie is currently working on a collection of short stories, as well as their first novel. More at charliejstephenswriting.com.

CAISEAS BLUES (A TERRIBLE RACKET)

gregory stephens

THE ESTHETIC APOSTLE

THE OLD MAN, SITTING in a big house up on the mountain, hollers, moans, bitches and groans. The yellow stucco house is on a hilltop street called Caiseas, looking out over the Caribbean, towards the Dominican. An idyllic, tropical setting from a proper distance, but up close Gabriel's vocalizations are unsettling. The zombie-ish groaning sounds like a man being crucified.

Some neighbors think Gabriel is senile. His wife Marta knows better. He makes a terrible racket but sometimes it is music to her ears. The symptoms of progressive supranuclear palsy include impulsive behaviors like "standing up without waiting for assistance," or "loss of interest in pleasurable activities," which Marta knows not to be true.

On the patio a Sun Parakeet is shrieking. The big bird cage hangs over the edge of the balustrade bordering the walk-around balcony, under the shade of an enormous mango tree.

"Cierre el pico, cotorra," Marta says, her voice raspy. Shut your mouth, chatterbox. But then in a more affectionate tone, she adds:

"I don't know why I keep feeding you." It is not clear if she is speaking to the parakeet, or to the invalid grunting out bestial noises. In fact, the bird seems to be mimicking the old man's bestial howls.

This aged parrot, its once splendid coat of many colors now faded, flew up from a ferry twenty-two years ago, back during boom days of Mayagüez. In that time, ferries stopped regularly, always an event. Tourists came on land and spent their money. New developments were pitched to investors sniffing around. Sometimes sexual fluids were exchanged.

Marta still remembers like yesterday how on that day, a young tropical bird escaped that ship. Maybe it belonged to a tourist or a crew member, ¿quién sabe? The brightly plumed bird flew straight up the steep slope into the house of Gabriel and Marta. It seemed like a harbinger then, presaging continued good fortune. Over time, however, the bird became a portent of something else. Nowadays this stretch of the island looks like a post-apocalyptic film.

Marta takes the tray out and dumps the bird waste onto the concrete slope, which Marta had poured all around the property about five years earlier, when Gabriel's health turned south. The concrete keeps the jungle somewhat at bay, now that the man of the house is no longer fit to fight it back. But it also amplifies the sounds coming up the slope: traffic on 102; the grinding and whining of a power plant; the docking of a freight ship. Then there are the island specials, jeeps with sound systems powerful enough to bring down the walls of Jericho. Pumping reggaeton at an incomprehensible volume, the whole mountain trembles.

"Ai, mi amor, que es mi amor," says Marta to her Sun Conure, in the same over-the-top sweet talk that she also uses for Gabriel, and the neighborhood dogs. She lays it on thick, and they all lap it up—dogs, men, aging birds. She gives the old parrot seeds, and looks the little guy in the eye, down in the bottom of the cage, from which he seldom strays now. Gabriel starts up again, and Marta shuffles back inside in a gown and slippers, gray hair now showing at the roots under the gold tint her beautician re-applied last visit.

The bird eats, the old man groans and the sky-scraping mango tree—towering up out of the poured concrete at its roots—is shedding its over-abundance of fruit at an alarming rate. It is April now and the mangos falling down on the concrete slope sound like mortar fire. Duds they may be, but the force of their fall still startles. They gather at a retaining wall where the concrete ends, and there they rot.

All around town the mangos sit and stink, evidence of the jungle's decadent affluence. Puerto Ricans are eating at Popeyes or some other fast food joint, and they don't have the time to pick up even the most beautifully formed brightly colored perfectly ripe mango. But the iguanas are having a field day. Up on Caiseas, below Marta's house, a giant of an iguana slithers up the mango tree to feast. The blue and avocado green of the iguana's scaly coat is somewhat of a camouflage when it moves from the long trunk into the foliage overburdened with fruit. The parakeet screeches at her.

"Cierre el pico," Marta calls out again, but not putting much effort into it this time.

The male nurse arrives, and Marta leaves for her volunteer work at a retirement home. For decades she was an enrollment officer at the University of Puerto Rico. Gabriel had an empire set up, travelling to distribute automobile parts, working out of an inventory in his shed right next to the homestead. They have money still, but Gabriel is not free to enjoy it. Marco, the young nurse, wheels him out to the patio to smell the ocean breeze. Gabriel is bald, and bare-chested. His bald head reflects the sunlight, giving the space around his head a halo-ish glow. His bare chest is surprisingly slender and well-formed for a man who has been an invalid for five years.

"Hey," he utters, the only word seemingly left in his vocabulary. He has pulled himself halfway up the banister, as if he might throw himself down to the concrete slope. Marco takes the hint and wheels Gabriel to the adjoining yard and storage space, where Gabriel once kept his inventory. The yard is a well-maintained island in the sea of junglish over-exuberance, a postcard stamp of tropical charm. But the yard is shadowed by huge power lines marching down to the sea. Marco helps raise Gabriel up to the metal bar atop the chain link fence, and Gabriel supports himself there a few minutes. The invalid is doing his version of pull-ups, keeping his body toned for his wife, who still hears music in his moans.

Gregory Stephens is Associate Professor of English, University of Puerto Rico-Mayagüez. His book *Three Birds Sing a New Song: A Puerto Rican trilogy about Dystopia, Precarity, and Resistance* was published by Intermezzo (2019). Short fiction from the novel-in-progress *A Terrible Racket: Making Do with the Residue* (2020) and *Close to the Bone* (2019) Literary nonfiction: *A Team of Mules; Spanking the Baby: Second Thoughts on Discipline; Voice, Conscience, Community; Integrative Ancestors redux—a Child's story from the past to the future* (2018); *Split-Screen Freedom*, and *Che's Boots: Discipline and the flawed hero.*

ONLY A LITTLE BIT LESS THAN I HATE MYSELF

amy stuber

LONGLEAF REVIEW

I'M SIX MONTHS OUT from my divorce, and my son Franklin and his boyfriend Alonso are waiting with me in an Outer Sunset restaurant kitchen with a sound guy, a cameraman, and a chef. I do a morning show ("Mornings On 2!"), which is not something I ever thought I'd do, but who can predict the future? Anyway, my producer thought it would be cute to have my high school son and his boyfriend cook something for a Mother's Day piece, and then at the last minute, literally, I'm standing there with two uncracked eggs in my hand next to a chef in a chef's hat, which is way too on the nose but whatever, and my producer calls and says, "Oh, by the way, you know that author, the blabby memoir dude, Karl Knaus-whatever the fuck his name is, something Scandinavian, he's going to make the egg shit with you. Sorry. He's on a book tour. I couldn't get out of it. It'll be great!"

Yes, I knew who he was. For the two years prior to our separation, my ex-husband read every word of Knausgård's endless volumes, and our conversations went like this: "What woman would be granted this ridiculous amount of page space to spew minutia?" (No woman.) "You barely speak. Why would you be drawn to someone who can't censor his banal thoughts?" (Can't explain it.) I saw Knausgård's bookback face more than I saw my husband's, which at that point was fine, I guess. It had been eighteen years. We were sick of each other and past being sad about it.

In person, Knausgård looks like the kind of man who would model an expensive watch on a windy beach in an NYT magazine ad. When he shows up, my son and Alonso are mock arguing like they do, playfully, this time about fonts for some reason (my son: "Garamond has a hideous light touch like it's constructed out of dried sticks and feathers. It makes me sick to my stomach." His boyfriend: "You are literally insane. Times New Roman is an ancient devil walking with a cane through a dead forest," etc.).

Knausgård smells like cigarettes and not just like he just smoked but more like he is actually made of ashtrays and then loosely covered with hair and skin. "I'm quitting, I know," he says and it's clear he is accustomed to being called charming, but I'm not falling for it.

I lean back against the half wall that separates the kitchen from the dining room, pull the sleeves of my shirt down, and put my hands in my pockets to cover the flora and fauna creeping down below my wrists, not because I give a single shit about Knausgård's opinion of me, but out of habit because, at 49, my tattoos embarrass me. I got them in my teens and 20s from my brother for whom my limbs and back were one big experiment. Now I find the entire genre of skin adornment boring and ugly and mainly I wear long-sleeved things from the 70s with giant neck bows and garish patterns to hide and distract.

Fuck it, I think. I stop leaning back and take my hands from my pockets. I stand up straight and take a step toward Knausgård, "Good, I say. Quit. You should quit." But, of course, I want nothing more than a cigarette right then.

He smiles a little but a kind of Norwegian half-smile that reminds me of sweaters and fog. I smile back not because I want to but because it's knee-jerk and human and I can't help myself.

And then, before any filming and small talk about eggs and mothers can start, Alonso is on the floor having a seizure. I know this about him. It happens sometimes, even with his medication, and Franklin and I know what to do: turn him on his side, get sharp objects out of the way, wait it out. Knausgard is closer to Alonso than we are somehow, but he just stands there immobilized as if he was sculpted strictly for adoration or amusement by Vikings. He's in the way, and I don't know why, but my instinct is to throw the eggs that are in my hand right at Knausgård's ridiculous head, so I do just that. People are moving around the restaurant kitchen. Metal chairs scrape concrete floors, and I yearn for a cushioned banquette. And then Franklin, my son, steps in and turns Alonso on his side. My son's eyes are almost the same caramely color as his hair. When he was younger, he had a series of tics: first it was throat clearing, which made my husband, my ex, and I almost lose our minds with its metronomic regularity. Then it was blinking, which was awkward but less unnerving overall. Then it was putting his hand over his heart every few seconds. Then it was tipping his head to the left in a series of sharp jerks. I can remember holding his head still between my palms to try to give him some respite. He is now practically a man who surely sometimes holds Alonso in sleep or after sex and holds him now right here until Alonso's body unclenches and moves toward stillness.

Am I surprised when I'm next in the hallway by the bathroom wiping raw egg off the side of Knausgård's sandpapery Norwegian face? Yes, a little. But I'm also thinking: I'm going to be 50 and soon my son will live elsewhere and then what? Who am I going to be? Do I hate myself more than I ever have when I lean in to kiss fucking Karl Ove Knausgård? Yes, I do. Do I keep doing it anyway? Yes. Tomorrow, I tell myself while I count to five and let Knausgård's broad tongue wander my teeth, tomorrow, I promise, I will be different, stronger, enviable, better. But for now: this.

Amy Stuber's fiction has appeared in *Copper Nickel*, *New England Review*, *Smokelong Quarterly*, *Wigleaf*, and elsewhere. She's print editor for *Split Lip Magazine* and is on Twitter @amy_stuber_ and online at www.amystuber.com.

THE TURN AROUND

mark terrill

BODY LITERATURE

I'M WALKING DOWN THE pedestrian-congested Bahrenfelder Straße in Hamburg just passing the Fabrik where I've seen John Cale, Lee "Scratch" Perry, the Mekons & so many other concerts over the last thirty years & then on past the big organic food supermarket swarming with all those super-hip politically correct couples paying horrendous prices for a bunch of grapes flown in from South Africa by a jet spewing its noxious exhaust all across the skies & just as I'm abreast of that big brick office complex housing all the medical practices a ground-floor door swings open & I see this young couple coming out—maybe in their early twenties if even that—looking smart & hip & handsome & well-to-do but not particularly snobby or uptight & maybe even somewhat sympathetic—& suddenly I notice that the girl's face is twisted into this contorted expression of sorrow & grief with tears running down her cheeks & the guy has his arm around her in this very possessive yet comforting way while biting his lower lip in a measured grimace of sheer determination obviously confronted with a whole new kind of challenge & in the very moment that they pass me by going in the other direction I turn & glance at the sign on the brick wall next to the door & see that they've just left the office of some gynecologist & immediately I'm speculating as to the source of all that grief & sorrow realizing that whatever it is it must be pretty serious maybe even major & while still walking I glance back & see the couple stopping on the sidewalk impervious to the throngs of passing pedestrians & the guy throwing both his arms around the girl in this big heartfelt real-deal embrace meant to palliate & assuage whatever can be palliated & assuaged by such a gesture in such a moment & I can see by the girl's body English & overall composure that the well-meant intention of his gesture is coming through loud & clear & I can feel my own lagging faith in mankind getting this sudden boost like a big shot of vitamin B complex for the soul & I can feel the iron grip of cynicism in which my psyche usually finds itself ensnared starting to loosen up

& I *know* that those two kids are going to make it & pull through & get beyond it all whatever it may be & who knows maybe we're *all* going to make it & pull through & get beyond it all but certainly not without the help of someone else who really & truly gives a shit someone determined not to get turned around by the vicissitudes & exigencies of human existence someone prepared to take the extra effort to try to turn those very vicissitudes & exigencies around & send them back to wherever they might have come from even if it's only one single fleeting gesture among all the countless others on the teeming Bahrenfelder Straße in Hamburg.

A native Californian and former merchant seaman, Mark Terrill was a participant in the School of Visual Arts Writing Workshop in Tangier, Morocco, conducted by Paul Bowles in 1982 and has lived in Germany since 1984, working as a shipyard welder, road manager for rock bands, cook, and postal worker. Forthcoming is a collection of poems and prose poems, *Great Balls of Doubt*, illustrated by Jon Langford (Verse Chorus Press); a collection of prose poems and flash fiction, *The Undying Guest* (Tract Home Publications); and a collaborative novel written with Francis Poole entitled *Ultrazone: A Tangier Ghost Story* (The Visible Spectrum).

HOW TO SPOT A WHALE

jacqui reiko teruya

THE MASTER'S REVIEW

DO NOT LOOK IMPRESSED when Roberta tells you about narwhals—the *Monodontidae*, the white whales. Do not bat an eye when she talks about their elongated canines, how they twist like candy out of the artic sea. When she says she's heard so much about you, look at your mother. Let her know you see her. When she reaches for a green olive, take one too. Roll the pit over your tongue, clean it on every side like your mother taught you. When Roberta talks about her work and your father's—the reason she's come all this way—clench the pit in your teeth and smile wide.

Do not pay attention to Roberta's red skirt flapping in the breeze or the cluster of orange freckles that dot her white-lady shoulders. Try not to notice the small flip of her nose, her full lips, or the crease of her eyelid. Do not admit you have dreamed of having that crease too. Do not compare your mother's face to her face. If you see the ivory pendant dangling at the line of Roberta's cleavage, look away. Fast. Do not think about the hollow of your mother's chest or the way she tries to hide it under baggy shirts and blouses. Make sure to ask Roberta questions. Questions that take time to answer, that fill space while your father orders lobsters from a silver airstream. Ask why she decided to study whales, if she still swims in the ocean, what she hopes to find off the coast of Maine. Do not listen to her answers. Hum inside your head. Do not picture the cobalt tributaries or the long stretches of ice that make up her Northern Territories. Look out at the wet, warm sand of Maine. Look down at the row of olive pits your mother is building. Do not make eye contact with either woman. Look at your watch, tap your sandaled foot on the cement.

When your father returns with steaming lobsters and clarified butter do not look excited. Do not let the thrill show on your face. When your mother stands and says she's going to walk the beach, let her go. Do not laugh when your father calls her a softy. Stare him down when he tells Roberta how your mother won't touch a lobster. How she cannot bring herself to crack their joints and tear them limb from limb. Make it clear Roberta should not laugh the way your father is laughing.

Know that—with your mother gone—you must sing for your dinner. Be ready to know their kingdom, their clade, down to their family, the part of the body you are about to eat. Start with the cheliped or your father will scold you. Pull the speckled meat from the cling of the exoskeleton; make it slick with butter. When the shell is picked clean, wipe your hands with a soapy wet nap, point out the yellow corn in Roberta's teeth, and ask your father if you may be excused.

Follow your mother from a distance, watch her blue dress flap at her ankles. Stay on the wet part of the sand and feel the chill of the foam at your feet. Watch your mother bend to pick up smoothed rocks and broken parts of a shell. Ignore how drab she looks against the gray of the sky; do not wonder if your father notices that too. When the wind blows your mother's straw hat into the water and she wades in—without grace—to retrieve it, love her more. Turn away, do not let her know you see her.

Go back to your father. Hear Roberta laughing at the picnic table. Watch them suck on small legs—the pereiopods—the last bits of the body that have yet to be eaten. Clear the tray of hollowed carcasses and remember that your mother ate only olives. When Roberta takes a thumb and wipes a smear of butter from your father's face, point to the breaking waves and shout, "Whales!" Be the first to say, "*Globicephala marcrorhynchus.*" Say it how your father taught you. Take your father's hand and rush him up the beach. Tell him you saw their dark grey bodies cutting through the blue curve of a wave. Tell him there are two, three, maybe five to the pod. Speak his language as you bring him to the water's edge, as you pull him back to you, to your mother. Make him look out at the sea. Stare at the ocean, hold your father's damp hand, and search the waves for the spray of a whale.

Jacqui Reiko Teruya is an MFA candidate at Boise State University where she teaches and is the Associate Editor for *The Idaho Review*. Winner of *The Masters Review*'s 2018 Summer Flash Fiction Contest, and second-place finalist for the 2019 *CRAFT* Short Fiction Prize judged by Elizabeth McCracken, her work has appeared in *The Masters Review*, *CRAFT*, and *Passages North*. She lives in Boise, Idaho where she is currently at work on a novel.

SWEET

robert tindall

NOON & HARPER'S MAGAZINE

GREGORY SPEEN LEARNS TO *not doubt himself and Mick Brenlan supports him wholeheartedly. A rhetoric of rapprochement does obtain. Maybe these two are taking stock, and that may be the story.*

She seemed sere of affect she was slim and her hair was mousy only she looked cruel—Speen did know that to object was not a viable reaction to such a one—she seemed to have made a life of being cruel toward her fellows but Brenlan wasn't having any of that today—the truth was, he was himself sick he was flawed maybe and that was the same thing.

Brenlan was silly inside only that made for a brilliance of perspective and he did sleep at night. He did take the others for granted that was the gist of it—Gregory Speen was alone in the world and Brenlan supported what he saw in the man—Speen was smart and happy and lucky.

Maybe there was a justice to it. What was right and what was wrong? That was the only question in his blood or in his eye. In the end it was all *verboten*.

Speen admired the unimpeachable quality that went with transportation workers in Chicago and the suburbs. The idea of men and women who worked the trains was a good one and they knew the secrets of life.

A man sat on a plastic crate in the tunnel to the train. Speen figured that the man was a prince. Such men had baskets of clothes or other goods and maybe they slept outside or knew a shelter somewhere. If they asked for money Speen would give them a dollar or so. The others were successful.

Speen remembered working until it proved that maybe he was an average fool.

And Speen was learning to respect the vague sorts carrying their belongings in wire carts on the bus. The drivers looked strong and smart and they were well paid. You had your foreigners and your hometown sorts. Women brought their young in strollers on the bus. Speen felt awful about that.

He defied the idea itself that maybe as a pariah he was blamable for anything and the nature of the afternoon did wipe his slate.

Yesterday was also a tidy thing—Speen loved the women and loved the men. The women were conservative looking and some of them were beautiful. The men were fashionable. The men wore beards and the women wore eye makeup.

If it was up to him they would share the wealth and he gave profusely to the homeless on the corner and it was nice in the morning on the road. He did have a minor sum from the government rolls.

When the snow fell Speen went to the Goodwill to buy clothes, then to ride the bus next was a treat.

The steady running of the CTA did offer answers to any puzzle as to whether Speen's life would end well. There were things Speen did not know but he was worth more than before.

Brenlan smoked with Speen at the drop-in center and it all made sense. Speen would go to the coffee shop in the majestic inertia that was his approaching age. Speen did not own a television set.

What was to be? Gregory Speen shaved and put on his suit. He rode the bus to the mall. The building where he entered was a happy place and that did justify an idle day.

If the others wanted it their way then Speen would concede—the next day he felt fine. He did not know any grief. He had used to carry a gun. And it was puzzling to be alone. The restaurant was full up. Speen sat at the bar with a bottle of beer.

Speen had fifty in his wallet and it was midnight. He left a tip and exited the place and he was paying his dues for later.

It was superb to be thumbing it on the highway until he could catch a ride south toward where he had gone to school in the years when he was plying his friends and he was coming up empty-handed only later he would know no real pain. In the end, who would remember?

Maybe Speen felt less than some others. Speen would respect others and that was genius—he entertained thoughts of a night when he exulted to ride in a friend's car and they were young.

With the money in his wallet Speen stood on the corner in the town where he had gone to school so many years before. He had a coffee cup to panhandle and it had come full circle so that now he felt a real and a durable winning state of mind in that nothing was wrong and life was sweet.

Robert Tindall lives in Evanston, Illinois. He studied fiction at University of Illinois and is a regular contributor to *NOON*. He was on the road for years and has now settled in Evanston.

BITE MUKO

adolphine umukobwa

AFREADA

HAS ANYONE CHECKED ON you since you told the elders that you could no longer bear the weight? I know it wasn't an easy conversation. They've raised us to bear it. Trained us, even. And you're the only one who has had the courage to tell them it is unbearable. Unmanageable.

The only one that we know of, at least.

Muko, I'm sure they weren't exactly surprised when you called the meeting. You are known for rocking the boat with your constant questions and interjections. Everyone thinks you speak your mind a little too freely, unsure of whether it's a blessing or a curse.

I too am uncomfortable with this weight, Muko.

Did they answer you when you asked them how they've been able to bear it for all this time? Did they give you any tips?

How about when you asked what the weight is? Did they tell you what it is that we all have to bear? I hope you didn't tell them your theory. They wouldn't take it kindly if you accused them of asking us to bear fear, pain, loss, secrets, and other dark things. Because what kind of elders would they be to pass those types of things down the family line? What kind of family would we be, harboring such darkness?

But what else could weigh so much, Muko?

My guess is that they don't even know what's in there. They were asked to carry the weight just like we were, but they were "good" kids and didn't ask questions.

Any chance you talked to them about releasing the burden? Understandable if you didn't.

Ever since we discovered this trick, I've done it a few times. I've let it go, little by little over time. Can you tell? I hope it's not too obvious. But, Muko, my shoulders aren't as tense, I stopped clenching my jaw, and I can sit up straight. Remember how they would comment on my posture? Shaming me for never sitting up straight and for never standing with my shoulders behind my ears.

I wonder if they were just mad that I couldn't discretely bear the family burden. I was never like you, Muko. You carried your share and the share of others and were still able to be a powerhouse. Standing upright, chest out, always smiling. That's why you got away with your questions, you know. That's why they tolerated your rebellion.

But, Muko, it's time for you to start releasing the burden. I can see how bearing this weight has affected you. Your eyes have bags underneath; they've lost their sparkle. You no longer walk with purpose. I can see you doubt every step. I see how the weight affects your relationships.

Please just release a little bit. I'll show you how. The elders won't even notice because you'll revert back to your old self. Please tell me you'll release it, Muko. Before you become what you are bearing.

Adolphine Umukobwa is a Rwandese-American writer who is based in New York. Umukobwa is a new writer who hopes to grow this skill while creating pieces that uncover questionable traditions and empower readers to make changes in their lives. She hopes her writing inspires provocative and important discourse on mental health issues, family dynamics, and the role of women in society.

WHAT HAPPENS ON SHABBOS

alisa ungar-sargon

JMWW

SHABBOS IS A DAY of rest. There are no cars on *Shabbos*. There are no computers. No television. No turning lights on and off, no cooking. Entertainment comes from elsewhere. Board games and card games and long conversations into the night. Adults are shocked when an epidemic comes to light, sweeping the teenagers of the community: texting on *Shabbos*. I once got a text from Shimon on *Shabbos*. I saw my phone light up and I ran over to where it was plugged in to see it before the screen went dark. It said: *I'm coming*. I thought he meant he was coming home and I waited for him all *Shabbos*. He didn't come home, though.

We got the call about Shimon on a Friday night. No one answered the phone, of course. Not on *Shabbos*. It wasn't until the police came up and rang the doorbell after midnight that we knew something was wrong.

Before that.

Before that, I was in college in Chicago. I went to school but not on Fridays. I went to school but not on holidays. I went to school but I never went anywhere with my friends. No drinks, no food, no music. It was easier than an explanation.

Shabbos is for socializing, but with people who eat kosher food and understand why we don't go to movies between *Pesach* and *Shavuos*. It's complicated to explain why these things are important. It's also complicated to explain why friends from college are important. It's important to understand why these things are complicated but I don't. Maybe by the time I'm gray and withered and no longer care about my frizzy hair or my chunky waistline I'll be able to explain. But my great-grandmother was still on a diet when she died, so maybe that'll never happen.

The unofficial *Shabbos* drink is a dessert wine in a blue bottle. The first time I got drunk was at a singles' dinner that was short on food but had plenty of alcohol. The blue bottle was bubbly and sweet. The boy sitting next to me was cute in the way a Labrador can be if it would stop barking for a second. He walked me home afterward. It took twenty minutes and every time we turned a corner I'd inhale his cologne and try not to notice too much when his arm brushed mine. At the end he reached out to touch my back and I had pulled away before I even realized I liked it.

It's less common for people to keep *Shabbos* in public and violate it in private, but it happens. The community is important. It's more important than "being true to yourself." The community invites us for *Shabbos* meals and arranges charity functions. The community celebrates our engagements and brings us low chairs when we sit *shiva*. We actually like being part of the community. If only the community weren't so judgmental about hemlines and PDA.

My parents sat *shiva* for Shimon after he died. I was supposed to, but I didn't leave my bed for ten days and by then it was over.

In summers, we take advantage of the warm weather to make lazy *Shabbos* rounds, collecting friends from across the neighborhood until we settle on a house and converge on the cool basement. In winters, during the long Friday nights, real plans must be made so that no one walks home alone in the dark without a friend.

Shimon was held up once on his way home. He had long hair at the time, underneath a big, colorful yarmulke that none of us took seriously. Since it was *Shabbos*, he didn't have any money, or a phone, or righteous indignation. All he had was a big shapeless coat with a hole that exhaled feathers whenever he moved his left arm. The mugger demanded his wallet. Shimon turned to him and said, "Hey man, I'm homeless." The mugger apologized and left him alone.

Shabbos can only be violated to save a life. The community EMTs carry around walkie-talkies that buzz at the *Shabbos* table, alerting us to the frailty of life amidst our conversation and talk of Torah. The community EMTs were the first ones in Shimon's apartment. His roommate was the one who found him, and that's what his roommate did. So they were there before the police came. They said he overdosed. They said it was an accident. These two facts refuse to coalesce. For a long time, whenever I saw an ambulance I would feel a wash of hate and it was such a relief to feel something that increases you instead of shriveling you up from the inside.

When we go to synagogue on *Shabbos*, we see classmates from high school, pushing babies in expensive carriages. They ask about our classes, about our siblings, which is usually when they remember I don't have any anymore.

When we let *Shabbos* out, the blessings are said over a single candle with many wicks. Artisans intertwine the wicks, connecting them to each other until they create a single flame. The ritual lasts about five minutes. The candle lasts about six months. We light it on fire and watch the wax burn down to a stub. Buying a new one has started to feel like a betrayal.

Shimon is gone. Shimon is gone and I lost eighteen pounds in tears. Shimon is gone and more than the sound of his laughter I'm trying to remember what made him laugh. Shimon is gone and am I the only one in the world who remembers him. Shimon is gone and when his *shloshim* comes I can't believe it's been a month, it was yesterday, how can it have been a month if my ribs are still cracked open exposing a heart that should give up beating but refuses to, I can't believe he's dead I can't believe he's dead I can't believe he's dead. Shimon is gone and it's been too long to be a mistake. Breathing is a mistake. Shimon is gone and if I let it become part of reality I won't be able to change it back. Shimon is gone and I can't taste food until three months later when I'm trying to study in a Starbucks and I order the biggest Frappuccino they have even though they aren't kosher anymore and I drink all 24 ounces while I stare at a map of Africa and my cheeks are already shiny and wet before I notice I'm crying again. Shimon is gone and I don't remember the flavor of the Frappuccino but it tasted like maybe someday I'll forget what this hurt feels like.

Once Shimon and I went for a walk on *Shabbos* afternoon to Lake Michigan, about seven miles away. Even though I'm dressed nice, I take off my shoes and socks and wade into the water. I thought I held my skirt out of the way but my hem dips in and suddenly the whole bottom is wet and clinging to my legs. Shimon sees me freaking out and he starts splashing around. We get soaked through. Afterward we sit on the sand and air-dry. By the time we leave the sun is setting and it takes us so long to get back that *Shabbos* is already out when we do.

Alisa Ungar-Sargon is a Chicago-based writer. She received her MFA from Northwestern University and her work has appeared in *TriQuarterly*, *Lilith Magazine* and *Image Journal*. "What Happens On Shabbos" originally appeared in *JMWW* and is nominated for The Pushcart Prize. For more information, please visit her personal website at www.alisaus.com.

OVER HEARD

anthony varallo

THE RUPTURE

MY GIRLFRIEND AND I were at a restaurant together, on the verge of breaking up again, when the man at the table next to ours leaned over and said, "Excuse me, but I couldn't help overhearing your conversation." He gave me a look that was meant to be conspiratorial or accusatory or both, I couldn't tell. "And I have to say that I agree with your girlfriend," the man said. "You really do spend too much time dwelling upon your childhood."

We hadn't been talking about me dwelling upon my childhood; we'd been discussing appetizers.

"It really is a form of self-pity," the man said, and dabbed at his lips with a white napkin. "In the final analysis."

I was about to ask him what right he thought he had to eavesdrop, when our waitress appeared, balancing two cocktails on a serving tray. "Excuse me," she said, placing my girlfriend's drink on the table, "but I couldn't help overhearing what this gentleman just said to you, and I have to say I think he's right: you shouldn't leave your bath towel hanging on the shower door." She set my drink in front of me. "It shows just how little you think about others."

I looked at my girlfriend. I wanted her to explain to the waitress that I hadn't left my towel on the shower door in weeks, months even, after we'd argued about it. And I think she would have explained if the maître d' hadn't tapped me on the shoulder and said, "Excuse me, but I couldn't help overhearing your conversation, and I have to say that I agree with your waitress: you can't keep accusing your parents of not paying enough attention to you, when you're the one who hasn't called them in months." The maître d' wore a black bowtie. "It's nothing more than projection."

I started to explain that, although I hadn't called my parents in a while, I texted them from time to time, and occasionally sent them pictures, but, at that moment the busboy materialized from wherever the busboy materialized from, and said, "Excuse me—"

"Don't tell me," I said.

"But I couldn't help overhearing your conversation, and I have to say—"

"That you agree with what the maître d' just said," I said.

The busboy nodded. "You really do make everything in this relationship about *you*," he said, "to the point where the relationship isn't really even a relationship, it's more like a movie playing inside your head." He took our silverware, although we hadn't even ordered yet. "It's a form of narcissism."

I would have refuted him, if the sous chef, sommelier, line cook, and hostess didn't arrive, each raising a questioning finger. "Excuse me," they said. "But I couldn't help overhearing—"

My girlfriend grabbed me by the hand and led me from the table, through the crowd, and through the front door.

Outside, I said, "Well."

"Well," my girlfriend said.

A week later, we were engaged.

Anthony Varallo is the author of a novel, *The Lines* (University of Iowa Press), as well as four short story collections: *This Day in History*, winner of the John Simmons Short Fiction Award; *Out Loud*, winner of the Drue Heinz Literature Prize; *Think of Me and I'll Know* (Northwestern University Press/TriQuarterly Books); and *Everyone Was There*, winner of the Elixir Press Fiction Award. He is a professor of English at the College of Charleston in Charleston, SC, where he teaches in the MFA Program in Creative Writing and serves as the Fiction Editor of *Crazyhorse*. Find him online at anthonyvarallo.com or Twitter @TheLines1979.

SMOKE GETS IN YOUR EYES

lavanya vasudevan

LOST BALLOON

AS WE DRIVE BACK east from Anacortes, we leave the heat and the haze behind. We listen to the rain as it bathes us in coolness, washes the soot out of the skies. You keep your eyes on the road, and I watch my own reflection in the window, the rivulets of water rolling down my cheeks. On the radio, they say that the flames have died; the smoke is clearing; that now, at last, we can breathe again.

The day before, we'd walked out to Crescent Beach with your mother. Ash from the wildfires lay in a black film over the water. "It's suffocating the poor creatures," she said. She showed me a starfish clinging to the bottom of a rock, abandoned by the tide. I picked up the empty shell of a shore crab. Perhaps it had moved on to better things. "It's so nice that he's found a friend at college," she told me. "A boy his own age. He never had a brother." The respirator muffled her voice, and her eyes, like yours, were unreadable. If you were ever going to tell her, the moment was now. But you had already moved on, turning over a different rock, and left us there, alone together, abandoned to the lie.

Three days ago, on the way out to your mother's house, the clouds had been tinged with red, the sun weak and struggling in the roiling skies. It was a long drive from the U to the ferry landing. I told you I was starving. You refused to stop. You said your mother would have made a big meal for us; she'd be waiting, hungry, so we could eat together; you couldn't disappoint her like that. When we arrived, after an hour of holding our breath on the boat so we wouldn't inhale the smoke, and more driving on the wandering island road, there was no one home. She'd left a note for us: she'd gone out to buy respirator masks, and then she was meeting a friend for lunch. You found rotis and warmed them on the stove, your black eyes flickering brown in the light of the flame. When I took a bite, my mouth caught fire. I could hardly breathe.

Lavanya Vasudevan is an engineer-turned-writer who lives in the Seattle area and reviews children's books for *Kirkus*. Her writing has been published in *Wigleaf, Paper Darts, The Masters Review Anthology,* and elsewhere, and selected for the Wigleaf Top 50. Find her online at lavanyavasudevan.com and on Twitter @vanyala.

BASKET BALL

siamak vossoughi

ATTICUS REVIEW

ONE DAY SHE REMEMBERED a young man she had known and loved for a little while when she was twenty-five. He would play basketball on Sunday afternoons and he would come to see her afterwards in the evening. He had been trying to tell her once how much he loved basketball and he'd said, "It feels like cheating."

It had been beautiful to hear it and she had thought that she could love him for a very long time when he'd said that. After it had ended, she'd remembered it and she'd wondered if she had something that felt like cheating. She had thought that she *would*, even if she didn't then, because she was only twenty-five. And she had not wanted to think that the only thing that could do that was love.

She was thirty-six now and there was a man, but he did not feel like cheating. He felt like playing the game correctly. But now at thirty-six it was hard to say what was cheating and what was playing the game correctly anyway. They blended together. The young man had not been talking of love anyway. He had been talking of basketball. Maybe if her mother and father had been the kind to sign their daughter up for sports, she would know what that meant. There was a basketball court near her house and now when she saw the little boys playing there and the little girls in the grass nearby, she felt angry.

When she remembered the young man, she wondered if she had shown him how much she loved that basketball felt like cheating to him. Maybe she had acted like it was only cute. It had been a funny age. There had been a lot of ways in which she'd tried to show that she was a woman and not a girl. Maybe she had made him think it was only cute. It was possible. It was possible she didn't know how to show someone that she took it seriously when they told her they had something that felt like cheating.

She wanted to ask the man she was with if he had something that felt like cheating. She did not think their relationship could bear it though if he did not know what that meant. It was the first sign that she should end it with him. She ended it soon after that.

Coming home from the last time of seeing him, she stopped next to the basketball court and watched the game. I want to cheat, she thought. I want to cheat with someone who wants to cheat as well. We are *here* to cheat, no matter what anyone says. She wondered what would happen if she were to run onto the court and tell the boys to make room for the girls in the grass.

Two years later, when she had met a man she was beginning to love, she decided she would tell him that she wanted to cheat, and that she wanted him to cheat with her as well. It would be her declaration. Men got to make declarations all the time. They had all the formal occasions to make them, but a woman had to make hers when she could.

On the way to see him it was very clear in her mind. I believe love should feel like cheating, she would say. It should feel like we are getting away with something we aren't supposed to have. And we should feel like bad criminals lifting our heads up when we shouldn't, and looking around us wondering if it's really true, if it's really true that nobody is going to stop us and say, just who do you think you are, acting as though you deserve happiness? And then she remembered the young man who had said that basketball felt like cheating, and for the first time she thought it was very foolish that basketball was the thing that felt like cheating to him. What a small and insignificant thing to feel like cheating. It wasn't even cute. No wonder she had ended it with him. She had known back then at twenty-five that there was only one thing that was the real cheating. She'd had to wait many years before she could explain to a man what the real cheating was. If boys and men could spend as much thinking of love as they did throwing a ball into a hoop, they could all start cheating together much sooner. She thought of the basketball court again and she did not want to bring the girls onto the court anymore; she wanted to bring the boys to the grass.

By the time she got to his house and sat down with him to talk, she knew it was going to come out angry. She had not planned for it to come out angry, but she thought it was better that it come out angry than not come out at all.

She told him how she believed that love was cheating, that it was the only cheating, and that she was looking for someone to cheat with, to cheat against all that was small and foolish and meaningless in life. It came out angry, but the anger was deserved. The man was moved by all of it, including the anger. He had never thought of love as cheating before, but he understood it and he told her he wanted to cheat with her as well.

The next day when she went past the basketball court, she thought it was a beautiful scene. It was the same as always—the boys on the court and the girls in the grass, and the only thing she felt compelled to do was to tell the boys to play, to play but to pay close attention to their playing, because if it ever felt so good that it felt like cheating, then the idea was that it was telling them about something else, and she imagined them asking her what that other thing was, and she imagined herself smiling and walking away.

———————————

Siamak Vossoughi is an Iranian-American writer living in Seattle. He has had stories published in *Glimmer Train*, *Kenyon Review*, *Missouri Review*, *Chattahoochee Review*, and *Columbia Journal*. His story "Basketball" originally appeared in *Atticus Review*. His first collection, *Better Than War*, received a 2014 Flannery O'Connor Award for Short Fiction, and his second collection, *A Sense of the Whole*, is due out from Orison Books in September 2020.

HUMAN BEING

joshua weiner

BODY LITERATURE

ALONG THE PERIMETER OF a busy compound, on a sidewalk in front of a high black iron fence, two women are standing in a drizzle without umbrellas. Early fall, before trees turn, with the stubborn warmth of summer holding off cooler weather. They are facing each other, one with head bowed, reading something to herself on her cell phone, the other watching her read. Tiny pearls of water collect on strands of hair. Slowly, the reading woman's face starts to change. The lips, starting at the center, slowly curl in a tight grimace, the brows bear down; cheek muscles push, reducing the eyes to slits. The whole face, for a flash, resists collapsing into unbelieving grief, then collapses. The reading woman's eyes stay trained on the words; she keeps reading through first tears, her shoulders shivering slightly, the tension of a lake troubled by growing wind.

The other woman speaks, her body strung in readiness, to lean in, to comfort. But something holds her back. The shock of impact, what the reading one is reading, an unexpected blow, keeps the other woman pushed outside of it, she's not *allowed* in. Even in public, the reading one's first intimacy is with herself. She must meet herself, as in a grove of thorns. She must stand there, still, in a silent settling of lengthening night, green thicket beginning to redden. To welcome in the other, she needs first to add time. You can see that it's already quickly re-forming, finding new direction, grief shifting to mourning. Only then does she somehow signal to the other woman, she can come in now, permission is granted. An inviolable public privacy has been turned inside out, like a shirt that one is still wearing.

The other woman takes a step towards her. A first tentative hand on a shoulder gives way to an embrace.

They are together, finally, in each other's arms, new lovers joined by the need to be consoled, the need to console. Seconds go by. Then a day, then years. And space opens between them even as they stay touching.

Joshua Weiner is the author of three books of poetry, most recently *The Figure of a Man Being Swallowed by a Fish*; he is also the editor of *At the Barriers: On the Poetry of Thom Gunn* (all from Chicago). His *Berlin Notebook*, reporting about the refugee crisis in Germany, was published by *Los Angeles Review of Books* in 2016 as a digital edition and supported with a Guggenheim fellowship. A chapbook, *Trumpoems*, is a free digital edition from Dispatches from the Poetry Wars (2018). His translation (with Linda B. Parshall) of Nelly Sachs' *Flight & Metamorphosis* will be published by Farrar Straus Giroux in 2021.

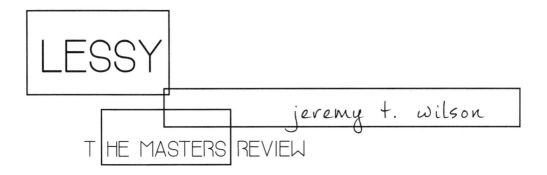

LESSY

jeremy t. wilson

THE MASTERS REVIEW

DELIA'S MOTHER FINALLY AGREED to get rid of her collection of ceramic mammies only after she saw the movie *The Help*. She'd told Delia she understood now why they "might possibly come across as offensive to some people." She'd lied. When her mother was dying of pancreatic cancer, Delia found a ceramic toothpick holder in the door of the fridge shadowed by ancient bottles of salad dressing and pepper sauce. The toothpick holder looked just like all the others: the cookie jar, the teapot, the spoon rest, the salt and pepper shakers; identical, except for the minor differences that fit their function. A red kerchief knotted atop their heads. Round, dark faces. Bright white eyes. Wide grins. A fat red dress covering an ample bosom, hands on sizable hips, and a starched white apron flowing to chunky shoes. Her mother had named them all, which somehow made an awful thing even worse. She called the toothpick holder Lessy.

Delia picked up the toothpick holder, ready to smash it on the kitchen tile, when her brother called her back to the bedroom and they watched their mother die. Delia was a hospice nurse, so was used to this, and even though it was her own mother, she approached the passing with a detached professionalism. She thought about curling the toothpick holder into her mother's hand as the men from the funeral home quietly took her body, but she didn't want to give her the satisfaction of being buried with this thing she was incapable of throwing away. Delia wrapped the toothpick holder in some dirty socks and put it in her suitcase and took it home with her when she left Georgia two days after the funeral.

Back at work, Delia developed a habit of checking her patients' refrigerators, curious about those things they might've told their own daughters they were getting rid of but held on to for God knows why. Mr. Sasaki kept a collection of Japanese coins in a small mason jar tucked in the corner of an empty vegetable drawer. Delia took them out and pressed the cold metal to her temples, imagining she might one day go to Japan and spend this man's money on sushi, circulating his coins back into the system where they'd lose their chill. Delia found a swatch of fabric from a baby blanket inside Mrs. Tierney's fridge, an ivory-handled butter knife at Mr. Cishek's, a snow globe of downtown Philadelphia at Mrs. Smith's, a Tupperware full of watermelon seeds at Mrs. Longenbach's, the shifter knob to a 1978 TransAm at Mr. Sherman's, what she thought was a human finger but turned out to be a fake inside a butter dish at Mr. Crandle's, and golf balls nestled inside an egg carton, each one of them dated with a black Sharpie at Mr. Dickman's. And the items she found that were small enough to take, Delia took. She kept them all in a shoebox along with her mother's toothpick holder. She didn't know why she stole these things from people. It wasn't so she could remember her patients or tally the numbers she'd helped usher to the other side. She felt like she deserved their things, or maybe like she was helping them unburden this part of themselves they'd kept buried in the cold. She told herself it wasn't even stealing.

Which is also what she told the hospice facility when they fired her for stealing.

Delia had a friend who urged her to move out to L.A. and start over. She found a sunny one-bedroom apartment scented with jasmine that always seemed to be in bloom. When Delia was unpacking, she opened the shoebox and went through all the objects. Junk now. A box of dead people's junk. Why had she brought this crap with her? She couldn't even remember all the patients who the objects belonged to, but she did remember her mother. She missed her. She dumped everything in the trash except for Lessy, whom the giddy perfume of jasmine now rendered laughable. Out here, Delia would not become a person who hid her secrets in the refrigerator. She was from the South. This had been her mother's. She would own it. So she put Lessy on the windowsill above the kitchen sink and filled the hole in her back with toothpicks like a quiver, and every time Delia washed her hands or rinsed off dishes, she saw Lessy smiling and thought of her mother without shame. Delia got a new job, made new friends, started a relationship with a man named Carl. He noticed the toothpick holder in her windowsill and asked her where she got such a thing and why she had it and why she kept it on display when it was so obviously racist and all their friends could see it at this very dinner party! Their black friends! She knew she couldn't answer the way that he wanted. She told him he had a fleck of pepper in his teeth.

Carl broke up with her. Her rent went up. The jasmine stopped blooming. One day she came home and the toothpick holder wasn't on the windowsill anymore. Delia would convince herself she'd finally summoned the strength to get rid of it, that she knew no matter how it kindled memories of her mother that it was unjustifiable, that it was mean and ugly and hateful. She would even call Carl and tell him she'd smashed the toothpick holder with a righteous hammer. But she knew the truth. She knew Lessy had finally had enough of waiting around for people to do the right thing and had simply walked away, her hollow body armed with tiny arrows.

Jeremy T. Wilson is the author of the short story collection *Adult Teeth* (Tortoise Books) and a former winner of the Chicago Tribune's Nelson Algren Award for short fiction. His stories have appeared in literary magazines such as *The Carolina Quarterly*, *The Florida Review*, *The Masters Review*, *Sonora Review*, *Third Coast* and other publications. He holds an MFA from Northwestern University and teaches creative writing at The Chicago High School for the Arts.

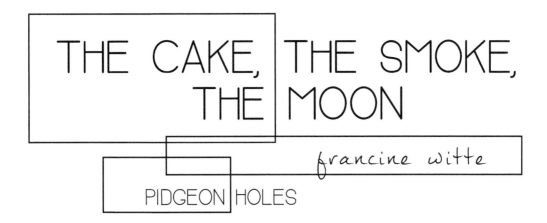

THE CAKE, THE SMOKE, THE MOON

francine witte

PIDGEON HOLES

IT IS THE FOURTH of July and the pop pop smoking the air, and the gray foggy fingers stretch way up into the humid night and dig down into the water. We sit there on the beach. We are lined up like questions. Where does smoke go when it dies?

One of us says we are children, and we don't need to know. Another of us decides it is time for cake.

We eat the cake and a third one says, we have to wait an hour now. She is the one who will follow the trail of the smoke fingers into the water. The water, that even an hour from now, will be lit up only by the moon.

The rest of us will wait safely on the beach, cake crumbs on the blanket. We will watch the water open its mouth and swallow. The one walking into the water, the one looking for the smoke, will never find it, and we can only watch as she never pops her head up like a firework dud. The lifeguards run their useless legs into the water. Even the moon knows it's too late.

Francine Witte is the author of the flash fiction collection, *Dressed All Wrong for This* (Bluelight Press), two flash fiction chapbooks, *The Wind Twirls Everything* (Musclehead Press) and *Cold June* (Ropewalk Press), and a novella-in-flash, *The Way of the Wind* (Ad Hoc Press). Her flash fiction has been in *Wigleaf, Gone Lawn, Mid-American Review, Milk Candy Review, Lost Balloon, New Flash Fiction Review, Journal of Compressed Matter, Cream City Review, Passages North,* the *W.W. Norton* anthology, *New Micro,* and others. She is also a poet and playwright. She lives in New York City.

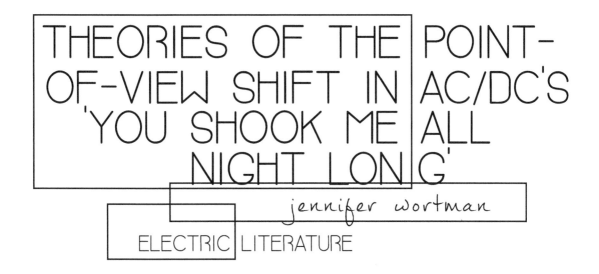

THEORIES OF THE POINT-OF-VIEW SHIFT IN AC/DC'S 'YOU SHOOK ME ALL NIGHT LONG'

jennifer wortman

ELECTRIC LITERATURE

1. THE SPEAKER—LET'S CALL him Brian—is documenting the shift, à la Buber, from I-It to I-Thou relations, from subject-object to intersubjectivity. Confronted with his lover's fast machine and clean motor, Brian can no longer maintain his stance as autonomous male subject gazing upon the Other. He and his lover merge; he is shaken.

Was I not a sufficiently fast machine? Did I not keep my motor clean? I cleansed assiduously for you, removed hairs, performed ablutions. True: over time I relaxed a little, cleansed and removed less of myself, slowed down. But is love not a sagging into each other, a softening of edges, an ooze? Was my dirt and languor not yours too?

2. The woman to whom Brian refers in the verse differs from the woman (or man or nonbinary individual) he addresses in the chorus. He uses talk of the woman in the verse to seduce, via titillation, jealousy, aspiration, etc., the choral "you." If I speak to you of a woman's ability to knock me out with her American thighs, Brian reasons, you will then want to knock me out with yours. His reasoning bears out: he is shaken.

You often spoke of how dumb she was. You didn't use that word, but you implied and I inferred. A groupie, you'd called her. A wannabe who imposed upon your time with toady tributes to your poetry. I'd seen her at parties: assertively busty, cosmetically lacquered, flagrantly blonde. After said parties, I'd follow your lead and mock her. After said parties, I'd follow your lead and fuck you hard.

3. After losing his lover, Brian can't bring himself to address her, yet much remains unsaid. He recounts their time together until, overcome by memories of their all-night shaking, he calls to

her across the ether. If he reminds her of their shaking, crows it over the roar of guitars, will she hear? Will she tell him to come even though, in a sense, he was already there?

Only later did I realize how much she resembled your ex. Later still I realized my once-careful grooming may have been a response to a photo I'd seen of your ex, who'd managed, in her appearance, to blend purity and smut, her perfection an invitation to blemish, to ravage and raid. Did you still love your ex? I called across the ether. Did you now love the groupie? Had you ever loved me?

4. Brian is masturbating. The woman is a product of his mind and "you" is himself. Her truth telling, her double-time on the seduction line, her meal making: these are all Brian's fabrications, his creation of an ideal woman who is fast, mechanical, immaculate, superlative, unseeing, authentic, strong, greedy, domineering, hard-working, inimitable, faithful, humble, ravenous, calming, violent. She doesn't exist, and Brian, unable to compromise his ideal, is left to shake himself.

Once I awoke and you weren't in bed. I found you in the living room, pleasuring yourself. How hard you'd shut your eyes, as if trapping whatever fantasy girl you'd formed in your brain. If I'd been working double-time on the seduction line, I would have shimmied over and joined in. But I'd been depressed. I didn't know why, but I knew it was my fault. How devoted you'd recently been. Yet I'd failed to satisfy you. What's more, I'd forgotten to shower. I stank of myself.

5. Brian is anxious because he has to fill the shoes of AC/DC's previous singer, Bon, who died of alcohol poisoning. A product of his anxiety and his cowriters' grief, the point-of-view shift is an oversight, a mistake that betrays subconscious feelings for Bon. Why did he leave them? If he returned, they would shake him all night long, each for their own reasons. Unable to acknowledge their pain, they cloak their urges in boasts of heterosexual intercourse, projecting their need to shake a dead man onto a feminized Other.

One day you disappeared. Ghosted, they call it: a misnomer. A ghost is a presence where there should be an absence. You were gone when you were supposed to be here. The morning you vanished, I flitted birdlike from room to room, my head jerking at strange angles, searching for you. When I understood what you'd done, I wanted to shake you until answers flew from your throat. Instead, I rammed myself against a wall, which gently shuddered, and left, on my shoulder, a chlorine-blue bruise.

6. Brian is documenting, per the Song of Songs, an encounter with the divine. Unable to evoke his sacred love with mundane language, he turns to the sensual, celebrating God's feminine aspects. However, Brian understands the vocabulary of masculine and feminine can be only metaphor. As the ultimate You, God transcends material forms and their signifiers. Yet God also

inhabits them. Brian's confrontation with this paradox unites him with the supreme mystery: he is shaken; he is shaker.

If you were my god, then whom did you worship? All poetry, you'd once said, entreats the divine. When you knelt before me and made me scream, was my pleasure a poem, a song to yourself? My idol, you smashed me. Yet I thank thee. I thank thee! Alone with the mess of me, I'm shaken and shaking. Shaking and shaken, I'm god of myself.

Jennifer Wortman is a 2020 National Endowment of the Arts fellow and the author of the short story collection *This. This. This. Is. Love. Love. Love.* (Split/Lip Press, 2019). Her work appears in *TriQuarterly, Copper Nickel, Glimmer Train, Electric Literature, SmokeLong Quarterly, Brevity,* and elsewhere. She lives with her family in Colorado, where she serves as associate fiction editor for Colorado Review and teaches at Lighthouse Writers Workshop.

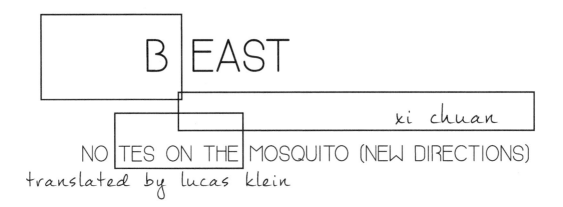

B EAST

xi chuan

NOTES ON THE MOSQUITO (NEW DIRECTIONS)

translated by lucas klein

THE BEAST, I SEE it. The beast, fur thick and stiff, teeth sharp, eyes nearly lifeless. The beast, gasping for breath, growling ill fortune, and from its feet, no sound. The beast, with no sense of humor, like a man straining to hide his poverty, like a man ruined by his mission, with no cradle to provide memories, no destination to locate yearning, not enough lies to plead for itself. It smacks a tree trunk and gathers infants; it is alive, like a cliff, and dead, like an avalanche.

A crow among scarecrows searches for a partner.

The beast, it despises my hairstyle, despises my scent, despises my repentance and reserve. In a word, it despises that I deck out happiness in baubles and jewels. It squeezes its way into my room, orders me to stand in the corner, and with no word of explanation collapses in my chair, shatters my mirror, shreds up my curtains and all that belongs to my spiritual defense. I beseech it: "Don't take my teacup when I'm thirsty!" Right there it digs up a spring, which I suppose must be some kind of response.

One ton of parrots, one ton of parrots' nonsense!

We call the tiger *tiger*, we call the donkey *donkey*. But the beast, what can you call it? Without a name, its flesh and shadow are a blur, and you can barely call it, can barely be sure of its location in broad daylight or divine its destiny. It should be given a name like "grief" or "embarrassment," should be given a pool to drink from, should be given shelter from the storm. A beast with no name is a fright.

A song thrush does away with the king's foot soldiers.

It knows temptation, but not by a palace, not by a woman, and not by a copious candlelit gala. It comes toward us, so is there something about our bodies that makes it drool? Does it want to slurp up the emptiness off our bodies? What kind of temptation is this! Sideways through the passageway of shadows, colliding head-on with the flash of a knife, the slightest hurt teaches it to moan—moaning, existence, who knows what stuff belief is made of; but once it settles down, you hear the sound of sesame at the jointing stage, you catch the scent of the rambler rose.

The great wild goose that clears a thousand mountains, too shy to talk about itself.

This metaphorical beast walks down the slope, plucks flowers, sees its reflection by the riverside, and wonders inside who it could be; it swims across the river, climbs ashore, and gazes back at the mist on the river, with nothing to discover or understand; it rushes into the city, chases girls, finds a piece of meat, and passes the night beneath the eaves, dreaming of a village and a companion; sleepwalking for fifty miles, knowing no fear, waking in the light of a new dawn, it finds itself returning to the location it had set out from: that same thick bed of leaves, the same bed of leaves still hiding that dagger—what's going to happen?

Pigeon in the sand, you are enlightened by the sheen of blood.
Oh, the age of flight is near!

Xi Chuan, poet, essayist, and translator, was born in Jiangsu in 1963 and raised in Beijing, where he still lives. A graduate of the English department at Peking University in 1985, he was formerly a professor of literature and head librarian at the Central Academy of Fine Arts (CAFA) and is now a professor at the International Writing Center of Beijing Normal University. In China he has been awarded the National Lu Xun Prize for Literature (2001), named Cultural China's Person of the Decade (2001–2011) by Shanghai's Oriental Morning Post, and been named Author of the Year by the Chinese Book Industry (2018). He has also one of the winners of the Germany's Weimar International Essay Prize Contest (1999), the recipient of Sweden's Cikada Prize (2018), and the winner of the Tokyo Poetry Prize (2018). His *Notes on the Mosquito: Selected Poems*, translated by Lucas Klein, was published by New Directions in 2012 and won the Lucien Stryk Asian Translation award.

Lucas Klein (PhD Yale) is a father, writer, and translator. He is executive editor of the Hsu-Tang Library of Classical Chinese Literature, from Oxford University Press, and his scholarship and criticism have appeared in the monograph *The Organization of Distance: Poetry, Translation, Chineseness* (Brill, 2018) and in *Chinese Poetry and Translation: Rights and Wrongs* (2019), which he co-edited with Maghiel van Crevel (downloadable for free from Amsterdam University Press), as well as in *Comparative Literature Studies*, *LARB*, *Jacket*, *CLEAR*, *PMLA*, and other venues. His translation *Notes on the Mosquito: Selected Poems of Xi Chuan* (New Directions, 2012) won the 2013 Lucien Stryk Prize; other translations include the poetry of Mang Ke, *October Dedications* (Zephyr and Chinese University Press, 2018), and contributions to *Li Shangyin* (New York Review Books, 2018). His translations of the poetry of Duo Duo, forthcoming from Yale University Press, won a PEN/Heim Translation Fund grant. He is currently an associate professor in the School of Chinese at the University of Hong Kong; as of 2021, he will be teaching at Arizona State University.

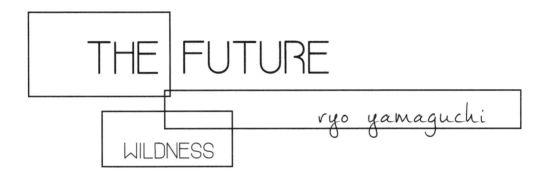

THE FUTURE
WILDNESS
ryo yamaguchi

PAST THE OLD ONE, and the little one. Past the painted ceiling, the scene of the dawn. Past numerical hemorrhages and worry, and tenuous light, stacks of chairs. Past the blustering color. Past a river carved into poverty. Past the javelin, past ceremony. Past what has been looked at until it could no longer be what it is. Past concrete, the raw matter spinning inside of it. Past news. Past posters. Past a lot of demolished cars sunken into the landscape, the way eyes are sunken when it's been days. Past days. Past all and past none. Past the one who knows what we must pass. Past television, conch, courtship, dimethyltryptamine. Past planar and columnar and spheroid, the bundle, the substratum, the ellipse invisible but for its effects. Past coffee and quiet reading, past conversation, flatware, crystal, and cloth. Past music. Past notifications. Past earnestness and tremors. Past manifestos and heights, the pyramid dizzied by birds. Past enforcement, presence. Past the horrible knowledge. Past the noise and past the muted. Past the predicate and thingness. Past the great cedars, the snow fields, the narrows. Past the fencepost and billboard, the cattle grate and fireweed. Past circumstance. Past what I am about to say next. Past it, and that, and this. Past past. Past present. Past future. Past the infinite overtones, past measure. Past eye and past voice. Past the horizon, the vanishing point, the swell, the frustum, the redshift. Past memory. Past dream. Past the gauzy light and the blue-tinted dark. Past the body, the self. Past effort. Past resignation. Past what has long been gone, and the yard, and the home, and the day in which we lived.

Ryo Yamaguchi is the author of *The Refusal of Suitors*, published by Noemi Press. His poetry has appeared in journals such as *Poetry Northwest*, *Gulf Coast*, and *American Poetry Review*, and his book reviews and other critical writings can be found in outlets such as *Jacket2*, *the Kenyon*

Review, and *Michigan Quarterly Review.* Currently traveling full-time, he was most recently based in Seattle where he was the publicity and marketing director for Wave Books. Please visit him at plotsandoaths.com.

AFTER THE DREAM, THE DREAM REMAINS

rich youmans

KYSO FLASH

THE CHEF WITH THE barbed wire tattoo is shouting for clean plates again. *C'mon, wetback, vamoose, vamoose!* Carlos feels the old snarl building in his throat, his *chamuco* temper ready to erupt. He grabs a rack of plates, shoves them into the dishwasher, brings down the door like a guillotine blade. Leans against the sink. The kitchen air smells of bleach and seared meat, and all the hanging metal pots reflect a smaller version of himself. The busboy booms through the swinging doors, carrying another clattering tray; Carlos takes the dishes, sprays off grease and chunks of fat. Yesterday his brother called: another raid, this time down at the carwash where his cousin worked. This is not how it was supposed to be. He pulls from the washer the now-clean plates, their round faces shining.

border crossing   saguaro arms raised toward the moon

Carlos washes the water glasses, rubs a rim until it sings. Marissa should be home from work by now, resting her swollen feet. Soon he will slip into bed next to her, her skin smelling of tree bark and cinnamon. If he's lucky, he won't have the bad dream—the crowd spilling from the funeral parlor onto Avenida Ruiz, the gang names spray-painted on corrugated shutters. Instead, he'll return to the plaza of their earlier days: children chasing pigeons from cobblestones, their voices a flutter of wings. The air sweet with the smell of *atole* and charred banana leaves. The high sun turning their skin to gleaming copper—*cobre reluciente*—as if it were the most ordinary thing in the world.

border crossing   night river flowing into its own sound.

Rich Youmans' haiku, haibun, and related essays have been published widely in various journals and anthologies. His books include *Shadow Lines* (Katsura Press, 2000), a collection of linked haibun with Margaret Chula; an e-book, *All the Windows Lit* (Snapshot Press, 2017), and *Head-On: Haibun Stories* (Red Bird Chapbooks, 2018). He is currently the editor in chief of *contemporary haibun online*. He and his wife, Alice, live on Cape Cod.

WHAT WE BE?

reza zareianjahromi

MORE OF US (LANDING PRESS)

WE BE PACK OF crow. Black bird perched upon scorched branch. Perched upon broken building. Perched upon snapped wire. Perched upon this doomscape.

We be pack of crow. Watched as bomb fell. Crow flew. Man could not fly. Man could not outrun it. Now it is all nest. Now it is all feed. Bodies of rotting and burnt flesh; once among living, but now just feed.

We be pack of crow. Watched as man burnt. Woman, child, infant, all burnt. Shadows etched into wall, as blinding light destroyed all.

We be pack of crow. Pick clean corpses. Woman's necklace. Child's buttons. Man's watch. All that was once of value, brought back to crow's nest.

We be pack of crow. Hay men in fields never inspired fear in pack of crow. Hay men did not kill or maim sheep. Hay men stuck to ground just as rows of corn they watched over. Arms stuck out for crow to rest. Farmers...men...were crow's source of fear. All past now. Rows of slowly rotting corn. Farmer's eyes blue as sky—now black and dull—all feed...all feed.

And when time for slumber comes, stars are once more seen. No more light but moon and stars. All buildings fallen. All noise suffocated. Just pack of crow, left to crow and crow and crow...

———————————————

Reza Zareianjahromi is a young artist from Iran, currently based in Wellington, New Zealand, with a passion for poetry, prose, and digital art. His works are influenced by new-age Persian poetry as well as some elements from performance poetry.

NOBODY KNEW MY MOTHER WAS A DRUNK

lisa zimmerman

APPLE VALLEY REVIEW

JEANNIE KIERNAN WAS MY best friend in 4th grade. Her big sister had a horse, a dark bay gelding who could fold his front legs and leap over painted rail fences, her sister balanced in the saddle, all poise and focus, capable hands holding the reins lightly, lightly. Jeannie had more Breyer model horses than I had—mares and grazing foals, elegant rearing stallions, dapples, chestnuts, prancing white-blazed ponies, a whole herd sweeping across the red carpet in her bedroom. We were allowed to eat snacks on her bed, Oreos which my mother never bought, and potato chips, caramel corn, the pound bag of M&Ms, salted peanuts in their shells. We could open the fridge without permission and pour Coke into tall glasses clinking with ice. We rode our bikes like fast horses up and down the ragged hill behind her house, each of us whinnying and snorting to each other. Dinner at Jeannie's house was served before dark by her tall graceful mother who circled the table like a musical note and we didn't have to sit and finish the food we didn't like. We didn't even have to put it on our plates.

Lisa Zimmerman's poetry and short stories have appeared in *Redbook*, *The Sun*, *Florida Review*, *Poet Lore*, *Chiron Review*, *Trampset*, *Amethyst Review*, *SWWIM Every Day* and other journals. Her first poetry collection won the Violet Reed Haas Poetry Award. Other collections include *The Light at the Edge of Everything* (Anhinga Press) and *The Hours I Keep* (Main Street Rag). Her poems have been nominated five times for the Pushcart Prize. Lisa is a professor of Creative Writing at the University of Northern Colorado and lives in Fort Collins, Colorado.

SPOTLIGHTED JOURNALS

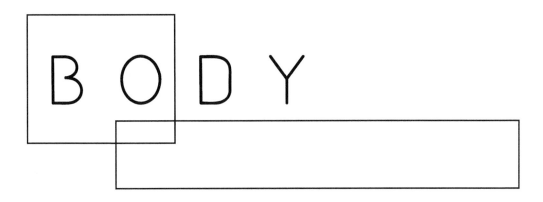

Best Small Fictions (Michelle Elvy): Congratulations! In this year's *BSF* volume, there are three inclusions from *B O D Y*: Lacie Semenovich's 'Daughter', Mark Terrill's 'The Turnaround' and Joshua Weiner's 'Human Being', all from the prose poem issue in June 2019. Tell us a bit about each of these pieces, and how you see the prose poem also as something that can be a perfectly formed small story? Where do you see the line between prose poetry and small fiction?

B O D Y: The line between prose poetry and short fiction—or even short non-fiction—is pretty permeable. While prose poetry, as a concentrated block of text, visually resembles a very short story, it tends to operate under different constraints, and has a different relationship to narrative than a story does. It doesn't require a plot, in the traditional sense, and is freer to operate by implication than action. The prose poem's form also represents a slackening of traditional poetic formal constraints, such as line breaks and metered forms, while introducing other, more amorphous constraints.

There's a gravitational shift from the line to the sentence, for example, where the sentence has to do the work of pulling the reader's eye forward. It also has to maintain the lyrical pressure that gives a poem its music. The process of preserving the perception of a poetic occasion while writing prose, or writing prose in a lyric mode, can give a prose poem a peculiar charm. In each of the prose poems you selected, one has the sense that what's being described, what's happening in the poem, operates within primarily a figurative space, even if a literal space, or occasion, is also present.

In Weiner's "Human Being," for example, the "plot" exists mostly within the speaker's mind. The literal action is very simple; it's the speaker's understanding of it that drives the narrative forward. The narrative arc is the speaker first observing then understanding what is happening, then understanding what it means, and it's that revelation that brings the narrative to its climax.

A similar thing happens in Terrill's "The Turnaround". In many ways, it's a classic Terrill poem, with fast-paced syntax and diction that combines colloquial accuracy with a heightened sensitivity of perception. The prose poem form helps him accomplish this even more elegantly, without the distractive trappings of enjambment and other features typical of poems. In a way, the prose form, in his poem, is just a container for what is essentially one very long line—a single, extended breath—that is conveniently wrapped into view by the margins of the page.

Lacie Semenovich's "Daughter" uses a similar rhetorical technique to Terrill, which is the kaleidoscopic view that pulls all of the fragments into one continuous stream and creates a breadth of observation within a very short space, but she breaks her observations up into short, staccato-like sentences. The sequence of hard facts builds the story; it's a simple plot. Also in contrast to Terrill: the speaker is not watching a concrete event unfold in the external world but relating a reality that unfolds over a much longer timeframe; the plot is not within her understanding of what's happening, but in ours. What Semenovich manages to do in this single sleek paragraph is almost novelistic.

BSF: How was the journal launched, and what were the original goals and meaning behind the name?

B O D Y: *B O D Y* was founded by Christopher Crawford, Stephan Delbos, and Joshua Mensch in 2012, and the name came from a reading series Chris had put together in Cambodia, where he was living at the time,. Michael Stein, who had interviewed us for another magazine, suggested a fiction in translation series among other interesting ideas, and soon joined us as an editor. Jan Zikmund came on board in 2015, first as a guest editor for our Czech Issue, which focused on contemporary Czech poetry in translation, and then as a regular editor.

The name *B O D Y* represents our appreciation for writing rooted in the world of objects and the physical world, an aesthetic that still drives the magazine today. In general, we're not huge fans of writing that's highly abstract or operates on a purely intellectual level. We like writing that's connected to a reality we can grasp with our senses—which doesn't preclude spiritual, or intellectual explorations of less tangible realities. The gaps between the letters was meant to visualize the openness and space that exists between the various realities we inhabit.

When we started the magazine, we weren't part of any dominant anglophone scene. We lived in a state of continuous translation, in a context in which we were exposed to a lot of non-English-language work that might never appear in English. We had also read enough literary magazines to know what we wanted to do, and what we wanted to avoid. Being from disparate places, such as Scotland, the US, and Canada, and knowing a lot of writers from those places, we felt we'd be able to solicit some great work to get us started. We also felt we could connect the readerships of those countries in ways they hadn't been before.

Bringing work to English-language readers through translation was something we knew we wanted to do early on, and it's a focus that has grown over time. We publish a great deal of translated writing in part because it keeps us connected to what's going on around us. To that end, we're fortunate to collaborate with some truly excellent translators. There is a special pleasure in introducing a writer to an English-language audience for the first time. It's like finally getting to share a secret you've been dying to tell someone.

BSF: Can you comment on the specificity of place and the universality of themes regarding writing from one geographical space—whether there is an aesthetic or approach to writing that reflects a particular place, or whether the themes explored in these special issues are relatable to a wide audience, no matter where the writer is from?

B O D Y: We'd say both are true. There's a famous quote by James Joyce that has become a kind of adage among writers: "In the particular is contained the universal." It's most often used to admonish those who think they can achieve the universal by writing something vague enough to sound lofty. So, while many of the works we've published are tied to a particular place and time, we think they stand apart from the particularities of geography and culture and find their place along the continuum of human experience, and in this way are relatable to anyone who has lived on this planet. Like most stories, they are stories about the experience of being alive.

Special issues are meant to highlight some of the writing coming out of a particular region, and while each piece is unique to the person who wrote it, the reader can get a sense of the imagination at work in those countries. It's a great way of drawing attention to work that might otherwise go unnoticed. When publishing a special issue of Serbian or Central European writers, for example, we're providing English-language readers with translations of some of the best writers they would never have likely heard of, let alone read. It also exposes them to stories that are fuelled by a different cultural imagination rooted in different histories and folklores.

The stories are as varied: a 17th century executioner, a Serbian punk rocker, talking snowmen, and drawings that come to life. If there is a difference this part of the world offers, it's that even relatively young writers from the Balkans, for example, have a direct experience of war, while those from Central and Eastern Europe have gone through occupation and regime change. One feels the presence of history happening in real time, while for many in the west, history is something that is more remote.

Interestingly, some of the best stories we've published as part of our special issues have not been set in the author's homeland, but in the places their own imaginations and experiences have taken them. A good example of this are the short stories of Hungarian journalist Sándor Jászberényi. Having worked for years as a war correspondent in the Middle East, his stories generally have much more to say about that part of the world than his native Hungary.

BSF: We'd love for you to share more about the translated work—and what is so special about bringing translated work to your readers?

B O D Y: Translation is integral to our existence as writers and literary participants in the Czech Republic. Part of that has to do with our own inherent transnationality, both in terms of where we live and what we read. There is a long tradition of translation in Europe. The Czech Republic is a small nation surrounded by other languages; here, there is a situational linguistic awareness that might be hard to imagine in other corners of the world. Our natural interests and daily reality took us toward featuring translation.

All of us are translators as well as writers and editors. Mike works closely with a number of presses that specialise in translated books, and curates our long-running Saturday European Fiction series, with translations of writers from Russia, Poland, and Hungary, as well as numerous underrepresented languages and countries such as Macedonia, Moldova and Yiddish, and has featured contemporary authors alongside writers from past eras, such as the pre-revolutionary Russian writers Teffi and Vlas Doroshevich. Jan, who is Czech, works for the Czech Literary Center and works directly with translators to bring new work into English, in *B O D Y* and other publications. Stephan recently co-translated a volume of poetry by Czech surrealist poet Vítězslav Nezval, titled *The Absolute Gravedigger*, with another book-length co-translation of Nezval coming out this year. Jan and Josh occasionally collaborate on translations of new Czech poetry, and Chris has translated a number of Czech poets as well.

BSF: Let's talk a bit about how you balance art and prose in the pages of your journal—and how the idea of looking forward and looking back might be specific to art that you feature.

B O D Y: The idea to start interviewing artists came from Jessica Mensch, our Art Editor. A visual artist who splits her time between New York and Montreal, she had the kind of access to artists that the rest of us had to writers and translators. She selected the work that would accompany their interviews and designed the layout of those pages.

All of the art interviews we've published have involved a degree of looking forward and looking back; the conversation is about work the artist has already produced, but we're talking about it in the context of where they're going—and that, inevitably, becomes part of a broader conversation on where they see the world going and how they want to respond to that.

In Richard Jackson's photo poems, for example, the photos function less as visual art than as visual cues for the poems. They aren't aesthetically constructed as "art" in the sense of something that stands on its own and exists purely within its own dimensions. Their value, rather, is in how they inform the poems, and the way in which they free the poems from the burden of description. The poems, then, have space to meditate on what the image shows, and describe that reality more deeply—they reveal what lies hidden beneath the surface of what you see in the photograph itself. The tension between the photo, which is a snapshot in time, and the poem, which constructs itself anew each time it is read, is what makes Jackson's photo poems so dynamic. The photo, in a way, is always looking back, while the poem pulls the subject into the future, even if its subject is the past.

In a way, this is a metaphor for what we have always tried to do with *B O D Y*.

Best Small Fictions (**Nathan Leslie**): I've been a fan of *The Cincinnati Review* for years now, but then you branched out into the *miCRo Series*, which made a great thing even greater. I'm hoping you can talk a bit about the genesis of the *miCRo Series* and how it has progressed over the past couple of years.

The Cincinnati Review (**Lisa Ampleman**): When we updated our website three years ago, we gained a lot of capability, since we were moving from an XML-based site (harder to update without expertise!) to a Wordpress platform. I knew we needed to increase the available content on our site, even as we remained committed to print, and I wanted us to go beyond just samples from the print issues.

At the same time, one of our assistant editors at the time, Gwen E. Kirby, suggested having an online flash series curated by graduate-student editors (who have always been part of the process of passing along promising pieces to the genre editors but at that point weren't curating any content in the print journal directly). This seemed like the perfect fit for our site.

The first set of graduate-student editors in the fall of 2017 helped set the guidelines for the series (once a week posts; ability to include audio; submissions 500 words or less for prose, 32 lines or less for poetry, 3 pieces per submission max). They also kept in mind how a piece would read online—it helps if it has some element that would attract additional readers, a social valence, a finger-on-the-pulse-of-the-moment. Successive groups of editors have kept that approach, and as a result, the series feels like it has grown organically but kept consistency. We've tweaked layouts a little over time, but the general ethos of the series remains the same.

BSF: How do you see the *miCRo Series* fitting in with the larger mission of *The Cincinnati Review*?

TCR (LA): Not everyone may know this, but we have a two-fold mission at *TCR*: connecting readers with the fabulous work of talented writers AND training graduate students at the University of Cincinnati in the art of literary publishing. The *miCRo Series* helps us do both; we're able to share more work, in a different medium, connecting those writers with even more audiences, and our editors have the chance to talk through the strengths and weaknesses of particular pieces, to experience the challenges and joys of curation.

BSF: May-lee Chai's "Telling" is an astounding piece. What do you admire about this particular work?

TCR (Caitlin Doyle): The tonal complexity in May-lee Chai's "Telling" is enormously compelling. While probing the nature of storytelling as a conduit for human connection across time, she prompts readers to consider the unspoken stories so often buried within narratives we inherit from those who have come before us. Through Chai's refusal to let the experiences of her mother and grandmother remain muted, she demonstrates that any truthful "telling" of the past must register the voices of those who have been silenced.

BSF: "Three Filipinas" by Harrison Geosits has an intriguing structure and presence. Talk a bit about what gravitated you to this particular piece.

TCR (Maggie Su): I was drawn to the seamless jumps in time and location in "Three Filipinas"—in just a 300-word piece, Geosits's prose spans two countries and decades of these sisters' lives. The structure works in opposition to the content—the list form implies easy categorization yet the sisters' paths are messy and spill outside of the 1-2-3 boundaries. The linear form's inability to encompass the complexity of the sisters' double identity, their "almost-white lives," reveals the false simplicity of the American dream.

BSF: The work "Kim" by Koss is described as a "gut-punch" by assistant editor Maggie Su. I agree. What makes this micro so powerful?

TCR (MS): Part of what makes Koss's micro so powerful is the simplicity of the premise: Kim is always falling, and we, the readers, are always watching her fall. Each time the story rewinds and plays itself over again, the fall changes forms, but the end result is always the same. As Kim's falls accumulate and build atop one another, the reader's grief turns into anger at the absurdity of the repetition. Koss implicates the reader in the spectacle as we act as witnesses to Kim's never-ending falls and the inexplicable gendered violence.

BSF: How have you seen flash as a form evolve over the past few years?

TCR (MS): The flash form has gained popularity in the last few years in large part due to the active and approachable flash community on social media. As a new writer, I was drawn to the form in part because of its accessibility. Micros don't take long to read and they're often available for free online—they're written to be shared and to connect writer to reader. The online nature of flash has had an impact on the form itself as micros have welcomed the experimental and strange. The field has evolved into a space that's open to writers whose work doesn't fit in traditional categories.

TCR (Jess Jelsma Masterton): One thing I've noticed, especially within our *miCRo* pieces, is that flash as a form has begun to really experiment with and test the limits of craft. More and more, we see hybrid work and pieces that break the "expected" conventions of the poem, essay, and short story. We also see authors who are tackling difficult subject matter from new angles—in part, because extreme compression forces them to do so. How do we talk about sexual assault in 500 words or less? How do we convey both the immediate violence and lasting trauma?

BSF: Micros seem more powerful than ever right now. How do you think flash is reflecting our current very strange and troubling time?

TCR (MS): Micros speak to the current moment because the form itself lacks rigidity. Flash fiction exists in that middle space between fiction and poetry, and thus the pieces are able to take on different shapes, to adapt to their content, and to function in both narrative and lyric modes. Flash fiction has always been interested in its own contradiction—in an immediacy that lingers. Now more than ever, we need those bursts of light and their reverberations to reflect back to us the problems of our world.

TCR (JJM): Like all narrative forms, flash has evolved—at least, in part—from our changing methods of communication and shifting definitions of storytelling. We live in an increasingly digital world in which, in an instant, we can share our most troubling moments or intimate secrets—all in 280 characters or less. I think the flash form reflects both the beauty and strangeness of that: the longing to share and connect while, at the same time, feeling the need to be pithy, witty, and direct when addressing an otherwise distant (and likely distracted) audience.

BSF: What does the future hold for *The Cincinnati Review* and the *miCRo Series* over the next few years?

TCR (LA): We're in the seventeenth year of the print magazine, so sometime in the next year or so, we'll start planning for our twentieth anniversary, including consideration of our design and content. It's possible we'll make some changes as part of that process, but we don't know exactly what yet. We'll also be in the fifth year of *miCRo* at that point, so perhaps we'll do a similar assessment. In the short term, we might consider some simple website redesign choices that might heighten the reader's experience. One other possible avenue: hosting a mini-reading series, either in-person or virtual (as we write, we're experiencing the coronavirus quarantine, which I think has changed everyone's perspective on how we interact with both each other and with texts . . .).

Best Small Fictions (Nathan Leslie): Let's talk about the genesis of *CRAFT* and your involvement with *CRAFT*.

CRAFT (Katelyn Keating): First of all, please let me say thank you to Nathan and the *Best Small Fictions* team. This is such an honor to be included as a spotlighted journal. *CRAFT* was founded in 2017 by Laura Spence-Ash and Kim Winternheimer, who had worked together for years at *The Masters Review*, which remains our sister journal. Laura served as editor in chief until October 2018 when I took the reins. The original concept was a journal that explores the art of fiction, that uses writing craft "as a focal point and a lens through which to present fiction." I had experience running several other online journals—I'd been EIC of *Lunch Ticket* and I work with the LA Review of Books Publishing Workshop each summer teaching/advising on the workshop's journal, *PubLab*—and spent a month under Laura's mentorship. I believe the transition appeared seamless and that our team has carried out the vision.

BSF: How has *CRAFT* evolved since its foundation?

CRAFT: The foundational work that Laura did cannot be understated—*CRAFT* hit the ground running with interviews, craft essays, and fiction by a dream team of literary fiction writers. This energy has generated so many outstanding submissions coming through our queues, I've never even considered soliciting fiction.

    The reading team had grown to ten volunteers right before I began. I knew I wanted (and needed) a bigger team and a more collaborative focus, so I created section editor roles for short fiction and flash fiction, an associate editor position, and doubled the reading team so we could consider more pieces in small groups instead of as individuals. The right balance right now is a team of thirty or so.

In 2019 we started publishing hybrid interviews, and opened the classroom corner as a resource for creative writing instructors. We increased the publication schedule to be able to share new work every week. We're always developing new craft column ideas and hope to have a few big announcements later this year. It was pure kismet that Tommy Dean had just started reading with us when I joined, and it was an easy promotion to make him our flash fiction section editor. With his wonderful community spirit and discerning eye, he has helped make *CRAFT* into a vibrant flash market.

BSF: I like the outlandish quality of Tyler Barton's "The Skins." Is this what caught your eye, or was it something else entirely?

CRAFT: "The Skins" is one where we were all drawn to the same aspects: the distinct voice, the rhythm of the piece, and the complex and original plot. And yes, it has an outlandish quality that sets it apart from much of what we typically read. I love what Tommy said about this story in our discussion, that it's "like watching a cooking competition: it's all about a perfect sound that we obviously can't hear." We agreed that the piece needed a few more lines of backstory about the MC. I didn't send that editorial note—when he confirmed acceptance, Tyler let us know he had a new edit of the piece with 100 words added. He had completely addressed our note about Ziegler before we even had to write it.

BSF: The story "Twelve-Step Program for Quitting My Life" by Kristen M. Ploetz uses form and concept brilliant. However, there is so much more to this flash. What else do you admire about this work?

CRAFT: When we first read and discussed the piece, we loved the control, the mystery, and how much space Kristen made for the reader. We edit extensively at *CRAFT*, and often go through several rounds of revision with an author. Working with Kristen on this story was an editorial dream. We asked her a series of questions to help sharpen the narrator's motivations and drive the tension. She absolutely nailed it, landing a perfect balance of mystery without confusion. What I think I admire most about this story is how generous it is, how open it is to study, to discussion—it's rich in sensory detail and language at the sentence level, but also in concept and form.

BSF: One of the aspects of *CRAFT* that is so appealing is the fact that it is so user-friendly for those of us who teach creative writing and literature in the classroom. Can you address how this came about?

CRAFT: Our foundational concept—explore how fiction works by combining an excellent short story with the author's discussion of craft and an editor's annotative introduction—is relatively simple and yet such a useful resource in the workshop or classroom. When we started hearing from many of our contributors that they use *CRAFT* to teach, we took the step of creating the Classroom Corner. The fiction archive was already spin the wheel to land on something you can dig into and teach, and we think the classroom designation helps collate essays and interviews into a single resource. We love being able to provide an accessible and free archive of original fiction and craft and critical content.

BSF: Do you find that *CRAFT* has a certain aesthetic? Is there a certain kind of story, for instance, that you find yourself gravitating towards in the fiction realm? I know this is not an easy question!

CRAFT: I am so grateful for our team and our collaborative process, because I look through our archives and see the influence of each of our readers and editors. We read to find excellence is craft: stories with technical precision and emotional resonance in balance. The mission is exploration of the art of fiction, so our aesthetic springs from our collective journey to find the work we can't stop talking about, thinking about, wanting to explain, wanting to learn from, and most definitely wanting to cite as influential in our own writing.

Best Small Fictions (Nathan Leslie): Tell me a bit about the origins of *Electric Literature* and how it has grown over the years.

Electric Literature (Halimah Marcus): *Electric Literature* started in 2009 as a quarterly anthology publishing to all platforms—print, ebook, pdf, etc. Everything *but* online, actually. It's hard to remember now, but in 2009 people were very wary of ebooks, and we were one of the first literary magazines, if not *the* first, to use them. In 2012, the founders moved on to another project and my former co-editor and I relaunched as an online-only non-profit. The centerpiece of EL 2.0 was *Recommended Reading*, which publishes longform fiction with a personal introduction by a top writer or editor online every week. Since then, EL's blog, which used to be called "The Outlet" (get it?), has grown into a robust literary website publishing essays, book recommendations, and interviews every day. EL went from about 100,000 readers in 2013 to 3.5 million today. *The Commuter*, where these three stories appear, launched in 2018 and publishes poetry, flash fiction, and graphic narrative under 1,500 words. In that short time *The Commuter* has built a devoted following; it seems to have filled a real need for a venue for brief, strange, humorous, and form-breaking writing online.

BSF: One of the things I admire about Electric Literature has to do with your eclecticism. Is this something you seek to actively foster?

Electric Lit (HM): Absolutely. That's why the different parts of EL—*Recommended Reading*, *The Commuter*, and our website proper—have such different parameters. When we launched *The*

Commuter, we didn't have a place for flash fiction, poetry, or graphic narrative on the site. *Recommended Reading* also cultivates eclecticism by publishing partner issues in which we excerpt a forthcoming novel, collection, or literary magazine's archives. This allows us to publish excellent work that may not necessarily come to us through submissions. Though it's worth noting that 75% of the work published in *The Commuter* is from open submissions!

BSF: What is your take on "Wishbone" by Rachel Heng? It is such a strong flash.

Electric Lit (**Kelly Luce**): This is a smart story that uses its central object incredibly well. By grounding us in the details of the wishbone proceedings, Heng buys herself room to travel through time—through generations and across continents—and tell not only the story of the siblings in that room that day, but of what in their family's past led them to that point. The voice is specific and dryly funny, as family dramas nearly always are, even and especially when they're underlaid by tragedy.

BSF: Jennifer Wortman's "Theories of the Point-of-View Shift in AC/DC's 'You Shook Me All Night Long'" is such an interesting and original story. What made you nominate this particular flash?

Electric Lit (KL): This story is about the end of a relationship and it's also an academic analysis of the lyrics of one of the most inane rock songs to ever blast from frat house speakers—what's not to love? Wortman gets the tone just right, a necessity for any parody, and the result is surprising and hilarious. It is hard to pull off this kind of story without seeming cutesy. She manages it with a combination of excellent sentence-level writing and by adding a parallel breakup narrative, making the piece more than just a clever mockery of lyrics.

BSF: What do you look for in a flash when considering it for publication?

Electric Lit (KL): The first thing I look for is excellence on the sentence level. Or rather, I don't look for it: I simply notice whether it's there. The second crucial element is voice. If a story nails the voice and has well-crafted sentences, all the higher-level stuff we love about reading can happen. These two elements of craft create space in the work for humor, sadness, absurdity, and any other number of complex, powerful emotional experiences. They lay the groundwork for one of reading's most delightful experiences, which is the experience of pleasant surprise.

BSF: Emily Everett's really original story takes on the form of a customer review. Its inventiveness really grabbed me as a reader. Was it the same for you?

Electric Lit (KL): Everett's inventiveness, format-wise, is only the beginning. Her genius comes in *how* she uses the review format. The slow reveal of the details of the review-writer's life and marriage, the heartbreaking way in which we learn, but are not actually told, that her husband has passed away, the matter-of-fact tone that is also somehow full of longing. In a story so full of grief, pain—but also joy and appreciation—it would be easy to go overboard. Everett's restraint, and the things she chooses not to say, are what make this piece unforgettable.

BSF: What are some of the other literary magazines currently publishing that you read and admire and why?

Electric Lit (KL): *Granta* always introduces me to great writers from outside the U.S. that I'd never have heard of otherwise. *POETRY* is such a consistent, important magazine that publishes both new and established writers, along with art and essays. It's one of the few "historic" lit mags (it was started in 1912) that still manages to feel fresh in its approach and aesthetic. And *Ecotone* is a well-edited journal that has impressed me every time I've read it.

BSF: What does the future hold for *Electric Literature* over the next few years?

Electric Lit (HM): Electric Literature's mission is to make literature more exciting, relevant, and inclusive. We do that in part by publishing work that is intelligent and unpretentious, investing in representation, and maintaining gender parity. We are also devoted to emerging writers, and are one of the few places online where writers who are just starting out can find a large audience. This mission will carry us through the next few years and beyond. But it's hard out there for literary non-profits, and as a free, online publication we can easily be taken for granted. EL is often mistaken for a much larger, better funded organization. We have fewer than ten staff members, only two of which are full time, and we are not backed by a university, publisher, or benefactor. So to make it for the long haul, we also need to mobilize our community to support us. If you enjoyed these stories, and believe in what we're doing, please visit electricliterature.com/support.

The Best Small Fictions (**Michelle Elvy**): *Wildness* was founded in 2015. Can you tell us about your goals when you first established the journal, and what has changed since you started reading and publishing literary prose and poetry? What were you looking for then? And what about now? And what of the name—how does it capture something about the inherent aesthetic goals of the journal?

Wildness (**Michelle Tudor**): Our primary reason for setting up *Wildness* was to enable us to publish as much exciting writing as possible. We had just set up Platypus and wanted another avenue (a more immediate one) to work within. In many ways, our initial reason for running *Wildness* hasn't changed all that much. We still see it as the most compelling way to discuss and dissect the current times, be that with personal themes or universal ones. Again, with regards to the kinds of work we were and are looking for, this has mostly remained the same—we always wanted to publish work by emerging writers, established ones, and anyone in between. We want work that speaks to our love of the environment as well as our personal relationship to it. In that respect, the name (which we took from a song title) perfectly personifies this: a reflection of the chaos that sometimes consumes a person, a movement, the world. A way to represent the very fact of what makes us human.

BSF: The journal operates as an imprint of Platypus Press. Please tell us a bit about the journal and the press—how they operate in conjunction with each other? Can you talk about the line between digital and print these days? What are the advantages or disadvantages of each?

Wildness: Whilst the press and journal operate separately (in the sense that one is more immediate, and the other is more of an ongoing process), as we (Peter and I) make the decisions, edit and present all of the content we publish, they're very much linked in their themes and motifs.

We have often thought about this—the distinction, if there is one, between digital and print. To us, there is less and less difference between the two, at least in the sense of the work itself. A physical book can be a thing of beauty, and the tactile relationship it can create between a writer and reader can be striking. However, we don't necessarily think this is always lost digitally, especially with the way digital content is now consumed more often than not (tablets, phones). What is more personal than a device you hold, decorate, and individualize as much as any other? In the long run, any means for a person to experience or be moved by the written word is a good thing.

BSF: You've said before you have a fondness of nature-based writing, as well as international contributions. Do you feel that nature-based writing a way to capture elements of a particular place, while also allowing for universal themes?

Wildness: I think we've found that the feeling of and towards nature tends to be echoed globally, with a deep sense of belonging expressed universally. Yes, we think so—we try to encourage this, and publish as broadly as possible. As with a lot of writing, the personal can be read universally, or at least empathically, and so the focus on nature can create an even more linked feeling between writer and reader, despite geographical distance and cultural differences.

BSF: *Poets & Writers* has said *Wildness* is a journal that 'embraces the mysteries of the self and the outside world'. Can you say a bit more about this? What is this relationship between inner and outer—an inward reflection and an outward gaze?

Wildness: I think what they picked up on was our desire to reflect both the internal discovery of the self, as well as the discussion of where a person belongs within the greater world. Again, the personal as the universal, and vice-versa. Any way to explore or investigate a person's feelings or failings (or any amount of other things) is always going to resonate.

BSF: There are two pieces from *Wildness* in this year's *BSF* pages: 'The Future' by Ryo Yamaguchi, 'What We Leave Undone' by Omotara James. Do you think these exemplify the writing in your journal for their themes or style?

Wildness: The two pieces chosen for inclusion do highlight the things we've discussed: the internal, the external, the personal, the universal. Obviously, as both are small pieces of prose-based poetry, they only reflect a small portion of the other work in the journal, but they definitely touch on the themes and tones we strive to publish.

EDITOR BIOGRAPHIES

Elena M. Stiehler is a graduate of SUNY Geneseo with a BA in English and Creative Writing. She is the Founder/Executive Editor of *The Sonder Review* and Sonder Press. She resides in Rochester, NY with her husband and a variety of four-legged creatures.

Nathan Leslie's ten books of fiction include *Three Men*, *Root and Shoot* and *The Tall Tale of Tommy Twice*. Nathan's poetry, fiction, essays and reviews have appeared in hundreds of literary magazines including *Boulevard*, *Shenandoah* and *North American Review*. Previously Nathan was series editor for *Best of the Web* anthology 2008 and 2009 and he edited fiction for *Pedestal Magazine*. He was also interviews editor at *Prick of the Spindle*. Nathan's latest work of fiction, *Hurry Up and Relax*, was just published by Washington Writer's Publishing House after winning its 2019 prize for fiction. He is the founder and host of the monthly Reston Readings Series and he teaches in Northern Virginia. Find Nathan on Facebook and Twitter as well as at Nathanleslie.net.

Michelle Elvy is a writer, editor and manuscript assessor. Her online editing work includes *52|250: A Year of Flash*, *Blue Five Notebook* and *Flash Frontier: An Adventure in Short Fiction*. In 2018, she co-edited *Bonsai: Best small stories from Aotearoa New Zealand*. She was also an associate editor for *Flash Fiction International*. Her poetry, fiction, travel writing, creative nonfiction and reviews have been widely published and anthologized. Her new collection, *the everrumble*, is a small novel in small forms, launched by Ad Hoc Fiction at the UK Flash Fiction Festival in June 2019. Find Michelle at michelleelvy.com.

Best Small Fictions Editors & Advisory Board 2020

Series Editor:
    Nathan Leslie
Guest Editor:
    Elena Stiehler
Assistant Editor:
    Michelle Elvy
Consulting Editors:
    Richard Peabody
    Tammy Ho
    Christopher Gonzalez
Senior General Advisory Board:
    Michael Cocchiarale
    Kathy Fish
    X. J. Kennedy
    Pamela Painter
    Robert Shapard
    James Thomas
    Clare MacQueen
General Advisory Board:
    Tara Campbell
    Elaine Chiew
    Jenny Drummey
    Jen Michalski
    Charles Rammelkamp
    Ryan Ridge
Interns:
    Gisele Gehre Bomfim
    John Strohl
    Michelle Stettner
Founding Editor:
    Tara Lynn Masih.

CPSIA information can be obtained
at www.ICGtesting.com
Printed in the USA
LVHW101435110221
679057LV00003B/242